▶ Medical Intuition

▶ Medical Intuition
Awakening to Wholeness

by C. Norman Shealy, M.D., Ph.D.

President, Holos Institutes of Health
Professor Emeritus of Energy Medicine
Holos University Graduate Seminary
Founding President, American Holistic Medical Association

4th Dimension Press   •   Virginia Beach   •   Virginia

Disclaimer

The information in this book is not intended to replace medical advice. You should consult your physician regarding any general or specific physical symptoms. The author and publisher disclaim any responsibility for adverse effects resulting from information in this book.

Cover design by Frame25 Productions

Contents

FOREWORD

MEDICAL INTUITION: A SCIENCE OF THE SOUL

I do not know one person who, when describing his or her state of health, does not fail to include a profile of his or her mental and emotional status. It is, in fact, incomprehensible these days to leave out those details. Who would even think to ignore their stress patterns or their heartaches or their business or life traumas when describing how they are feeling? I can honestly say that I cannot even imagine such a conversation these days. Over the past fifty years, we have made great strides into re-awakening the Divine design of the natural order of the body/mind/emotions/spirit coordinates that support life. This inherent intelligence about the natural harmony between the soul and the body was lost over the centuries as the Age of Reason or the Enlightenment fell in love with the scientific approach to life, but we now stand on the threshold of both a Mystical and a Medical Renaissance. We have crossed the psychic Rubicon and entered into the era of the intuitive mind, the cosmic heart, and mystical consciousness. We have not yet fully arrived in this new place, make no mistake. But we have made the crossing. We are pilgrims, en route to our potential, a potential we will never fulfill in this lifetime. But we are the pilgrims who have begun the journey.

The field of holistic medicine is, of course, a central part of the energy paradigm. And the need for medical intuition to be recognized as a science within this emerging paradigm of energy, or mystical consciousness, is not an option so far as I am concerned. It is a necessity. We have years of research ahead of us to mature this field into a well-respected science that can stand alongside other sciences, and like other new fields, this, too, must earn its stripes. But that is a worthy scrutiny, as medical intuition needs to come into its own as a legitimate field. As an energy-based science, medical intuition has an enormous amount of vital data that it is capable of providing to the physical world of science, data that quite frankly makes a standard diagnosis incomplete. Yet, because medical intuition is not yet subject to the rigors of an authentic science and does not yet have an agreed upon education program for medical intuitives, much less a national board that licenses them to practice, and because we have yet to formulate controlled means to validate "energy data" or to work with it in a reliable manner, the field has not yet earned the credibility that it so urgently needs.

While Norm brilliantly addresses these concerns within the pages of this book, as a practicing medical intuitive for over two decades, I know from long experience that the field of holistic health, including the science of medical intuition, is confronting several obstacles that will take years to resolve, as they are not mere problems. Problems have solutions. What we are confronted with as we truly come to grips with the vast difference between the physical world of medicine and the philosophical core of energy medicine is a predicament—namely, a collision of realities and all that such a collision portends. And predicaments, unlike problems, do not have solutions. Rather, they call for the emergence of new perceptions in order to move forward.

Let me offer just a few examples of what the challenge is to which I am referring. What makes "science" a science is repeated research that, in turn, produces reliable data. Such data becomes a building block, a given piece of information that can then be applied to a problem toward arriving at a solution. Energy information is an entirely different type of data. It is "kairos" data as opposed to "chronos," meaning that it is reflective of the "here and now" or having a more "timeless" quality to it, whereas physical, or chronos, data is concrete and forensic-friendly.

A person may be emotionally upset today, in the "here and now," but not yesterday and perhaps not tomorrow. That doesn't make the "here and now" data invalid or useless, but it does make it exactly what it is—good for the "here and now" and not measurable. A person's energy is "off" today but "on" yesterday. Such information is valid but how exactly does that translate to hard–core healing information? People talk about the influence of attitudes and beliefs. That's true, but which ones? Have you any idea whatsoever how many beliefs you have in that head of yours? And exactly which ones are causing you stress? Which precise negative patterns do you think are at the root of your crisis? Now that's what I call a fishing expedition if there ever was one.

All science evolved and inherent to the evolution of all sciences was the evolution of the vocabulary of each science. There was a time when the words "bacteria" and "infection" and "germs" and "virus" and "molecules" and "atoms" did not exist. Words are the telescopes and periscopes and microscopes of the imagination and intuition. Without an adequate vocabulary, we can see nothing. We can articulate nothing. We can "sense" that something is "out there" or "in there," longing to makes its presence known and its significance realized, but we are helpless until we name it. Language and *naming something* are as significant a building block to any science as the discoveries are themselves. Our challenge at this point is that we lack an adequate vocabulary that carries us between the dimensions of the physical body and the full force of the energetic anatomy and all the mysteries and power of that domain. We are at a loss to find a way that actually animates in measurable, real terms the connection between First Chakra issues and their everyday fetishes or fears. For example, the influence inherited tribal superstitions have on a person's emotional maturity are huge—not small—huge. They are as influential as the religious myths a person grows up with because they are often intertwined. Try to measure the "energetic intensity" of that subtle thread within a psyche and then delicately track that thread as it went from a superstitious thought form into a behavioral pattern that resulted in a control fetish so intense that the person becomes incapable of intimacy. Can physical medicine do something like that? Not likely.

The role of power and our relationship to power is, so far as I am concerned, basic to a health evaluation. People hemorrhage power for all manner of reasons—power plays in relationships, low self-esteem, lack of social clout, fear of rejection, personal finances, compulsive need for approval, a chronic fear of being humiliated—it's an endless list. And that's the point when it comes to your health—your health is intimately connected to your sense of power. The powerless find it nearly impossible to follow a health program. The empowered get right back on track. Can a person's sense of power be measured in a lab? Of course not. But it most certainly can be intuitively assessed by a competent medical intuitive, and through my work with Norm, we learned early on that factors of personal, emotional, psychic, and mental power were as significant to a health analysis as blood work.

I can continue to list the many obstacles I see ahead for the field of medical intuition and energy medicine—and there are many—but I can also sum them all up in explaining that the science practiced in allopathic medicine, for the most part, is objective. Lab tests are lab tests. Energy medicine and the role of the medical intuitive provide subjective data, data that has many more variables than quantifiable data in the physical world. Every memory has an emotional thread, for example, and the fact is, you alter the intensity of the emotional current that you transmit through that thread moment by moment. Thus, the significance of my earlier statement: the role that medical intuition faces is not so much as a problem within the field of science as a predicament. Its field of reality is fundamentally mystical in design. Its data is energetic and of the substance of mystical consciousness. That does not make it any less valid. In fact, if a person truly grasps the significance of this rich domain of soul dialogue, then you know you are engaged with the core of a person's true being. But, as I say, that leads to the predicament of translating that subtle field of data into the practical world of hard-core illness and treatment. And the obstacles in that world are equally complex in that patients rarely want to do the arduous work of soul transformation. Though they want the information, they are often under the impression that such information is like a release valve, as if it's a secret, dark memory that you unlock, and poof, health is returned. Healing just doesn't work like that.

Yet another variable that exists within the field of the medical intuitive is what the client believes the intuitive can actually do. It must be understood that the maturity of the medical intuitive, the attitudes and beliefs of that person and that individual's inner discipline, play the leading role in the quality of a medical intuitive reading. An immature, arrogant, untrained person who claims to be a medical intuitive will give a person a defensive reading; that is, he or she will have to be right and will argue to prove a point lest he or she be thought of as inadequate. I've seen that more often than I can count. Clients (medical intuitives may not refer to individuals requesting their help as patients) are vulnerable people. They often make the mistake of thinking that a medical intuitive has a tech lab for a mind instead of a mere intuitive system. Clients always imagine that an intuitive of any kind can answer questions that he or she simply cannot. They want their fortunes told. They want their life problems resolved. They want all their mysteries unfolded and not just about them. They usually come with a list of family members or a lover. A medical intuitive is not a street psychic or a carnival barker who can "see the future." A medical intuitive is exactly that—a person who has the ability to interpret energetic data as it relates specifically to health–related crises. This data often includes behavioral patterns, archetypal patterns that govern the soul's path, life traumas, and then there is the presence of physical illness as well as the illnesses that are in the process of developing. A profile of the individual's relationship to power as profiled within the Divine order of the chakras provides a map of how and why and where a person is losing power. Stepping out of those parameters and discussing other relationships and what a person might be able to psychically pick up about another person or discussing investments or business dealings during a medical intuitive reading is, so far as I am concerned, "energy malpractice," a crossing of the lines of the appropriate use of one's intuitive skills. If you are a medical intuitive, you must be governed by the ethics and parameters of what "medical" means. It means you are devoting your intuitive abilities toward assisting people to heal. If you want to be a street fair psychic and do romance readings, then list yourself as such but do not call yourself a medical intuitive.

Here comes the next logical question: Can people be taught to do medical intuitive readings with that same precision? First, the false belief that intuition is a gift needs to be completely shattered. Intuition is not a gift. Everyone is naturally intuitive, beginning with our inherent survival gut instinct, which operates in us as a function of our animal nature—not our higher consciousness, but our lower one. However, as a second point, let me say that our intuitive senses evolve not because we are gifted with them but because we seek an inner life. The trigger mechanism or launch pad for the beginnings—and note I said beginnings—of sharp intuitive abilities is to develop a strong sense of self-esteem. By that I mean a sense of who you are without being controlled or influenced by the fear of being humiliated. If you can get a grip on that one fear—the fear of being humiliated—then you will have the courage to hear your intuitive voice, the deep, clear, Divine voice that is not driven by your fear of survival. That's the beginning of mystical intuition, the core of what it takes to be a master medical intuitive.

Norm addresses a chapter of our history together and our effort to train a group of devoted students in the science of medical intuition. From that came Norm's brilliant idea to found the American Board of Scientific Medical Intuition. His intention in creating ABSMI was to establish a national standard of excellence. I say "his" because, even though I am on the Board, the fact is, it was Norm who envisioned the need for the creation of the American Board of Scientific Medical Intuition. It was Norm who first realized years ago that we had entered the energetic age, an age that would call forth practitioners of the energetic arts of healing. Up until now, we have named ourselves without testing, without having to prove these abilities to a Board of qualified authorities who, in turn, would grant us a license to practice our science. Through such a process of standardization, this intuitive skill is matured into an energetic healing science. This is the route medical intuition must follow in order to emerge as a mainstream science. So far, very few medical intuitives have stepped forward to be tested. Hopefully, that will change in the years to come. Hopefully, medical intuitives will feel confident enough in their skills to believe that they qualify to step up to the ranks as members of an emerging science. Hopefully, that time will come soon.

Norm's book on medical intuition is a textbook on this new science, a book that combines his history as a scientist examining this skill and as a physician urging the common sense of personal health care. Energy medicine and allopathic medicine are teamwork, but neither compensate for negligent health habits, as he is quick to point out. Norm Shealy has always been a visionary in the field of medicine and human consciousness, and I have been blessed to be a part of his life's work. I would not have become the medical intuitive I am today had we not met so many years ago. And I can also say that it was precisely because of my skill as a medical intuitive that the inner world of human consciousness opened up to me. I know that this is a science, but it is a science of the soul, not the mind. And it requires the utmost inner training on the part of the practitioner to become a precise instrument. I was more than lucky in finding Norm as my mentor; I was blessed. And this I know to be true above all else—you cannot walk into the territory of the soul unescorted. A mentor is essential. I am grateful my mentor wrote this book.

Caroline Myss
Oak Park, Illinois
September 2009

1

MY JOURNEY FROM PARAPSYCHOLOGY TO NEUROSURGERY AND MEDICAL INTUITION

While I was growing up my mother visited a little black lady outside our town, Lil Brown, known throughout the southeast as an excellent psychic. Supposedly, she had been consulted by our governor and various prominent people. Her technique was to have a client tell the problem. Lil would then dream on the solution and come up with a passage from the Bible. She then used that passage to give a practical answer. A remarkable use of scripture as a metaphor! In fact, just before I left for college, my mother had Lil do a "reading" for me. Lil told me, "You will be well known, but you will never be president of the United States." I do not remember ever wanting to be president! Indeed, I cannot understand why anyone would want that position.

Three years later, while I was an undergraduate at Duke University, I was asked by the director of "The University Players," to write a radio skit on Dr. J.B. Rhine's work in parapsychology. I spent three months interviewing this first professor of parapsychology and observing in his lab. I was convinced that he had exhaustively proven that individuals could "guess" correctly the contents of closed envelopes, precognitively know what was coming next, and do psychokinesis—influence the rolling of dice. The work was fascinating but left me frustrated—why did he not do something *useful* with this parapsychological wisdom?

The terms used in those days were *psychic, clairvoyant, psychokinesis, viewing,* and *precognition*—all anathema to "academic" psychologists! The skit was produced in the spring of the year, and I went on to medical school in the fall of 1952. For the next eighteen years I was preoccupied with medical school and graduate training in neurological surgery and my beginning clinical practice. Actually, I chose that field because I thought somehow it would help me understand the brain-mind. In medical school I had two major experiences with what I later would recognize as intuition. In my sophomore year, in Physical Diagnosis class, I made a diagnosis, which was correct, but which the professor felt I should not have been capable of making! He accused me of cheating and wrote a scathing report for my student file. Two years later, he apologized and asked me to intern in the Department of Medicine. He said he had withdrawn his earlier report from my file. In my junior year, I made a diagnosis of sarcoidosis of the pituitary gland in a patient who had entered the hospital over the weekend. Sarcoidosis is an autoimmune disorder that can be very serious, especially when it involves the brain or master gland. The professor of endocrinology was shocked when I presented my diagnosis and said to me, "You are a medical student. You can't make such a diagnosis." It was the first case of sarcoidosis of the master gland seen at Duke, and Professor Engel and I wrote a definitive paper on the subject.

Meanwhile, my research throughout medical school was investigating the physiology of the amagydala of the cat. The amagydala is strongly tied to emotions. Then, during my neurosurgery residency, I developed interest in the physiology of pain and continued that when I joined the faculty at Western Reserve Medical School. There I discovered the physiological foundation for pain mechanisms, a paper for which I was given the first Harold G. Wolff Award for Research in Pain. Remember this event, as it later became one of numerous *synchronicity* aspects of my life, a concept or term which, at that time, would have had no meaning! I met, at that meeting of The American Headache Society, Dr. Janet Travell, President Kennedy's physician, and a leading expert in myofascial pain. Out of my work came also my first two inventions—TENS, Transcutaneous Electrical Nerve Stimulation, and DCS, Dorsal Column Stimulation—both now used worldwide. Again, a beginning of what I would later know as *intuition* at work!

From age sixteen, I had planned to be a professor of neurosurgery. In early 1966, I was offered an opportunity to be interviewed to take over a major department of neurosurgery. As I had experienced by that time major meetings with a large number of chairs of Departments of Neurosurgery, I suddenly realized that I really did not like many of them. They were often arrogant, rude, or alcoholics and not individuals with whom I wanted to socialize! In fact, neurosurgeons had a reputation from the early days in the twentieth century of being the rudest of all specialists! I phoned Dr. Talmage Peele, my mentor since I entered medical school; I had done my amagydala research in his lab; and his response was, "Junior, you are ruining your career."

Suddenly, I made a critical decision—to leave academia. I took a position as chair of the new department of neuroscience at the Gundersen Clinic in LaCrosse, Wisconsin. The Gundersen Clinic was at that time the tenth largest private clinic in the United States. One of its founders had been president of the American Medical Association, and my position at Gundersen Clinic would allow me an opportunity to be clinically active but do some continuing research. Over the next five years, I was by far the busiest I have ever been, often working eighteen–hour days and seeing hundreds of patients with the broadest variety of neurosurgical problems. During that time our department expanded to include three neurosurgeons, three neurologists, and a neuropsychologist. I was able to have wonderful laboratory assistants who could carry out the research protocols that I developed. I even worked with a palsied orangutan, Shakey, in whom I demonstrated that electrical stimulation could indeed control tremor. In collaboration with Dr. Ted Tetzlaff, a neuroscientist at the University of Wisconsin, LaCrosse, we demonstrated electrical control of seizures in rats as well as control of penile erections in monkeys.

Meanwhile, my research with chronic stimulation of the spinal cord in cats and monkeys had proven successful enough that in 1968 I presented my work at the American Association of Neurological Surgeons in St. Louis. The paper was so controversial that physicians jumped up on the stage and grabbed my microphone. The paper was the first ever given at that meeting that was turned down for publication in the *Jour-*

nal of Neurosurgery as too controversial. It was subsequently published in *Analgesia & Anesthesia*. Two years later, I presented my first eight cases of DCS in human patients with advanced, incurable pain. Suddenly neurosurgeons wanted to jump on the bandwagon and do the procedure!

I had developed the original equipment with Tom Mortimer, who had done his master's and doctoral research in my lab. When he graduated, he joined the faculty at Case Institute of Technology and went on to become a famous biomedical engineer. He suggested that I invite Medtronic, the leading manufacturer of pacemakers, to manufacture the Dorsal Column Stimulator (DCS) devices. They agreed initially to support the Dorsal Column Study Group, a consortium of neurosurgeons who planned to operate on a total of five hundred patients and follow up on them, over five years, before we made the procedure publicly available. I tried from the beginning to interest Medtronic also in TENS, but they refused until one of their research engineers left the company and began manufacturing the first TENS devices. Two weeks later, his replacement at Medtronic produced a smaller device, using the electronics I recommended! As so often happens in industry, greed crept in. Another company started advertising DCS to the neurosurgical community and Medtronic followed suit. The study group had barely inserted stimulators in 480 patients, but few followed five years. And, unfortunately, the design of the electrode was changed from my initial design. That led to many complications and forced me to abandon the approach. Forty years after my first DCS patient, I was invited to receive a "Lifetime Achievement Award" for the creation of DCS, even though I have not inserted a DCS since 1973!

Meanwhile, in the fall of 1969, my family moved to a farm outside LaCrosse and began our work with Appaloosa horses. My wife has been the major force in that work, but our involvement with horses opened the door to my old, dormant interest in psychic phenomena! In October 1970, I flew to Colorado to visit Sun Appaloosa Ranch, where the owners were retiring and had some champion horses for sale. I drove down from Denver to Castle Rock, and when Joyce Cannon opened the door, I knew her at a deep soul level! We spent a couple of hours discussing psychic phenomena and even past lives, which I had never before even thought about! I wound up purchasing eight of Ralph and Joyce's horses, and we became good friends.

Two weeks later, I received *Psychic Discoveries Behind the Iron Curtain* from Joyce. *Wow!* That really did the trick. I was excited to see how far parapsychology had come in eighteen years. Another week passed and Joyce sent me Shafica Karagulla's book *Breakthrough to Creativity.* Here was proof of *practical* application of clairvoyance! I wrote to Shafica and asked for an address of Kay, who had been mentioned in the book as highly accurate in making medical diagnoses just by seeing the patient. She told me to "find your own psychic." I was disappointed but began asking colleagues if they knew any good psychics! I was lucky to stay out of the insane asylum.

In November 1970, on my monthly visit to the University of Minnesota, where I had a teaching appointment, I said to one of my colleagues, "Pain is the most common symptom that takes patients to a physician, but no one has specialized in pain management." His response was, "An interesting idea, but who would ruin his career doing that!" I was immediately convinced that I should found a comprehensive pain management clinic. Over the next nine months, the idea incubated. In July, I visited Dr. Wilbert Fordyce at the University of Washington to see his five-year-old Behavioral Modification, or Operant Conditioning, Program. Working with just one hundred patients in the five years, he hospitalized them for two months. His program was what I would call passive behavioral modification. But he had a 60 percent success rate doing little but ignoring their pain and weaning them from drugs, as well as a modicum of physical activity. He felt that if he had only a 10 percent success rate with these chronic pain patients, then society would break even. The cost of these patients to the medical system is enormous! In August 1971, I made the decision to leave Gundersen Clinic, as I needed space in which to develop my ideas. I went across town to St. Francis Hospital, where I was allowed to take over an entire floor in the oldest part of the hospital to develop an inpatient pain management program. Not being born Catholic, little did I suspect at that time how strongly I would be attracted to St. Francis— and have been for many centuries. More about that in a later chapter.

I was already being sent four hundred chronic pain patients from around the world to consider DCS. I was selecting only 6 percent, re-jecting the other 94 percent as too disturbed emotionally to have even this relatively benign procedure. Now, you have to realize that I knew virtually nothing about psychology or psychiatry. The worst course I ever took anywhere was psychiatry at Duke. On the final exam, they gave this asinine directive: "List five qualities of a good psychiatrist." I wrote "Crazy as Hell" five times. They threatened to flunk me until I replied, "Do you want me in this class again next year?"

In October 1971, I opened the world's first comprehensive pain clinic, The Pain Rehabilitation Clinic. Those four hundred patients I was being sent each year were the first to experience my form of "active" behav-ioral modification. They were hospitalized and gotten out of bed at 7 a.m. and not allowed to return to bed until 9 p.m. They were assigned many active physical activities, sent to the YMCA five days a week for water exercise, treated with my intuitively received electroacupuncture, the old crude electrical stimulator patented in 1919 by C.W. Kent, a naturopath from Illinois, and ignored when they mentioned or demon-strated pain behavior. I enlisted a young psychiatrist to do "Group Therapy" with my key insistence that they must not be allowed to com-plain about anything. Little did I know! A year later, I sat in on one of his sessions that I found appalling—it was largely a bitch/moan party. I have never since indulged such pandering in group wallowing!

In January 1972, Dr. Janet Travell was quoted in the *Wall Street Journal*, stating that all the publicity over James Reston's control of pain in China after his December appendectomy wasn't that important. "There's a young neurosurgeon in Wisconsin who has a Western form of acu-puncture!" Acupuncture was suddenly a hot item. I had been doing my totally spontaneous form of electroacupuncture since 1966! (*Synchronicity* number 2). Soon thereafter I was invited by Dr. Paul Dudley White, Eisenhower's physician, to visit him to discuss my Western form of acu-puncture —major beginning of *Synchronicity* number 3! In April 1972, I flew to Boston to consult with Dr. White, truly one of the great Brah-mins of American Medicine. At 84, having just flown in from Greece, he was busy seeing patients. We spent two hours enthusiastically discuss-ing my work and I flew home.

A month later I received a phone call: "I am Bob Matson, president of

the American Academy of Parapsychology and Medicine. We are holding a symposium on acupuncture in June at Stanford University. Dr.
Paul Dudley White is to speak, and he said you know much more about
acupuncture than he does. Would you replace him on the program?"
Who could refuse that?

I went to the symposium, which was attended by twelve hundred
physicians. I met many who became lifelong friends, among others:

• Dr. William Tiller, chair of the Department of Physics and a leading materials scientist interested in parapsychology

• Drs. Bill and Gladys McGarey of the A.R.E. Clinic in Phoenix

• Olga Worrall, renowned spiritual healer

• Dr. Felix Mann, British physician specializing for twelve years in
acupuncture

• Dr. Phil Toyama, Japanese/American physician and acupuncturist

I learned from Dr. Toyama that the technique I had been using, of
placing a needle in the center of pain and stimulating a needle below
the pain to one above the pain, was one basic principle of traditional
acupuncture—although they had been twisting the needles for manual
stimulation. Later, I was to learn also that the Chinese began using electrical stimulation of needles in 1966—the same year I began doing that—
another synchronicity! But perhaps the most important life-changing
event at Stanford was talking with the McGareys. I told them I was
planning a symposium on pain at the end of September. They said, "You
should meet Dr. Bob Brewer. He is a surgeon who thinks like you. He is
planning a symposium in Virginia Beach, at the A.R.E. the end of August."

Thus began what for me became the "rupturing of the mental hy-
men," as I learned later from Dr. Andria Puharich. Now you need to
know that I had never heard of the A.R.E. or Edgar Cayce! "The Week of
Attunement" symposium was a highlight of this life. I learned about
colonics, color therapy, trance mediumship and, above all, reincarnation. I also met Dr. Genevieve Haller, a wonderful chiropractor and dear
friend. Her husband, Jeffrey Furst, had just written *The Return of Frances
Willard*. When I asked for a referral to a good psychic, he suggested
Henry Rucker. That led me full steam ahead into medical intuition!

I learned that, off the program, Dr. Lindsay Jacobs was going to do a past–life therapy session. I was able to get in to watch it, and it literally blew my mind! I said to myself, "I must try this but I can't do it in front of anyone else—maybe I was a prostitute in a Greek war camp!" I have to assume I was! Otherwise, it would not have entered my mind! Dr. Jacobs agreed to do a private session. It was indeed transformative. I saw myself as a physician in Egypt three thousand years ago during a cholera epidemic. We stopped the epidemic by burning the bodies. *I recognized my wife and my son of that life as people in my current life—friends.* I also realized that, despite my concerns about the path of modern medicine, it was my journey to help change it. For two hours after that experience, I wandered on the beach, lost in my first true "peak" experience, seeing in those ineffable moments the interrelationship of all.

That evening, Joel Andrews, a trance–medium harpist, played a concert for the entire audience, and I had my first out–of–body experience, floating above the crowd! Indeed, the "Week of Attunement" thrust me well into another world. A few weeks later, Joel visited me and did a harp concert in the chapel at St. Francis Hospital, and I did my first recording of a guided imagery exercise for past life therapy. That was part of the first holistic medical meeting, with four hundred attendees! We also had Dr. Wilburt Fordyce; Dr. Richard Sternberg, a leading chiropractor; Dr. Fred Barge, a Christian Scientist expert; and a few others outside "convention." The local medical society spent two hours attempting to get me censored for having the chiropractor on the program! Fortunately, I had more friends than enemies and it was not passed.

In the fall, I visited Olga Worrall at Mt. Washington United Methodist Church in Baltimore, where, for over thirty–five years, Olga and her husband, Ambrose (who died in 1971), conducted spiritual healing services every Thursday morning. Three hundred people crowded into the tiny church for the laying on of hands. Among the miracles that began that day, I was allowed, after the service, to examine a professor of English from a major university. She had advanced breast cancer, eroding through the skin as a black, gangrenous malignancy. One month later, a letter from her stated that her cancer had totally disappeared! This began my interest in spiritual healing. I wanted to publish a book, *Twenty-five Cases Suggestive of Spiritual Healing.* I began to have Olga send me letters so that I could get permission from the patients to obtain their medical records.

Eventually, my interest in spiritual healing became the book *Sacred Healing*. Equally important, Olga shared with me one of my favorite all-time booklets, *Essay on Prayer*, written by Ambrose in the '50s. Several other booklets by Ambrose were also treasures, and Olga gave me permission to reproduce the booklet to keep it in print. She also approved my doing a guided meditative tape of the *Essay on Prayer*. Much later that booklet became the foundation for my DVD on holistic healing, *Medical Renaissance—The Secret Code*. Olga also introduced me to Religious Science and Science of Mind.

Shortly after that week, I phoned Henry Rucker and arranged a one-hour consultation with him for December 19th. As I walked into his office, Henry said, "I've been waiting nineteen years for you. My teacher told me you would come." I spent three hours with Henry, who told me much more about me than I could have dreamed! At the conclusion of our visit, I invited Henry to come to LaCrosse to see how well he could diagnose patients.

One month later, Henry arrived with eight other psychics, eight of the nine being black. I noted that they had just doubled the black population of LaCrosse! Meanwhile, I had told my twenty-five in-hospital patients what I had in mind, and all were quite eager to participate. One at a time they were brought into my office, and each of the psychics looked at them or a handwriting specimen. They were not allowed to ask any questions. When they all were in agreement, their diagnoses were 98 percent accurate. There were three paraplegic patients—all from different causes—gunshot wound, trauma, and infection. The team correctly gave the cause of paralysis! I took Henry on rounds in the hospital. One of my patients had had surgery a few days earlier and had spiked a white blood count to forty-two thousand. We were concerned that a latent leukemia had been evoked by the stress of surgery. Henry stated that there was just a problem with the liver and that the patient would be fine. Two days later, the results of the bone marrow exam came back, and it turned out that he had a leukemoid reaction to the anesthetic—a very rare event. The patient left the hospital well within a couple of days!

I was hooked! I wanted Henry to work with me. At the time, I was a consultant with a Fortune 500 company, and I asked them for a $50,000 grant to study psychic diagnosis. They gave it with the caveat that I must never mention their name in association with the study! I had a ball! Going on word-of-mouth referrals, I visited a total of seventy-five "psychics" around the country. They were given only a photograph of patients with name and birth date. I had designed a form that could, at best, give a 10 percent chance of making a correct diagnosis by chance. Most of the psychics were 50 percent accurate—five times chance and highly statistically significant!

Five of those I studied were 70 to 75 percent accurate; truly amazing. Incidentally, physicians are said to be 80 percent accurate with an initial history and physical exam of the patient. The results were published in the *A.R.E. Journal*, (Shealy, C.N. "Perspectives on psychic diagnosis." *A.R.E. Journal*, September 1976; 11, pp. 208–217), which may be read in Appendix A.

Among the notable intuitives I studied was Jack Schwartz, who was 75 percent accurate and who told me that I was trying to cram seven lives into this one. He also introduced me to photostimulation with his I.S.I.S. I was intrigued enough to purchase twelve of his units and have an electronics person change them from flashing alternatively into right and left eye to flashing them simultaneously into both eyes, to enhance relaxation. Eventually, this led to my later devices, The Shealy RelaxMate I and II, and my first patent. Incidentally, Medtronic told me my ideas for DCS and TENS were not patentable, and in my naïve early days, I believed them! They actually patented both devices. I now patent all my discoveries and currently have applied for number 12. Incidentally, *all* of my inventions are related to my own medical intuition. More on that later!

By April 1973, I wanted Henry Rucker to become a counselor at my clinic at St. Francis Hospital. The problems—he was black, had no college degree (two years at a junior college), and had created his own metaphysical church, something like, The Holy Essence of the Wisdom of the Light of Hermes! I said, "It won't fly, Henry." By this time, I had become quite acquainted with Unity, Religious Science, and Science of Mind and learned that all Science of Mind churches are independent.

So Henry and I formed the Science of Mind Church of Chicago. Philosophically, we were totally compatible with Ernest Holmes' philosophy. I was ordained. I figured that I was so far out on a twig that if my physician colleagues objected to my research, I could truthfully say it was part of my religion. Henry was immediately accepted as a pastoral counselor in my clinic at St. Francis! Many of the nuns and physicians consulted him. And, of course, the creation of the church was a remarkable intuitive (synchronistic) foresight, as it became the foundation for our school, Holos University Graduate Seminary.

Henry was the best one–on–one counselor I have ever known. Although he was 70 to 75 percent accurate in making a medical diagnosis, his forte was counseling. The son of our congregational minister had had severe drug and behavioral problems for years. One hour with Henry and that young man came out saying, "Why didn't anyone talk to me like that before." He has been free of drugs and behavioral problems for the subsequent thirty–six years! Henry was also a healer. One of the most striking situations was a six–year–old whose skull fracture had not healed in over a year. One session with Henry and the fracture healed rapidly. Later, we demonstrated that his healing could raise DHEA (dehydroepiandrosterone) with a single session. Henry worked with us until his retirement. He was a friend and confidant throughout the rest of his life. My children looked upon him as a major friend and counselor. He died at age eighty–four.

In January 1974 I was told by a friend that I should meet Dr. Robert Leichtman, a board–certified internist, who was quite psychic—by far the best of all those I studied initially and who will be discussed in a later chapter about the best Medical Intuitives. Suffice it for now to say that he was 80 percent accurate in physical diagnoses and 96 percent accurate in evaluating the psychological status of patients. Bob has also become a lifelong friend and advisor.

In 1974, I also entered my Ph.D. in psychology (which I completed in 1977) at the Humanistic Psychology Institute. It was one of the great learning experiences of my life. I focused on creating what I call the software of biofeedback, Biogenics. My first major public book, *90 Days to Self-Health*, based upon my dissertation, was published the week I passed my defense of dissertation.

Bob Leichtman and Henry became for many years my major consultants when I had a problem with making a diagnosis or "getting through" to patients. Bob remains so today. Meanwhile, in May 1978, I was responsible for founding The American Holistic Medical Association. The major reason for this was my hope that spirituality would become a major factor in medicine. And, to me, medical intuition, intuition, synchronicity, and reincarnation are essential elements in the broad field of spirituality.

In April 1984, at the "Council Grove Meeting," I met Caroline Myss, who introduced herself as "one of those," when I had been discussing psychic diagnosis. I asked her how good she was, and of course she did not know. A few months later, I began calling her and eventually I demonstrated that she was 93 percent accurate in making a diagnosis physically or psychologically. We have worked together since that time, doing workshops all over this country, Canada, and Europe. In 1998 we began collaboration on *The Creation of Health*. In writing that book, I decided that we should not use the terms *clairvoyant* and *psychic* and we created the term *Medical Intuitive*. Although the concept had existed at least since the 1830s, this was the first known use of the term. So the birth of Medical Intuitive was officially in the fall of 1988. Since that birth, the term has become extremely popular.

Unfortunately, it has been all too popular. At one time there were 1,200,000 listings for Medical Intuitive on Google. At least 99.99 percent of those listed have had little or no training or documentation. Many have written to me but with evaluation have been *zero* accurate. Other sociopaths who claim to be Medical Intuitives have told me that I had leukemia (1988) and lots of other inaccurate garbage. Indeed, I consider this type of nonsense *intuitive malpractice!*

The main reason I am writing this book is to document the great benefit of accurate medical intuition! It is a field of great importance, which deserves qualified and competent Medical Intuitives. But first, we need to lay the foundation for the broad field of intuition.

2

INTUITION AS THE FOUNDATION
OF CREATIVITY, SCIENCE, AND HEALTH

On January 8, 1990, Buck Charlson wrote:

> Intuition is an innate capability, specific for each individual serving
> as a guide, counselor and informer. It is an abstract quality of mind,
> programmed with a higher level of consciousness. It is a segment of
> a Universal Mind from which all knowing and physical manifesta-
> tions are derived. Each and all of our bodily cells and systems re-
> spond to this direction. It possesses an intelligence we use
> intuitively and this may be expanded if we sense and believe in it.
> Training for this capability is needed, just as is necessary for all
> exercises.

Buck Charlson is the creative genius who discovered hydraulic brakes,
hydraulic steering, and held eighty–eight patents in the field of hydraulics. He had a high school diploma, no college, and yet discovered great
principles of physics, which had eluded some of the most famous academic individuals.

A couple of decades ago, the *International Tribune* had an interesting
editorial on creativity and vision. At that time, two of the great giant

corporations were floundering, and the editorial emphasized that it was because of lack of creativity and vision on the part of the leaders. I realized then that all creativity and vision are really the result of intuition. Art, music, poetry, every scientific discovery, and even the Industrial Revolution are all the result of intuitive knowledge put into play. There are numerous stories of famous individuals who have had unusual relations with their creativity. Schubert is said to have slept with his glasses on and a candle lighted by his bed so that he could awaken from a dream and quickly write down a new musical score that he had dreamt. With that *International Tribune* editorial and having worked with Caroline Myss for several years, I felt the time had come to evaluate how easy it is to "teach" intuition. Unfortunately, there is no known psychometric test that measures intuition itself, but there are several that measure creativity. So I taught a class at Drury University in Springfield, Missouri. The course attracted some two dozen students and was carried out over a full semester. At the beginning of the semester, each individual was tested with the Agor AIM survey, Alternate Uses Form C, Christensen–Guilford Fluency Test, Ideational Fluency, Association Fluency, Expressional Fluency, Guilford's Consequences Forms A1 and A2, Myers–Briggs Type Indicator, and the Stanford Hypnotic Susceptibility Scale. Actually, the Ideational Fluency Scale gave the best results of all, with 70 percent of the students having an increase on that particular test. The Taggart Management Style Inventory also showed that 70 percent of the students had an increase. During the course of the semester, we concentrated on the following:
- Deep relaxation training
- Creative guided imagery
- Brain synchronization techniques
- Self-hypnosis
- Music
- Guided intuitive testing

Midsemester we "tested" the students with experiential intuitive ability such as sensing the major illnesses in a given individual, and sending and receiving certain thoughts, words, or ideas from one person to another, and so on.
- Creative imagery, symbology and affirmation

The results of the semester were quite striking, with significant improvement in most of the students on at least several of the creativity tests. Following that, Caroline and I began our series of workshops, Vision, Creativity, and Intuition. Our initial enrollment was eighty-four students, and we had a plan of a four-year program with two long, weekend courses each year. Essentially, in its broadest form, Caroline and I alternated our input with Caroline giving her very broad view of the Human Energy System, Archetypes, and so on, which have been integrated into her book. I revised the "Medical Intuition, Intuitive Intuition Diagnostic Check" sheet and each month, the students were sent names of six individuals, generally with only one significant medical problem, or people who were healthy. It was obvious that the vast majority of the students would not practice. They did not send in their monthly reports, and they only wanted to come to the classes. Halfway through the program, it was therefore obviously clear that most students would not become Medical Intuitives but would develop significant skills as counselors. So we created the term "Counseling Intuitive" at that point.

Over the four-year period, the class gradually dwindled to thirty-seven individuals. At the end of that time, out of twenty-one who took the "Counseling Intuitive Exam," only six took the "Medical Intuition Exam," in which they were to give a true medical diagnosis on forty individuals, presented over five days, or to conduct a personal counseling intuitive session with a client provided by us. The session was observed by a member of the Board of the American Board of Scientific Medical Intuition, which Caroline and I had formed during the course of this four-year course in order to certify competent individuals. None of the students passed the "Medical Intuition Exam" with a 75 percent accuracy rate, which would have been required for certification, but all of them were quite competent and were certified as Counseling Intuitives.

I remain convinced that individuals can enhance their medical intuitive ability, but it takes great practice unless one somehow is born the rare genius to whom this comes spontaneously. Many can learn to play Chopin's music, but it is only the rare genius of a Chopin who can create it.

I have no idea whether I could pass the Medical Intuitive Exam, be-cause I am not the least bit interested in being a medical intuitive. My own medical training and certainly my clinical skill provide me with the ability to make a diagnosis at least 99 percent of the time. On the other hand, getting across to an individual patient what the problem is and what the underlying psychological, emotional, and spiritual prob-lems are, is often a challenge. I would like to relate just a couple of cases in which I have used Caroline Myss or Bob Leichtman to assist me.

A mid-forties-aged woman who was overweight and diabetic pre-sented with pain in her throat. She actually had total numbness on the right side of her throat with no gag response whatsoever. This is one of the complications of diabetes, a neuropathy of a cranial nerve in this particular case. With her permission and with the patient sitting in the room but not listening to what I was saying on the phone, I called Caroline. Caroline stated, and this was the first time she had ever men-tioned a past life, "I see this being related to a past life. She died with a blunt object across her throat. Do a past-life therapy session on her." So without telling the patient anything other than that Caroline had rec-ommended a past-life therapy session, I did the session. She gave me a vision of seeing herself as a teenage Polynesian girl who was kidnapped by pirates. She was in the bottom of a ship when the pirates were at-tacked by another pirate ship. The ship began to sink, and as it did, a beam came lose and struck her across her throat, killing her in that way. Following the session, the patient admitted to me that she had had a serious concern that her husband was sexually molesting their two sons. She divorced her husband and both her pain and the numbness in her throat disappeared completely. By medical standards, that is a miracle.

On another occasion, a woman came in wanting me to help her with her problem of excessive and prolonged menstrual bleeding. I did a complete workup and history, and at her request, called Caroline. Caroline asked, "What did she tell you about her two abortions?" The patient had never mentioned the two abortions, and when I asked her about that, she got up and ran out of the room and was not interested in any further therapy. Denial is not a river in Africa!

On an earlier occasion, I was working with a fifty-year-old man who had severe, chronic, low back pain. Physically, he had had surgery on his lower back at the fourth and fifth lumbar discs, which was where, along with the upper sacrum, he experienced pain. Theoretically and medically, the pain should have come from the facet joints on either side, between L4 and L5. But, when I needled those areas, it did not reproduce his pain. I called Bob Leichtman, and he said, "I think you ought to try at L2." When I put the needles onto the facets at L2-3, the patient said, "That's it, Doc," and I was then able to relieve his pain by numbing those two joints.

Finally, and perhaps this is one of the most striking cases that I treated, was a man in his early sixties who was exquisitely depressed. He had some pain but depression was much more of a problem than the pain. His history was that he had been driving along an interstate highway, came up over a hill, and ran into a car that was actually parked across his path. The man in the car was already dead, having hit five head of cattle before my patient arrived there; and although the police and coroner determined that the man in the car had been dead before my patient hit that car, he had extreme guilt. I tried everything in my power to help him out of his depression, with no success. So, I called Caroline, again with the patient present, as I have always done, and she said, "If he does not come out of this funk within a year, he will have bowel cancer." That was in July. He had no symptoms, but in November of that year, he was operated on for cancer of the bowel. He recovered. He was still depressed the following February, and I called Caroline again. She said, "If he does not come out of his depression, he will die in August." After my discussion with Caroline, I told him exactly what she said. I shook him and told him that he was going to be sitting next to a widow if he didn't come out of it and did not respond any more than he had to everything else we had done. August of that year came, and the patient was admitted to the hospital with a pulmonary embolus, a blood clot from the legs to the chest, but he did not die. One year later, on August 31, he died. I had not asked her *which* August!

These are striking examples of excellent intuitive medical diagnoses. I would like to discuss my own major intuitive ability, which I think is creating scientific solutions to various health problems. In the late 1970s, I was invited to drive from La Crosse up to Minneapolis to discuss consciousness with Buck Charlson, the wonderful genius of hydraulics, with which we began this chapter. Once a month I would drive up for a long afternoon of discussions about the broad field of consciousness. In 1982, when I moved form La Crosse to Springfield, those visits ceased, but in 1987, Buck wrote a letter, stating, "If you would do a study to determine whether crystals could be helpful in healing, I will fund it." I spent almost a year and one half wondering how to study crystals, and then, with sudden intuitive insight, it was obvious: quartz crystals are piezo-electric. *Piezoelectric* means that when you put physical pressure on a substance, it responds with an electrical current. Quartz crystal is one of the premier piezoelectric materials, but our skeleton, muscles, tendons, and even intestines are also highly piezoelectric. I reasoned that if we gave individuals a programmed quartz crystal, it would help keep them out of depression. We already knew by that time that one of my earlier intuitive hits would treat depression with great success.

In 1975, I discovered that one of the electrical stimulators, called the Pain Suppressor, developed by Saul Liss, created a sense of a visual flicker when applied transcranially. We did studies on it and demonstrated that this stimulus significantly raised both serotonin and endorphins. At the same time, we were using photostimulation to help such patients relax, and we found that in more than thirty thousand patients, when we combined the Liss stimulator transcranially and the photostimulation (which later became the Shealy RelaxMate), we could get 85 percent of patients out of depression successfully within two weeks without drugs. So, we put the patients through our typical treatment for depression, daily stimulation with the Liss stimulator, and education of the various aspects of stress management, and so on. At the end of the two weeks, at least 80 percent of the patients were out of depression. On the last day, in a double-blind study, they were given either a quartz crystal or a glass crystal. They programmed the crystal by passing it through a flame, to get rid of any stored energy, and then blowing into the crystal three times while imagining their ideal of being free of depression. They also used a short healing phrase, not more than six words, which we had worked with them on during the two-week program. They went home with no further therapy. At the end of three months, they came back. Seventy percent of those who had quartz crystals, but only 28 percent of those who had glass crystals, were still out of depression. That is statistically significant at the 0.001 level. Over the next ten years, Buck continued to fund research projects that grew out of that particular one and led to my discovering that 90 percent of individuals are deficient in magnesium; initially we gave everyone intravenous magnesium. Much later, I discovered through my own intuition that magnesium chloride is absorbed through the skin better than it is orally. We discovered that virtually all depressed people are deficient in 1 to 7 essential amino acids and 86 percent are deficient in taurine— one of the most important amino acids— which works synergistically with magnesium to maintain the electrical charge on cells.

In the early 90s, I was told by a guide with whom I had verbal communication that "within five years you will have tools to regrow an eye, a limb, or the spinal cord." Now, you know you are crazy when you get that kind of message! Shortly thereafter, I was invited to go to Kiev in the Ukraine to study microwave resonance therapy, which they had been using since 1982, treating more than 200,000 patients with a wide variety of disorders. They stated that they had "discovered" that human DNA resonates at 54 to 78 billion cycles/second, or Giga Hertz (GHz). I was trained in their technology, but they wanted $700,000 for fourteen of the devices to bring back to the United States. When I got home, I called my friend Saul Liss, an engineer, and asked him how to produce giga frequencies. He said that all you have to do is pass a high voltage through a spark gap. Here again is how intuition works. In that instant, I suddenly recalled the work of Georges Lakhovsky, which I had read back in the 70s. At least twenty years earlier, I had had his book *The Secret of Life* (published originally in this country in 1935). I looked it up and saw the Lakhovsky multiwave oscillator, which consisted of two coils of coiled copper tubing, placed three feet apart, looking like a maze. He attached to that a Tesla Coil and treated more than three hundred patients between 1939 and 1942. He reported great success in curing cancer and other illnesses. He was killed in 1942 and the work had never been restarted.

Shortly after that, while I was in Holland doing a couple of workshops, I was out jogging and suddenly had an image of a copper pyramid above a small copper room. The next night my guide came and said, "Where do you think that image you got yesterday came from?" I replied that I thought it was mine. The guide replied, "I put it there." When I got home, I got permission from our Institutional Review Board to treat seventy-five patients in a small room that I had constructed with copper on the lower walls and a copper pyramid above, with quartz and amethyst at the top of the pyramid. Then the copper pyramid was activated by a Tesla Coil attached to the copper tubing. We treated seventy-five patients; twenty-five each with chronic back pain, rheumatoid arthritis, or depression—all of which had failed conventional therapy. We had them sit in the pyramid for one hour, five days a week, for two weeks. At the end of that time, 70 percent of them were remarkably improved; but my thinking at that point was, well, this is all great, but we would never get this approved by the FDA! Coupling this with my information from the Ukraine, I set about constructing a modern, solid-state electrical stimulator to reproduce the output of one of the first electrical stimulators in this country, the Electreat, patented in 1919. It turned out that it was not only very successful in treating pain but also in producing human DNA frequencies of 54 to 78 GHz, the exact same frequency and intensity as the devices from the Ukraine—50 to 78 decibels. The copper room and pyramid produced exactly those same frequencies when a Tesla Coil was turned on.

Eventually, with the help of several individuals, we were able to develop the Shealy Pain Pro. While I was working on that over a period of five years, my guide gave me five specific electrical circuits in the human body. Actually, the beginning of this goes back to another earlier intuitive hit. In the early 90s, I had become quite interested in DHEA, or dehydroepiandrosterone. It is the most important hormone in the body and the most prominent, in terms of concentration, and one which decreases from age twenty-five on. The average eighty-year-old has less than 10 percent of the average twenty-year-old. My intuition said that if we would use natural progesterone cream, it would raise DHEA. We did the experiment in seven men initially, and it raised DHEA from 60 to 100 percent. But if you start with only 100 nanograms/deciliter and you need 750 or more in a man to be optimal, doubling doesn't do a great deal. One day I sat down and asked the question, What else can I do to raise DHEA? My guide said, "If you stimulate the acupuncture points that connect the kidneys with the gonads, with the thyroid, adrenals, and the pituitary, through a Window of the Sky acupuncture point, it will raise DHEA." Having practiced acupuncture since 1967, I knew a great deal of the meaning of what I was told. Kidneys, in Chinese cosmology, are the area where you concentrate your ancestral "chi," or energy. My response was that there was no acupuncture point for the pituitary. The guide said, "Find one." So I got out my acupuncture atlas and chose Governing Vessel 20 to activate the pineal because it directly overlies the pineal gland, which then controls the pituitary. The points I chose were Kidney 3, bilaterally; Conception Vessels 2, 6, and 18; Master of the Heart 6, bilaterally; Large Intestine 18, bilaterally; and Governing Vessel 20. I asked the guide whether these were right, and he said, "Try it." We did our initial experiments and found that, over a three-month period, with stimulation of these points, three minutes per pair of points daily, DHEA was raised an average of 60 percent with some individuals, getting an increase of up to 100 percent.

Shortly after that, I began to receive from the guide more descriptions of circuits, including the Ring of Air, which he said would stimulate simultaneity of thought or holographic thinking (which I consider intuition). Next came the Ring of Water, which he said would open the crystological heart, or help balance emotions. Next came the Ring of Earth, which he said would recreate the physical body; and finally, the Ring of Crystal, which I was told would lead to actual regeneration. Now I was not told the names of the points to use—I had to develop those points based upon general physical sites that the guide mentioned, and I was given no further information about the chemistry involved. That required work and intuition on my part.

We found that the Ring of Air strikingly increases neurotensin, a brain-produced neurochemical that is a neuroleptic. That means that it really allows one to detach from the body and feel somewhat spacey but very alert. The Ring of Water significantly normalizes aldosterone, the adrenal hormone that controls water and potassium metabolism. The Ring of Earth controls or raises calcitonin up to several hundred percent. Calcitonin is a thyroid hormone that is essential for depositing calcium in bone. And, finally, the Ring of Crystal, stimulated three days in a row with the Shealy Pain Pro, reduces free radicals an average of 85 percent. This led to my writing the book *Life Beyond 100*, because I felt that if, when I had completed the work on the five circuits, individuals could restore their DHEA and calcitonin and keep free radicals low, the average person with good habits could live an average of 140 years. And I still believe that to be true, but when I started presenting this to the public, I learned that most people do not want to live to be 100, let alone 140; and they would not take the twenty minutes or so a day necessary to stimulate even one of the Rings.

In January 2007, I awoke at 4 a.m. with an image of the old copper pyramid on top of a copper wall. I knew this was a message from my guide that I had not completed the work on that approach, so we reconstructed the pyramid without the walls and just put a copper mat under the pyramid. We began to measure telomeres, which are the end of the DNA. Telomeres are key to both health and longevity. They ordinarily shrink by one percent every year of life, starting at birth, and those with bad habits have them shrink much faster. We had six individuals who agreed to participate in the project and use the pyramid with a Tesla Coil for a minimum of thirty minutes, five days a week. At the end of three months, we found that their telomeres had regrown by one percent. That was very exciting, but as I began talking with individuals about it, most people didn't want a pyramid in their house. I then intuitively felt that the only alternative was to create the giga frequencies needed in a mat that could go on top of a mattress so that the whole process could take place while you were sleeping. We created this mat and named it the RejuvaMatrix®, as I had already been calling the copper pyramid that. The six individuals then used the mats instead of the pyramid over the next seven months. At that time, telomeres had grown 2.5 percent, which would have averaged a bit over 3 percent in a year, and I was very excited. We now have some fifty individuals involved in a five-year study of telomere regrowth. To date the RM is leading to an average of 2.6 percent regrowth of telomeres per year.

I have gone through my own process of intuition in some detail because I think each individual has his or her own unique ability. If you "listen," you are aware of symbols and messages that come spontaneously or in dreams; then vision (images) becomes creativity, which is the fruit of intuition. Every individual has the ability to strengthen creativity by observing, using, and honoring intuition.

BIBLIOGRAPHY

1. Agor, W. "Intuition as a brain skill in management." *Public Personnel Management Journal*, 1985; 14(1):15–24.

2. _____. "Test your intuitive powers: AIM survey. Test Your Intuitive Ability." El Paso, TX: ENFP Enterprises, 1989: 133–144.

3. Briggs, K.C., and I.B. Myers. *Myers-Briggs Type Indicator, Form G.* Palo Alto, CA: Consulting Psychologists Press, 1976.

4. Carlson, R., and J. Williams. "Studies of Jungian Typology: III Personality and Marriage." *Journal of Personality Assessment*, 1984; 48(1):87–94.

5. Cayce E. "A new look at the Edgar Cayce Readings." *Intuition, Visions, and Dreams*, 1987; 2(6).

6. Chinen, A.B., A.M. Spielvogel, and D. Farrel. "The experience of intuition." *Psychological Perspectives*, 1985; 16(2): 186–197.

7. Coman-Johnson, C. "Intuition: A bona fide occupational requirement in the management consulting profession?" *Consultation*, 1985; Fall: 189–198.

8. Foster, D. "EEG and subjective correlates of alpha frequency binaural beats stimulation combined with alpha biofeedback." Dissertation presented to the Faculty of the Graduate School of Memphis State University, 1989.

9. Goldsmith, R. "Sensation seeking and the sensing–intuition scale of the Myers–Briggs Type Indicator." *Psychological Reports*, 1985: 581–582.

10. Fallick, B. and J. Eliot. "Relation between intuition and college majors." *Perceptual and Motor Skills*, 1986: 63:328.

11. Goldstein, M., D. Scholthauer, and B.H. Kleiner. "Management on the right side of the brain." *Personnel Journal*, 1985: 40–45.

12. Guilford, J.P., J.S. Guilford, P.R. Christensen, and P.R. Merrifield. *Forms A-1 and A-2.* Palo Alto, CA: Consulting Psychologists Press, 1958.

13. Guilford, J.P., J.S. Guilford, and P.R. Christensen. *Christensen-Guilford Fluency Tests: Word Fluency, Ideational Fluency, Associational Fluency Forms A & B, Expressional Fluency.* Palo Alto, CA: Consulting Psychologists Press, 1958.

14. Guilford, J.P., P.R. Christensen, P.R. Merrifield, and R.C. Wilson. *Alter-*

nate Uses, Forms B & C. Palo Alto, CA: Consulting Psychologists Press, 1960.

15. Hanson, J.R., H.F. Silver, and R. Strong. "Research on the roles of intuition and feeling." *Roeper Review*, 1984: 167–170.

16. Havens, L.L., and H.L. Palmer. "Forms, difficulties and tests of empathy." *Hillside Journal of Clinical Psychiatry*, 1984; 6(2): 285–291.

17. Hill, O.W. "Intuition: Inferential heuristic or epistemic mode?" *Imagination, Cognition and Personality, 1987-88*; 7(2): 137–154.

18. Hummel, R.P. "Intuition and the public manager." Book review of Weston Agor's *Intuition in Organizations: Leading and Managing Productivity*. Public Administration Review, 1990; July/August: 458–460.

19. Kaiser, M.K., D.R. Proffit, and M. McCloskey. "Development of intuitive theories of motion: Curvilinear motion in the absence of external forces." *Developmental Psychology*, 1966; 22(1):67–71.

20. Kieren, T.E., and T.O. Alton. "Imagination, intuition and computing in school algebra." *Mathematics Teacher*, 1989 (January): 14–17.

21. Raina, M.K., and A. Vats. "Style of learning and thinking (hemisphericity), openness to inner experience, sex and subject choice." *Psychological Studies*, 1983; 28(2): 85–89.

22. Norris, C.J, and C.M. Achilles. "Intuition leadership: A new dimension for education leadership." *Planning and Changing*, 1988; 19(2): 108–117.

23. O'Regan, P.J. "Intuition and logic." *Mathematics Teacher*, 1988; (November): 664–668.

24. Rew, L. "Intuition: A concept analysis of a group phenomenon." *Advances in Nursing Science*, 1986; 8(2): 21–28.

25. Schultz, H.S. and B. Leonard. "Probability and intuition." *Mathematics Teacher*, 1989; January: 52–53.

26. Weitzenhoffer, A.M., and E.R. Hilgard. *Stanford Hypnotic Susceptibility Scale, Forms A & B*. Palo Alto, CA: Consulting Psychology Press, 1959.

27. Nadel, L., J. Haims, and R. Stempson. *Sixth Sense: The Whole Brain Book of Intuition, Hunches, Gut Feelings and Their Place in Your Everyday Life*. NY: Prentice-Hall, 1990.

28. Westman, A.S., and F.M. Canter. "Diurnal changes on the Myers–Briggs Type Indicator: A pilot study." *Psychological Reports*, 1984; 54: 431–434.

29. Witkin, S. "Cognitive processes in clinical practice." *Social Work*, 1982; September: 389–395.

30. Page, I.H. "Science, intuition and medical practice." *Post Graduate Medicine*, 1978; 64(5): 217–221.

3

EDGAR CAYCE—
THE GREATEST MEDICAL INTUITIVE

The first major book on the abilities of Edgar Cayce was written in 1931, *There is a River* by Thomas Sugrue, originally copyrighted in 1942 by Ault, Rinehart, and Winston. My own copy is the 50th Anniversary Issue printed in 1981. Sugrue actually first met Edgar Cayce in 1927 and spent the summers of 1929, 1930, and 1931 interviewing Cayce every day and examining materials from the files. But the story that is so appropriate, even today, is that told in chapter one of a stranger appearing in Hopkinsville, Kentucky, in January 1912. A professor from Harvard, Dr. Hugo Munsterberg was arrogant and insulting, despite his impressive M.D. and Ph.D. degrees! At that time, for the previous year there had been stories appearing in news media about "Edgar Cayce— Psychic Diagnostician." Edgar Cayce's mother-in-law was quoted as saying, "Well, you've got to expect that sort of thing from Yankees. They don't know any better, poor souls." Fortunately, during the time that the arrogant Munsterberg was visiting Cayce, Dr. Ketchum, the first licensed physician to work with Cayce, also came in for one of the "readings." It appears that watching the effect of that one reading actually noticeably changed Munsterberg. Nevertheless, Dr. Ketchum was received even less graciously by his fellow physicians.

Dr. Wesley H. Ketchum was a homeopathic physician. He was an

M.D. but his specialty was homeopathy. At the time, homeopaths were generally at least reasonably well accepted in this country, but not by other physicians! Interestingly, at the time Ketchum first visited Edgar Cayce, Ketchum himself thought he had appendicitis and his physicians thought so. Cayce, on the other hand, recommended a spinal adjustment by an osteopath. In fact, Ketchum's original impression was that Cayce was a fake; however, he went to the osteopath that Cayce had recommended. After the osteopathic treatment, Ketchum is quoted as saying to Edgar, "You are not a fake. I have just been a damned fool." Ketchum went on to report on some of his excellent patient results and even had a paper of his presented in Boston at the American Society for Clinical Research.

Shortly after that, Gertrude Cayce, Edgar's wife, became very ill with tuberculosis. Physicians had given up "hope" and Cayce recommended heroin, which other M.D.s would not prescribe, but Dr. Ketchum wrote the prescription and, perhaps most importantly, Cayce recommended inhaling the fumes of apple brandy placed in a charred keg. And, of course, although it was almost miraculous, Gertrude truly recovered from a disease that should have led to her death.

During his entire career, which lasted until 1945 at the time of his death, Cayce delivered more than fourteen thousand readings, of which more than nine thousand were related to the treatment of diseases or related to health itself.

Of significant interest is that Cayce helped Dr. Ketchum treat a patient who had severe malnutrition from "too much hominy and grits." Cayce's recommendation of a well-balanced diet with plenty of green vegetables worked beautifully. This was well before we knew about B vitamins! Numerous cases with individual details are well described in both *There is a River* and another of the bestselling books about Cayce, *Edgar Cayce –The Sleeping Prophet* by Jess Stearn. Among the scores of books about Cayce, another of the most interesting is *The Outer Limits of Edgar Cayce's Power* by Edgar Evans Cayce and Hugh Lynn Cayce, Harper and Row 1971. More than nine thousand medically related readings were done for more than five thousand people. Some individuals had more than one reading (more than 50,000 pages and about 200,000 different topics covered).

In a small survey for their book, the authors report that, out of seventy-six readings for which they could find outcomes, 14.8 percent were negative and 65, or 85.5 percent, were positive. They stated, "Assuming that the ratio of positive to negative results remains the same in the cases not reported and applying the random survey to the 14,246 readings on file, Cayce's accuracy of 85 percent compares favorably to that of modern physicians." Interestingly, there have been studies showing that the average physician, with a patient's history and physical exam, is about 80 percent accurate!

Shortly after returning from my 1972 visit to the A.R.E., one of our Appaloosa horses had a severe cut around the entire foot just above the hoof. At the time, it was winter and the veterinarian felt that the horse should be put down because it would be impossible to heal. I suggested instead that we should use a castor oil pack. To make a long story short, the horse recovered totally and our veterinarian, thereafter, was likely to recommend castor oil packs in such situations! In the ensuing thirty-seven years, I have recommended castor oil packs numerous times, and in the 1980s, a study was done at George Washington University on the effectiveness of castor oil packs on the abdomen in healthy people. Application of a castor oil pack to the abdomen for one hour yielded statistically significant results with a very objective test of immune function. To me, if Cayce had recommended nothing else in his entire career, his contribution of castor oil packs is one of his greatest and most useful "discoveries."

The late Dr. William McGarey of the A.R.E. Clinic in Phoenix has written extensively on the clinical results of castor oil packs. These include the following:

• Five drops of castor oil orally each morning to control allergies.

• Puncture wounds, cuts, and bruises heal rapidly when rubbed with castor oil.

• Prevention of pregnancy stretch marks when abdomens are rubbed with castor oil during the last two months of pregnancy.

• Rapid healing of a sprained ankle rubbed overnight in castor oil.

• Marked reduction in tinnitus and hearing loss by applying castor oil drops in the ears.

• Rapid healing of hepatitis using daily castor oil packs.

- Clearing of cataracts using one drop of castor oil in each eye at bedtime (use U.S.P. castor oil).
- Healing of a pilonidal cyst after use of castor oil packs.
- Clearing of brown skin aging spots using castor oil plus baking soda.
- Relief of severe eye allergies by rubbing eyelids with castor oil at bedtime.
- Relief of low back pain with one week's application of castor oil packs.
- Relief of chronic diarrhea using abdominal castor oil packs.
- Clearing of vocal cord nodes in horses, using castor oil packs applied daily on the neck for three months.
- Complete clearing of tinnitus with six-eight drops of castor oil orally each day for 4 weeks.
- Clearing of hyperactivity using castor oil packs.
- Removal of a wart after four weeks of application of castor oil.
- Resolution of a calcium deposit from the sole of the foot using daily castor oil massage.
- Clearing of skin cancer using castor oil plus baking soda.
- Clearing of snoring after two weeks of abdominal castor oil packs.
- Improvement of a bee sting by application of castor oil.
- Increased hair growth through daily scalp massage with castor oil 20 minutes before shampooing.
- Clearing of nail fungus after four months of castor oil packs on the nail.

All of these can be found at: http://www.edgarcayce.org/th4/tharchive/therapies/castor1/html.

These have been my own experiences:

- Marked reduction of swelling of the knee in a number of patients who wrapped the knee in a castor oil cloth overnight.
- Excellent and rapid relief of acute abdominal pain with acute intestinal flu.
- Healing of deep wounds on the pastern of horses.
- Rapid recovery from viral infections with a 30-minute soak in the bathtub in hot water, using one cup castor oil, or applying castor oil over the entire body after a shower and then putting on an old sweat

suit or winter long johns underwear, top and bottom. The castor oil bath or suit is clearly the most effective and rapid approach for treating acute flu.

• Clearing of early cataracts with the use of one drop of castor oil in the eye at bedtime.

• Rapid recovery from a cold or flu by taking a castor oil bath or using a castor oil suit.

Cayce recommended white wool flannel, but even old cotton flannel works well. Or, in a pinch while traveling, I have used just facial tissues and castor oil. The entire abdomen should be covered, especially over the liver (or around a joint or neck), and cover this with plastic. The abdomen is best wrapped using plastic wrap around the body to absorb any leaking castor oil. Cover the area with a towel, and use a warm heating pad for 1 hour, or leave on overnight without the heating pad.

A castor oil bath consists of putting a cup of castor oil into a bathtub with adequate, comfortably hot water and soaking for thirty minutes. If you choose to do a castor oil bath, *please* be sure to let all the water out of the tub and wash off carefully with a cheap shampoo, rinse off, wash off a second time with the shampoo, and rinse yourself and the tub very thoroughly before getting out of the tub!

For a castor oil suit, after a bath or shower, rub castor oil over the entire body from neck to ankles. Put on an old sweat suit or pair of long johns and sleep in it overnight.

All of the medical advice given by Cayce might be considered by many to be anecdotal. There have been numerous uses of many of the approaches. It is also worthwhile mentioning that in certain situations, Cayce specifically stated that his recommendations would be useful for "this body," meaning that this was not the case for everyone. One such example, which became very popular, was the statement that eating three almonds a day would prevent cancer. But this was said to only two people, and in both cases, this recommendation was specifically said "for this body." Not that three almonds would harm anyone else, but it is important not to generalize unless Cayce did!

In addition to these fairly widely known aspects of castor oil, individuals have sent the following reports to me:

• One individual reported that she had such severe pain during her menstrual cycle that physicians investigated. During a laparoscopic exam they discovered that she had adhesions between her fallopian tube, uterus, and intestine. She used castor oil packs for six weeks. The pain went away and has never returned in sixteen years.

• An ankle sprain with great swelling and discoloration was cured within a week of using castor oil packs.

• One individual noted that castor oil mixed with baking soda and applied to a mole leads to their shrinking and disappearing.

• Castor oil plus baking soda not only removes moles but also removes age spots.

• Castor oil rubbed on a neuroma in the foot cured the pain.

• One individual reported that, in three generations of his family, castor oil had been very helpful for knee arthritis.

• A Reiki master reported that massaging castor oil into irritated varicose veins helped them virtually disappear.

• Castor oil packs relieved symptoms of gall bladder disease.

• Another individual reported that a mole disappeared within five nights with just the application of castor oil.

• Castor oil packs for acute low back pain have been reported as useful.

• Application of a castor oil pack to someone with scleroderma led to a total cure.

• Wounds to the abdomen left behind a blood clot, and the patient was told that the wound would have to be drained surgically if it did not heal within a month. Castor oil packs led to total resolution.

• Although I have not had cataracts, I have recommended one drop of castor oil in each eye at bedtime and had numerous individuals report that their cataracts had disappeared.

• "My husband has had great relief from the castor oil packs. He used to end up at the hospital with his severe pain in the abdominal area from complications with adhesions, etc. Now when he feels the pain coming on, we apply the castor oil packs. He no longer has to go on the painkillers or have the tube put down his nose to relieve the pressure on his stomach."

And, of course, there are many other reports of benefits from the Cayce readings. The following are some that I have received from individuals:

• An individual used the Wet Cell appliance recommended by Cayce. Twenty-one years later, her electromyographic studies revealed that her nerves were better than they were twenty-one years ago. She had a hereditary nerve degenerative disease.

• Another individual reported using yellow saffron and slippery elm tea for serious skin problems. Incidentally, Cayce also recommended this for stomach ulcers and any indigestion problems.

• IPSAB toothpowder cured diseased gums.

• IPSAB cured severe tooth sensitivity.

• "The moment I have an inkling of a cold coming on, I drink grape juice, eat raw vegetables, lots of salads, and stay away from acid-producing foods. The virus does not seem to take hold when I do that."

• Another individual reported hearing a voice say, "Be still and know who is here." She knew that it was Edgar Cayce. She was instructed to apply cold compresses to the left wrist when she had had trauma to her head, causing an energy block in the left hand. After three nights of applying the cold compresses, energy went up the left arm and "left," and she has been healed for many years.

• Dramatic cures from tendonitis have been reported with the application of iodized salt, vinegar, and heat.

• "In the summer of 1991, I developed multiple sclerosis, a chronic disease of the brain and spinal cord that can gradually result in total debility. My symptoms manifested in a relapsing/remitting pattern, and included numbness, blurred vision, difficulty swallowing, tremors, muscle spasms, depression, fatigue, failing memory, slurred speech, and bladder dysfunction.

"In the fall of 1991, I began using an alternative treatment suggested by Edgar Cayce. It involved dietary measures, massage, maintaining a positive mental attitude, keeping a high spiritual ideal and, in particular, consistent use of a very mild, usually imperceptible, mode of electrotherapy. Over a period of about two years, all my MS-related symptoms gradually disappeared."

• "I'm an 84-year-old geezer with a couple of Cayce method healing experiences. Way back when I was in my thirties, I had skin problems that manifested with a hivelike rash on my chest after showers, and thin skin on my hands. The hands cracked and bled slightly from hard use. The hand problem showed when I used a golf club for a couple of hours or other such continual grip-type use.

"I also had trouble with IBS at that time, which I considered a minor disturbance—gas and irregular bowel movements.

We moved to Virginia Beach in 1976, and the problem became more acute. So I began having colonics and that helped somewhat, so I added psyllium husks once daily to my diet. The problem remained a little, so I ultimately consulted a gastroenterologist (non-Cayce), who suggested increasing the psyllium husks to twice daily. That, along with occasional colonics, cleared up the problem completely. I now follow this routine fairly closely, with the colonics only about once a year.

"During the past ten years, I've had other health problems (peripheral neuropathy and inoperable spine deterioration) and have been taking medications. I developed a severe rash on my buttocks, which I assumed was caused by the medications, so I went to a skin doctor, who prescribed a cortisone cream. It made the rash worse. That doctor said the problem may have been psoriasis, so I had about four colonics in a row. This didn't solve the problem, so I went on the Pagano diet (which is based mainly on the Cayce readings), and the rash eventually disappeared.

"Other than having a diet that adheres mostly (we indulge occasionally) to the Cayce recommendations and keeps me relatively healthy, I don't have any other healings to report."

• "Although I already sent you a Cayce success story for your book about my Charcot-Marie-Tooth (CMT) disease, I want to share some other success stories with you.

1. "Having CMT, I used to be plagued with killer leg cramps at night in my calf muscles. I had to wake my husband up so he could push down on my knee to force my heel back down to the floor. The cramps were so strong and painful that I couldn't work them out myself. Dr. Genevieve Haller told me that I needed to take more minerals. Taking the Cayce product Calcios, which is a highly absorptive mineral paste, a couple of times a week has worked miracles. It completely banished the cramps. This was about 25 years ago, and the cramps have never returned."

2. "For years I suffered recurrent sinus infections. For example, from

2002 to 2004 I had four sinus infections that required antibiotics. Wanting to cure this problem without taking medication, I turned to a gargle that Edgar Cayce frequently recommended, Glyco Thymoline, as an alkalizer. I was already gargling with it daily and knew that Cayce had recommended it for all of the mucous membrane linings in the body, so I thought it would be helpful to my sinuses. I began sniffing a few drops of Glyco, diluted with a small amount of water, from the palm of my hand up into my nostrils each morning and evening. I also tilted my head back and gently rolled it around to distribute the liquid into as many sinus passages as possible. Since that time, I've not had another major sinus flare-up."

3. "Like many middle-aged, overweight Americans, my doctor told me that I was hypoglycemic, which meant I was a candidate for diabetes. I had seen my father-in-law lose both legs to this insidious disease, and I knew that I definitely did not want this to happen to me. Again I turned to a suggestion in the Cayce readings—Jerusalem artichokes. They are not actually artichokes but are part of the sunflower family, so they are often called sunchokes in health food stores. Cayce said they contained insulin, which would help the pancreas to resume its normal function. I began to snack on raw sunchokes a couple of times each week. They are rather bland and look like small potatoes or ginger root. They can also be cooked. As a vegetable, I assumed they were harmless. I thought that they may help my body chemistry in some subtle way, but I never expected to feel so much better. I was often at the mercy of blood sugar swings where, if I didn't eat soon, I felt like I would faint. After eating a couple of sunchokes each week for about six months, I realized one day that I was feeling hungry, but it was a *normal* hungry feeling, not a frightening sense that I might faint. This return to normal hunger also meant that I could eat less often and therefore diet to lose weight."

Numerous simple responses have been received, such as these:

• "For instance, using the Cayce diet, massage, and cleansing suggestion *regularly*, my blood pressure and weight are those of a 20-year-old; I am 71. My skin, too, is quite smooth for my age, so that was not the object of my efforts. Finally, my emotional and spiritual health have improved over the years."

- A 66-year-old man reported that he had been diagnosed with Hodgkin's lymphoma some 8 years earlier, had tried one dose of chemotherapy, and was quite ill from it. Therefore, he ceased using any conventional therapy. He was in total remission 8 years later, which was 8 years after the original diagnosis, using carbon ash and the Ultra Violet lamp shining through a green glass light, the Cayce diet, and Essiac tea. The Essiac tea was not specifically recommended by Cayce, but all the others were, and the gentleman attributes his cure primarily to the use of the Cayce approach.

- "I had just turned 80 in December 2007 when I started to experience 60–70 black floaters, large, medium, and small, coming from my right eye. I was referred to a doctor who specialized in the retina. Upon examination I was diagnosed with hemorrhaging behind the right retina.

"I was told that there is no known treatment for this condition except group therapy.

"The first week in February 2008, I attended a conference in Virginia Beach at Edgar Cayce's foundation [A.R.E.]. I went to the library and read materials pertaining to my eye condition.

"I spoke with a librarian who told me of Vibra Tonic 3810 [also sold under the name Optikade Eye Tonic], found in the Edgar Cayce readings. I purchased it right away and started to use it from February 2008 up to the present, January 2009, one tablespoon three times a day before meals and at bedtime.

"One month after taking Vibra Tonic 3810, I was seen again by my doctor, who was surprised to see the great change since December 2007. He stated, 'No one has recovered that quickly.'

"I am now being checked every three months. The bleeding and floaters are down to a small amount and, at times, none appear.

"My thanks and appreciation to Edgar Cayce's foundation [A.R.E.] and to the librarian who so lovingly told me of the tonic.

"P.S. Cause of hemorrhage: occlusion of vein between heart and eye."

Another, more striking, case is that my wife learned in the early 90s that she had scleroderma. Being life members of the A.R.E., we immediately obtained the circulating file, and she began following his recommendations. When she began having problems with her lungs, we bought her a charred oak keg and ordered the 100-proof Laird's brandy. It completely helped her lungs and she discontinued that therapy. Her lungs have been fine ever since and the scleroderma has apparently gone into remission for almost two decades. It is interesting, of course, that one of the things that Cayce recommended for scleroderma was the apple brandy inhalation from the oak keg. For more information on the oak keg–apple brandy therapy go to: http://www.edgarcayce.org/health/database/chdata/data/theoakkeg.html.

- "I have had asthma since about 1960. At times it is triggered by exercise, being active in cold weather, or when stressed. An inhaler (Albuterol) usually took care of it. About one and one-half years ago, I decided to try the keg, the oak keg with apple brandy. I have not used the inhaler one time since. I haven't needed to. I am believing that unlike the inhaler, which merely relieves symptoms, the brandy fumes heal."

Of considerable interest is that Cayce recommended cinnamon for treatment of diabetes. Certainly at the time that he was alive, we did not know that cinnamon is a remarkable source of chromium. Today many people with mild adult onset diabetes are cured just by taking 1 mg. of chromium daily. I have many reports of individuals using that for their adult onset diabetes.

In a marvelous book, *The Edgar Cayce Products—Thirty-Five Years Ago*, published by the Heritage Store in Virginia Beach, a chart on page 160 reports that 72 to 100 percent of individuals had reported good or excellent results with IPSAB, Formula 636, Crudoleum, Atomadine, Dermaglow, Formula 208, TIM, Scar Massage, Wet Cell Appliance, Formula 545, Slippery Elm Bark, and Egyptian Oil.

The unique aspect of Cayce's intuitive readings was not only his ability to diagnose without seeing the individual but also to recommend treatment with a phenomenal variety of approaches. Sometimes this involved current medical drugs, and other times it required drugs that were hard to find but had been used in the past. In addition to this is the use of the Wet Cell Appliance and the impedance device, for balancing the electrical system and the physiology of the body, which were certainly presages of what we now call energy medicine.

Cayce's expertise extended well beyond the wide application to medical problems. I first became acquainted with the broad Cayce approach to psychological and spiritual issues with Jeffrey Furst's book *Edgar Cayce's Story of Attitude and Emotions:* (published by Coward, McCann, and Geoghegan, Inc. New York, 1972). Jeffrey's book addresses such crucial issues as these:

- Attitude is more important than fact.
- We make ourselves sick.
- Four aspects of mental, emotional growth.
- Understanding past-life experiences.
- Interpersonal relationships.
- Home and family.
- Balanced living.
- The problem of extremes.
- Changing attitudes and emotions.
- Health and healing.
- Love and forgiveness.

As a neurosurgeon, I was most impressed with "A General Reading on Multiple Sclerosis Itself." Cayce repeatedly indicated that multiple sclerosis was a problem of "the general mental and spiritual attitude of the entity." He often said it was a "case of the entity meeting self." I found that particularly interesting, since the question of autoimmune diseases had not been raised in medicine at that time. It was many years later that we in the medical field recognized that multiple sclerosis is a true autoimmune disease in which the body's own immune system attacks the brain and spinal cord.

Cayce emphasized "consideration of the whole person" and our relationship to our spiritual being. He emphasized that there are no incurable diseases, only incurable, stubborn minds and bodies.

- Some individuals can only face the reality of their past-life era by "having their noses rubbed in it."
- Serious diseases require serious changes in attitude with "faith, acceptance, optimism and cooperation, etc."
- All healing comes from God.
- No one should call themselves a healer. Individuals can only be channels for healing.
- Prayer heals (certainly, this has been remarkably emphasized in

the work of Dr. Larry Dossey in the last two decades).

Cayce truly was a fountainhead of holistic concepts, emphasizing the interrelationship between diet, especially proper balance of alkaline and acid foods; water intake; detoxification; castor oil packs; massage; herbs, tonics, and inhalants; vibrational therapy with color, sound, music, and electrical appliances; and spinal manipulation.

Finally, from the psychospiritual point of view, the three-volume work *Attitudes and Emotions* is truly an encyclopedia that far surpasses any psychological text of which I am aware. Cayce covers everything from attitudes and emotions in general but also every emotional concept that one can imagine, from anger to zealousness. Here we have almost thirteen hundred pages with detailed descriptions of the attitudinal, and sometimes karmic, foundations for both positive and negative emotions. I know of no one in history with a wider range of correct intuitive information that not only was useful at the time it was suggested and through the time of Cayce's death in 1945, but obviously, from the many current case reports, there remains a fountainhead of appropriate complementary, alternative, and holistic approaches to health. The only conclusion one can make from this body of information is that Edgar Cayce was truly the Einstein of medical intuition!

Edgar Cayce genuinely has been the role model for the broadest and most comprehensive medical intuitive but also a counseling intuitive and a spiritual counselor. The wisdom that he brought into the world will continue to be a light for many centuries to come.

For a collection of Web sites that deal with Edgar Cayce's approach to treating sixty-three common conditions and diseases, you can find it online: http://www.webspawner.com/users/ecstreatments/index.html.

Wherever possible, each ailment includes not only the treatment overviews featured on the main A.R.E. Web site but also relevant research, testimonials, treatment protocols, circulating files, related books, and supplemental e-books. These extra features make "The Directory of Edgar Cayce's Treatments" quite a useful and comprehensive source of information relative to the diseases and conditions in question.

4

WHO'S THE MATTER WITH ME? ORIGINS OF DISEASE—ILLNESS AS A METAPHOR

▶Several years before I first visited the A.R.E., I had come across a wonderful book called *Who's the Matter With Me?* by Alice Steadman, which was originally copyrighted in 1966 and again in 1968 and 1969. It was published by DeVorss and Company of Marina Del Ray, California, and has long been out of print, although you can find a few used copies available on Amazon. "People of different temperaments are predisposed to different ailments, because their 'druthers' and their 'bothers' are different." Steadman emphasizes that we begin learning very early on in life, sometimes through relatively insignificant events. Of course, we all know the common phrases, such as, "he or she is a pain in the neck;" "that makes me sick at my stomach;" "it makes my heart ache;" "that will be the death of me;" "I can't stand it;" and many others—all of which are negative suggestions to that brat that lives in all of us, the subconscious. She goes on to say, "Every thought we have has an instant effect on some part of our body." She quotes Emerson, who said, "If you see a person's soul, look at his body." She, therefore, then goes on to discuss disease as a "friction." That is, "stress between two of your cells, between the body and the soul." She also quotes Emerson as saying, "Each soul builds itself a body." These statements are remarkably similar to one of my most favorite Cayce quotations, "Mind is the builder." I must admit that she mentions Edgar Cayce on page ten, and even though I had read the book, I didn't look up Edgar Cayce at that time or discover him until my visit to A.R.E. in 1972! She emphasizes that even imagined fears or unhealthy emotions of hate, envy, grief, guilt, or resentment, even if planted in our dreams, can potentially lead to disease.

Interestingly, other than these physical body/mind emotion interactions, we appear to be well organized in ways that are even more unconscious. Eric Berne, in his wonderful book *Games People Play*, emphasized a variety of ways in which people may avoid getting well. For instance, I think that one of the most common that he mentioned in *Games People Play* is "cure me if you can." I have certainly seen patients who appear to fulfill that role very well. In addition, his student Claude Steiner wrote the book *Scripts People Live*. Among other stories of scripts that seem comparable to a *Gone With the Wind* play, Berne said that we set both the age and the cause of our death, usually in childhood. For ten years before he died, he told an inner group of friends that his script called for him to die at age sixty of a heart attack, and he did. For one so brilliant, I used to say, Why does this brilliant man, once he had that insight, not change his script? until a psychologist visiting me said, "But Norm, what better way to prove his point!" I have worked with scripts with different people, and I will mention just one here.

In 1974 a patient with advanced metastatic breast cancer was sent to me for help with her persistent pain. She had totally failed to respond to chemotherapy and twice the usual dose of radiation. She could hardly keep any food or drink down, was very frail, and moved around in a wheelchair or on a stretcher. As we began teaching her the principles of self-regulation, which I will get to in the chapter on stress management, she kept saying to me, "I didn't come here to be brainwashed. I came here to get rid of my pain." To which I replied, "If you would just shut up and listen, I am teaching you how to control your pain." On the 17th day of our working intensely in this program, this woman was brought into the room on a stretcher. I did a twenty-minute exercise with a group of patients, and at the end of that, she got up and walked out of the room without pain. It was like a scene from Lourdes. A year and a half later, I flew to Los Angeles to give a talk at the hospital where she had been unsuccessfully treated. She picked me up at the airport, and we were driving down the highway when she said, "Norm, I want to tell you what happened last year. During that exercise I suddenly realized how much I hated my family, and I decided, I am not going to let the bastards kill me." It is not what I call perfect insight, but it appeared to be adequate for her. She went on to say, "I came home and within three months, my cancer was gone and my husband committed suicide." Another year passed and her dog died. She became very depressed and her pain returned. When she came back to see me, we could not find any evidence of recurrent cancer, and in working with her this time, we discovered that she had scripted at age sixteen to die at the same age that her grandmother had died. At the conclusion of this second period of treatment, she said, "I now realize that I cannot afford the luxury of depression."

Scripts, games, and all of the reactions to our day-to-day environment and relationships ultimately create *Who's the Matter with Me?*

In popular metaphysical literature, the right side of the body "thinks" in response to the left brain, which is rational, and the right side of the body, called the male side, energetically. The left side of the body responds to the right brain, which is the area of our feelings, our true cognitive and subconscious feelings; and it is the female side energetically. There is also a common belief that the subconscious mind does not understand the difference between negative and positive, so that one has to be careful stating such things as "I will not smoke." That actually could be programmed through the subconscious to mean that I will smoke.

From a more metaphysical point of view, the brain is the center of the sixth chakra, the chakra of knowledge and wisdom. Thus, disorders of the brain, in any form whatsoever, may be the result of unexpressed fear and negativity and, in the ultimate situation—when a person has essentially consciously lied—may set the energetic potential for developing a malignant brain tumor. This does not necessarily mean that every person who goes through life lying will develop a malignant brain tumor, but my suspicion is that if it is not related to this life, it may be the result of unfinished business from a previous life. We will discuss that in the chapter on reincarnation and past-life therapy.

The fifth chakra includes the mouth, ears, eyes, nose, cervical spine, throat, arms, and hands and is the center of will. Here is a personal story that emphasizes the fifth chakra:

In 1957 I played a serious practical joke on a very dear friend. Fortunately, it did not cause him any residual problem. Six months later, while a group of us were horsing around at a lake, he jumped off my right shoulder with both feet, instead of one foot on each shoulder, and I developed a severe, right neck pain that mostly cleared within a few weeks but kept recurring. Eventually, in 1960 I just turned my head to the right, and the pain returned and spread all the way down into my thumb. Gradually I began to lose adequate sensation, which could lead to serious numbness in my right thumb or hand. That would be a big problem for a neurosurgeon. So I had the usual test of that day, a cervical myelogram, and had a very large ruptured disc pressing on the nerve to my right thumb. This led to the first surgery on my neck, what I would say was a 95 percent recovery, although there always remained a dull and easily aggravated pain just above my right shoulder blade.

In 1966, in the operating room, a nurse tripped over my headlight cord and gave me a reverse whiplash. The pain became increasingly worse, so much so that I was having trouble sleeping. So, in 1967, because of the degenerative changes at that disc space where the disc had been ruptured, I flew to Cleveland and had an anterior fusion between the fifth and sixth vertebral bodies. I recovered reasonably uneventfully but still had some nagging pain problem on the right, just above my shoulder blade over near the spine. In 1976 a physician who came to show me his "hot hands" jerked my neck 180 degrees in both directions and dislocated my spine between the sixth and seventh vertebrae. I was so ill over the next six months that I paid very little attention to changes that began to take place over the next few years, ignoring neurologic symptoms up to the point that I began falling easily. On June 16, 1995, I awoke about 75 percent paralyzed in the legs. I will come back to this story in the chapter on reincarnation. Suffice it to say, that was my third major "illness" in the fifth chakra. My right vocal cord was paralyzed for some five or six months after the surgery and is only about 85 percent recovered at this point. Interestingly, however, for the first time since my original injury in 1957, the right suprascapular pain was gone and has remained so.

How does this relate to the fifth chakra? Well, in early 1974, I had my first consultation with Dr. Robert Leichtman, who did not know me at all. He started off with something like, "You have a few warts but not very big ones. You have such a strong will that some people think your parents must have been robots." Interestingly, I have always pushed to have greater will, thinking my will was not strong enough! To finish that story, which is obviously one of the great lessons of this life, my father died in December 1962. In November 1994 my father came back to visit, and he said, "I am tired of you saying I committed suicide smoking. My contract was to die at age fifty-three. My contract with you was to present you with someone you would consider weak-willed because you came into this life stating you wanted a very strong will. You have a very strong-willed mother so that you could make the choice." I responded, "You have been dead thirty-two years. Why didn't you tell me this earlier?" He responded, "You weren't ready to hear it." I would guess that at least *one* of the most major lessons for me in this life is *not* to use my reasonably strong will to impose it upon others!

Obviously, there are many other things that can happen in the fifth chakra, but in general, diseases affect the eyes, ears, nose, throat, arms, and hands. All undoubtedly have some relationship to issues of will. Probably much more common than an extra strong will is too weak a will, an inability or unwillingness to express one's own personal needs and desires. And, of course, I could look back to age seven, when my will took me up too high in a tree and I fell, breaking my right arm.

Interestingly, Alice Steadman says that pimples in an adolescent are the result of parents and teachers that don't think an adolescent is mature enough to make decisions. The teenager "doesn't dare give voice to his irritations and it breaks forth on the face." She also says, "Is the flaw on your nose because you are looking down your nose at someone else or because you fear another is looking down on you!" Steadman also mentions such remarkably small things as children who lose a dime or their gloves and they feel so frustrated that they wake up the next morning with a sore throat or a stiff neck. She also feels that individuals who are more rigid and fixed in their ways are more likely to complain of stiffness and soreness. And, of course, we all remember that Cayce started his career as a medical intuitive diagnosing his own difficulty in speaking! Chemists believe that "germs and viruses do not cause colds any more than cockroaches cause the kitchen to be unclean." He felt that germs are scavengers who reduce dead cells. Others think that these are detoxification processes that allow one who is exhausted and not paying attention an opportunity to rest and get well. To be sure, there have been several experiments in which volunteers were exposed to the cold virus, physically "infected" with it, and even though they were exposed to a harsh environment, they did not come down with a cold. They had no great stress at the time and therefore did not develop these "infections."

Steadman's feeling was that the thieves of health represented the "hidden side of your personality," since they are your foundation. She felt that they "represent your secret hopes and desires, your inner most dreams, waking and sleeping, your fears and limitations, etc." Remember that "Death and life *are* in the power of the tongue," Proverbs 18:21.

Moving beyond Alice Steadman and my own experience, Edgar Cayce's story of *Attitudes and Emotions* by Jeffrey Furst is one of the books that I have revisited perhaps more frequently than any other. The chapter in which he discusses several cases of multiple sclerosis is particularly valuable. First he quotes Cayce as frequently saying, "This is a case of the entity meeting self." At the time this reading was given, we did not even know what autoimmune diseases were. There certainly is a case of the "entity" meeting itself and, in fact, attempting to destroy itself by attacking certain tissues in the body as if they were foreign agents. In general, this wonderful little book emphasizes seven cardinal virtues in attaining self discipline:
1. "Dedication (a decision)"
2. "Motivation (a commitment)"
3. "Willpower (the desire)"
4. "Persistence (the application)"
5. "Consistency (being steady and habitual)"
6. "Patients attaining acceptance (expectancy in maintaining faith)"

From page 132 of the book, these are quotes from the book extracted from readings by Cayce:

Question: Is marriage as we have necessary and advisable?
Answer: It is.
Question: Should divorce be encouraged by making them easier to obtain?
Answer: This depends first upon the education of the body. Once united, once understood that the relationships are to be as one, less and less is there the necessity of such conditions. Man may learn a great deal from the study of the goose in this direction. Once it has mated, never is there a mating with any other—either the male or female, no matter how soon the destruction of the mate may occur—unless forced by man's interventions.   826-6

Furst also said, "What we are intimating here is that our illnesses and imbalances seem to arrive as bait—enticing our soul's awareness to surface and confront the conscious mind with inner truths which cry out for attention as the possible prelude to our spiritual awakenings."

In looking at emotions, it is also important to recognize that there is a place for expressing one's emotions. "We find from Mars that the entity has a very good temper; but good temper! One without a temper is in very bad shape, but one who can't control his temper is in still worse shape!" (1857-2). Although I have personally emphasized that the major negative emotions are anger, guilt, anxiety, depression, and love, there are huge numbers of antonyms and synonyms that fit into one or combinations of these. These include the following:

Healthy, joyful happiness.

Faith, success, growing, brotherhood, masculine/feminine.

Abundance, trust, ability, humility, generosity, elevating patience, peace, strong, flexible, giving/sharing, forgiving, power seeking, indifference, unbalanced, envious, misery, fear, failure, depleting, prejudice, feminine, restrictions, ties, poverty, worry, inferiority, pride, greed, criticizing, ill tempered, tension/war, weak, rigid, grasping, resentful, loving, selfless, selfish, and so on.

Another wonderful quotation from Cayce: "For selfishness is the real sin, and as we become less and less conscious of self and more aware of being at an onement with *Him,* greater may be the possibilities . . . " (5265-1)

Personally, in looking at the problems that I have encountered with thousands of patients, it appears to me that the most prevalent imbalance is an unwillingness to be forgiving, and one must always remember that holding a grudge is like taking poison and expecting it to kill the other person!

The second most important seems to be tolerance, and nowhere is there greater intolerance than there is in many religions. There are also great intolerances, again mostly within religions, against individuals of different race, different creed, different sexuality, different political parties, and so on.

The third greatest problem appears to be a lack of serenity and an inability to be at peace with what is happening around you that you cannot change. There are many other imbalances in emotions and attitudes, but eventually, they all rise to the top—problems with will, problems with reason, and the inability to love. As stated in the *Urantia Book*, "Love is the desire to do good to others." It is my firm belief that our most intense *need* is to nurture other people. If we have not been adequately nurtured, if we have failed, been abused or abandoned, then we are likely to wind up either angry or depressed. We still crave, at some level, helping others, and often it is in helping others that we save ourselves and redeem ourselves from the greatest problems that we have.

Enough about my own *Who's the Matter With Me?* The fourth chakra, which is sometimes called the heart and sometimes called the thymus chakra, is basically the chest and all of its entities, ranging from the breasts to the rib cage, the spine and surrounding area, and the lungs, the heart, and so on. In general, the issues of the fourth chakra have to do with love, or lack thereof, with injustice vs. justice, acceptance or rejection of others, and what not. When Caroline Myss and I wrote the book *The Creation of Health*, I called heart disease the number one choice way to die. How does this relate to *Who's the Matter With Me?* In my opinion, some of the most brilliant work of the psychic aspects of disease has been done by Dr. Hans Eysenck. Eysenck demonstrated that a huge majority of patients who die of heart disease have lifelong anger. Those who die of cancer have lifelong depression. Of course, looking at another major disease, lung cancer, obviously there are subtle individual aspects of emotions gone astray or unfinished that can lead to diseases of various kinds. Long before I evolved into looking at the psychic or emotional foundations for disease, I noticed, back in the mid-60s, that some of my colleagues had wives that developed breast cancer. I said to my wife that I always felt that they were married to cold fish and did not have any emotional nurturing. That fits in extremely well with Dr. Eysenck's concept that those people who die of cancer of any origin have been hopelessly depressed throughout their lives, wanting someone who really cannot give them the nurturing and positive affirmations that they wish for.

The third chakra is, of course, the area of self-esteem and responsibility, either taking or resenting responsibility and feeling angry that someone has not taken the proper responsibility, and so on. The major disease of the third chakra is obviously today adult-onset diabetes. There is no question that there are many other factors involved in any of these illnesses, and please do not misunderstand and think that there is nothing behind a disease except unfinished emotional business. Even, however, in Diabetes Type I, in which we believe that the cause is a viral infection, my suspicion is that there is a self-esteem problem in these children that makes them more vulnerable. In adults, since 90+ percent of adult-onset diabetics are overweight significantly, self-esteem is obviously one of the biggest problems. And our society as a whole has moved into remarkable abandonment of personal responsibility. Increasingly, a huge number of people, soon to be a majority, are dependent on someone else for much of their life.

Moving down into the second chakra, the issue of sexuality, security, and finances, we find perhaps a greater variety of illnesses than in any of the Chakras. Cancers of the ovaries, uterus, and prostate are among the most serious issues in these areas. Erectile dysfunction, although unequivocally associated with both problems in blood flow and often atherosclerosis, changes in nitric oxide, and so on, there are probably almost invariably some issues related to money; feelings of security, mostly financial; or sexuality.

Finally, we come to the first chakra, the chakra of safety, grounding and, particularly, connectedness—both with life itself and one's family. Remember that "I can't stand it" phrase that some people use? Now there are other aspects, of course, than just emotions. There are also astrological influences. And the hips, for instance, are the physical part of the body that is associated with vegetarians. I have had two first chakra issues: one at age nine, when I fell between two boards and cracked the upper medial part of my tibia and developed a huge abscess. This was before the advent of antibiotics, and the wound was left open to drain. I was told that I would never walk without a limp. I became very angry at the thought, and when the wound was healed within about three months, I walked normally for me. Now I have to admit, I have been called "duck waddle" and a few other things because I am "slew-footed," and have been all of my life. Then in 1971, on a Sunday afternoon, I got extremely "careless" and did not pay attention to what I was doing. I attempted to get on a "green-broke" horse that had not been ridden in three months and which I had not exercised. I got one foot in the stirrup and ended up on a rock on the opposite side suffering a fractured right hip. Who's the matter with me in this situation? Carelessness!

A British researcher "found that smart girls with smart looking legs and that heavy and well shaped legs mean you are sure of yourself and know what it is all about." One of my favorite statements from the Steadman book is, "Don't use your stomach [third chakra] as an emergency pantry" (page 61). She also found a reported research that showed that individuals with a low income are seven times more likely to become overweight than those with a high income. Again, the problem of poor self-esteem!

Note that I did not start at the very top of the chakras in looking at the issues related to them. The seventh chakra is the nonphysical chakra, the connectedness with God, Soul, and the Divine. In general, issues of the seventh chakra have to do with what I prefer to call existential crises. These are problems of purpose, meaning, why me? and so on. I have to admit that I have only had one brief, significant issue with the seventh chakra. I have never had any doubt about God. I have always "known" that we have a soul and that it survives physical death. One of my earliest memories is of climbing at age four, upon a rather large lard can in my grandmother's kitchen, watching an uncle outside making a snowman. I was a little unhappy because my mother wouldn't let her "four-year-old-baby" go out and play in the snow. My grandmother walked in and said, "Son, be careful. You will hurt yourself." To which I responded, "Grandma, don't worry. If you are going to die, you are going to die." She responded, "That may be true but you can certainly shorten your life." I have never feared death, because I know it is not the end of life. On the other hand, exactly one week after my 1995 neck surgery, I had what I call my Job day. I spent six or eight hours moaning and groaning about "why me?" I didn't do anything to deserve this. Just wait until you find out what I did do in a previous life! At any rate, after that period of time, I said to myself, "This is nonsense and I will never get well if I stay in this funk." And that was the end of it. I have been very blessed to have no lingering issues with existence, purpose, meaning, or connectedness with the divine.

Most metaphysically oriented experts believe that rheumatism, arthritis, and the like, are primarily the result of too rigid a personality. Obviously, there are also problems with the pH of the body, as often emphasized by Cayce, as well as diet. Ultimately, in every dis-ease, it is important to look at the metaphors and the *who* that is the root cause!

5

BLOCKS TO HEALING AND
BUILDING SELF-ESTEEM

Abraham Maslow emphasized the essentials for self-actualization, or as he called it, a Hierarchy of Needs. First and foremost are physiological needs:

- Air. We can live approximately three minutes without air.
- Water. Depending upon the temperature and a few other things, we can live approximately two weeks without water.
- Food. Depending upon one's weight and caloric "reserves," one can live four weeks or more without food.
- Sleep. In experiments in which individuals are awakened every time they fall asleep, individuals become psychotic within seven days. Sleep deprivation and inadequate sleep are associated with numerous illnesses and are even one of the contributing factors to obesity.
- Clothes. In most climates, one needs a variety of clothes.
- Shelter. In many climates, individuals will not survive very well without some form of shelter.
- Psychological—Nurturing. Giving and receiving love.

Having worked with well over thirty thousand individuals who have disabling pain and/or chronic depression that has not responded to conventional medical care, I am convinced that the vast majority of people who are having problems functioning have had

one of two problems in childhood:
- Abuse—verbal, physical, or sexual.
- Abandonment—mental, emotional, social; inadequacy of parenting.

Many of my patients have told me that they cannot remember ever being truly happy. In the 1970s my wife and I wrote a book, *To Parent or Not*. This was our reaction to a series of articles in an Ann Landers column. She wrote that she had had many thousands of people write to tell her that they wished they had never been a parent. At least 70 percent of the people who wrote stated this. If we look at the problems that are prevalent throughout our society, abusive or negligent parenting appears to be the foundation for most psychological/emotional problems.

In addition to working with people who have truly failed to be able to function adequately in our current society, I have had the experience of working with numerous students, friends, and associates and am impressed that many people carry with them, throughout life, a feeling of poor self-esteem that arose because of feelings of abandonment or abuse in childhood. Most often this leads to anger or depression. In general, for most people, anger is the result of feeling abused and depression is the result of feeling abandoned. Obviously, we are all individuals, and some people have both those problems, with various degrees of dominance. This fits in very well with Hans Eysenck's work mentioned earlier. Hans Eysenck was a psychiatrist who did most of his clinical work in England, but he and a colleague from Heidelberg, Germany, analyzed more than thirteen thousand individuals who were healthy adults, ranging in age from twenty-five to fifty when they first started the survey. They followed them over the next twenty years using extensive psychometric testing. They categorized the individuals into four types:

Type 1 individuals have lifelong feelings of hopeless depression. Basically, they wanted nurturing, which probably began with a parent but was transferred in adulthood to another individual who was not the least bit interested in a relationship or nurturing. These individuals feel hopelessly depressed because they can never receive the nurturing that they need. Over the next twenty years, roughly 75 percent of those who died of cancer had a Type 1 personality, 15 percent had a Type 2 personality, and 9 percent had a Type 3 personality.

Type 2 individuals have been angry throughout life and have never been able to deal with their anger. Over the next twenty years, approximately 75 percent of those who died of heart disease had a Type 2 personality, about 15 percent had a Type 1 personality, and approximately 9 percent had a Type 3 personality.

Type 3 individuals can't make up their mind. I often call them "bi" because they flip between depression and anger. Interestingly, however, this is healthier than either one of them alone. Type 3 individuals die only seven years earlier than Type 4, whereas Type 1 individuals die approximately 35 years earlier than Type 4.

Type 4 individuals are what I would call self-actualized, although Eysenck called them autonomous. Basically, they say, You can't make me happy and you can't make me unhappy. I am responsible for my own happiness or, as *In a Course in Miracles*, "Happiness is an inside job." Only 0.8 percent of Type 4 individuals during that next twenty years died of cancer, and Type 4 individuals live an average of 35 years longer than Type 1.

Another way of looking at problems is to address the emotional and, ultimately, physical problems that arise related to the energies of the seven chakras.

As one who has focused on the functions of the brain and the nervous system and particularly physiology, I have always considered the energy centers to be anatomically real. For instance, the first chakra is the sciatic plexus, which essentially feeds the major nerve supply to the leg. This chakra, of course, is primarily associated with problems of relationships with family and one's physical environment, and ultimately, that means one's feelings of being alive and in the world.

The second chakra involves issues of security, both financial and physical, as well as sexuality. The second chakra is the pelvic plexus, which feeds the low back and genitalia.

The third chakra is the chakra of self-esteem. It is the area of the body and psyche that has to do with feeling "I am okay." Resentments of being forced to take too much responsibility or feeling that someone else is not taking adequate responsibility, and particularly the feelings of rejection and abuse, may well dominate the issues of the third chakra. The third chakra is the solar plexus, and even in medicine it is called that, as it is in metaphysics. The third chakra involves all of the organs in the upper abdomen.

The fourth chakra is neurologically the cardiac plexus and the issues of the fourth chakra are those related to love and judgmentalism.

The fifth chakra is the cervical plexus. This is the chakra of will, one's ability to express one's needs and desires or to suppress them.

The sixth chakra is the brain itself, and this is the area for reason, knowledge, and "knowing." It is, of course, the area of the brain/mind and, ultimately, integrative processes of intuition.

The seventh chakra is the only chakra that does not have a neurologic component. I think of it as the connection between mind/brain and the soul and God. The issues of the seventh chakra are those of meaning, purpose, and justice.

We have, therefore, not only the problems of abuse or abandonment but also the ones related to the issues of the etheric and physical nervous system and bonding. My impression is that the particular abuse and abandonment that an individual may feel is colored to a huge extent by past-life experiences interrelated with the current parents and others that one meets early in life.

In order for one to function optimally—physically, mentally and emotionally—in a career or job and, most particularly, as an intuitive, one has to clear as much unfinished business from childhood and, in many people, from previous lives as possible. Anger, doubt, depression, guilt, and anxiety all inhibit the natural flow of intuition. Essentials for health, self-esteem, and intuition are these:

- Self-esteem
- I'm okay
- Respect for others
- You're okay
- True, unconditional love—"The desire to do good to others."

Ultimately, the path to self-actualization and that of optimal intuition involve the path toward unconditional love. The single most important issue is forgiveness. Remember, holding a grudge is like taking poison and expecting it to kill the other person. As long as there is a grudge, it is not possible for one to discern accurately what is going on, not only in oneself but also in others, because one is always looking for the defects in others.

The second requirement is tolerance. One does not have to believe or like everything that everyone else does, but as long as it is not harmful to you individually, it is important to tolerate the vast variety of beliefs and activities of human beings.

The third most critical issue is serenity and being able to be at peace despite the chaos in the world around us. When we have these three, we can build the other steps toward unconditional love. These include the following:

- Compassion. Compassion for those less fortunate than we and for those who may have been more abused than we.
- Charity. As part of one's need to help others, there is the drive to contribute to and help those less fortunate.
- Motivation. Next on the stairway to self-esteem is motivation. Certainly, anger, guilt, anxiety, and depression are great inhibitors of motivation, but motivation to develop one's optimal ability is a key in the growth toward self-actualization.
- Joy. Joy is also critical. Although it may be impossible to feel joy all of the time, it is important to see, feel, and sense the joy of being alive and to see the beauty in nature and to smile and laugh as frequently as possible, especially at the incongruities of the world.
- Faith. Faith is a critical issue. Faith requires belief that no matter how bad the situation is, justice and light ultimately prevail. Hope is the recognition that no matter how good or bad the current situation is, the future will be better.
- Confidence. Confidence, of course, is the ultimate self-esteem requirement. Knowing that you are confident and capable of success is a critical factor.
- Courage. This is the courage to face the present and the future with the inherent belief that good will prevail.
- Will. There are three aspects of will. Basic will, of course, is the will to survive. I have often said I believe that if someone were threatening suicide and to jump off the top of the Empire State Building, if you tried to push them they would fight back. That is how strong the

basic will to live is. Obviously, some people lose that and stay in life-long depression or do commit suicide. The internal will is activated when one realizes that seeking something that is not possible is painful, yet the person continues to play the broken record. Wanting something you cannot conceivably have will only perpetuate anger, guilt, anxiety, or depression.

- Transcendent will. The transcendent will is the will of the soul. At this level of understanding, you recognize that not everything can be changed, and even though some things might be changeable, you may not have the energy or the passion to try to change them. Therefore, you accept those things you cannot or will not change and detach from them. You have no need to know why. You are not judgmental and you are at peace.

- Reason. Reason, of course, is the function primarily of our left brain. Logic and understanding the logistics of our beliefs and actions are critical. It is always a question of balancing this reason and logic with wisdom.

- Wisdom. Wisdom is the primary function of the right brain, the knowing brain, but it can be "fooled" if we have not done all of the intervening work necessary to clear unfinished business and recognize the wisdom of focusing on the positive.

- Love. Ultimately, love truly is the unconditional ability, not to like but to need, to help and nurture others. I think that *innately and intuitively*, we are born with a need to help others. With love, all things are possible, including miracles; and with true love, intuition can flower.

The following is the "Love Attitude Inventory," which I created many years ago. You might see where you have unfinished business related to any of these. In addition, to have another way of looking at the blocks that you might have, include "The Human Potential Attitude Inventory." Again, this is not a question of right or wrong. This issue is, "How good do I feel about myself and others? How forgiving, tolerant, and serene am I?"

Love Attitude Inventory

1. Define love in one sentence.

For all other questions, grade *your* reaction/belief from strongly disagree
—; disagree –; neutral 0; agree +; strongly agree ++.

2. I am loved   _____

3. I am loving   _____

4. God is love   _____

5. Love is . . .

giving	_____	receiving	_____
being	_____	God	_____
a matter of chance	_____	sexual gratification	_____
a pleasant sensation	_____	the desire to help others	_____
the desire to do good to others	_____	a pleasant sensation/event	_____
		an art	_____
communication with others	_____	understanding	_____

6. Sexual gratification may be love _____

7. My degree of ability to . . .

forgive	_____	be tolerant	_____
be at peace	_____	be confident	_____
feel good about myself	_____	be wise	_____
		feel joy	_____
be logical	_____	feel hope	_____
express joy	_____	express my will	_____
have faith	_____	express love	_____
feel love	_____	receive love	_____
give love	_____	be courageous	_____

accept responsibility	_____	respect others	_____
be daring	_____	be at one with God	_____
learn	_____	love animals	_____
love all people	_____	love minerals	_____
love plants	_____	love the universe	_____
love the earth	_____	be self-reliant	_____
love God	_____	love unconditionally	_____
accept myself	_____	integrate and see the whole picture	_____

8. Masturbation can be self-love _____

9. My level of personal development . . .

discipline	_____	patience	_____
concentration	_____	concern for others	_____
self-esteem	_____		

There is no right or wrong, but introspection will assist you in knowing where you have work to do!

6

SYNCHRONICITY, VISION, AND CREATIVITY

Synchronicity was first brought into prominence by Carl Jung. Essentially, one way of looking at it is that events that seem to be of critical importance in life are somehow connected. It often occurs without a clear cause, as if a polar magnet draws two people together in an invisible way. Arthur Koestler, in his book *The Roots of Coincidence*, describes this phenomenon more clearly than anyone that I have read. In the absence of a proven law of nature or science, synchronicity appears to be a minor (and sometimes major) miracle. I have already talked about some of the synchronous events, but it is important enough to repeat at least the beginning of my awareness of synchronicity. Some of these were mentioned earlier, but they are so critical to my own understanding of synchronicity that I will summarize in this chapter.

As mentioned in chapter one, in the fall of 1970, one year after we had started raising Appaloosas, I visited an Appaloosa Ranch in Colorado. When Joyce C., wife of the owner, opened the door at the ranch, I instantly knew her, as she did me. It was not at that time a recognition of having known one another in a previous life but a feeling of connectedness that had to come from something not explainable to us. We, therefore, spent an hour discussing this unusual sense and its relation to parapsychology. A week later, Joyce sent me *Psychic Discoveries Behind the Iron Curtain*, and another week later, *Breakthrough to Creativity*. These books, after my meeting with Joyce, rekindled my early life interest in extrasensory perception, or psychic phenomena. In terms of career, this synchronicity experience has had one of the most powerful influences; it changed everything after that time!

Even earlier, without my being initially aware of the synchronicity of events, I moved to Boston, after my internship and year of General Surgery to enter the Neurosurgical Residency at Massachusetts General Hospital. I knew only one person in Boston, someone with whom I had interned. I wrote and asked David if he would like to get an apartment together. He said yes and, when I arrived, found that he was dating "Chardy" Bayles. Without recognizing it consciously, I was jealous of their relationship from our first meeting. A couple of months later, after double-dating a few times, I asked David to stop dating her because I knew he would never marry a skiksa. His parents were Orthodox Jews. Several months later, he agreed, on the condition that I could not date her for a full month after he ceased dating her. One month after that— December 4th, my birthday—we began dating and five weeks later, I asked her to marry me.

That experience is one of those synchronous events that is, in most respects, a minor miracle. The miracle of our three children, the first conceived on our first night without using contraceptives, is another. Another synchronous event took place when, after eighteen years of dedicating myself toward being a professor of neurosurgery, I chose to "ruin my career" by leaving those hallowed halls. And then, only five years later, I decided to ruin my career a second time by discontinuing my practice of neurosurgery to concentrate on pain management. Those two "ruin" statements were made by two very close friends.

There have been numerous other synchronous events in my life. All of them actually involve a significant degree of intuition. At the beginning of this book, I discussed my intuitive development of transcutaneous electrical nerve stimulation and dorsal column stimulation. And then there is the concept of establishing the Pain and Rehabilitation Center, the first concept of rehabilitating pain patients. It quickly became a popular concept. And there is the synchronous event of Dr. Janet Travell, John F. Kennedy's physician, being quoted in the *Wall Street*

Journal in January 1972. This led to my meeting Dr. Paul Dudley White, Dwight Eisenhower's physician, to discuss my work, and then in 1972 being asked to replace Dr. White at an acupuncture symposium. This, of course, led to my "discovery" and introduction to the Association of Research and Enlightenment and the work of Edgar Cayce.

That meeting in which I replaced Dr. White exposed me to the broad field of alternative medicine, Kirlian photography, subtle energy, spiritual healing, homeopathy, the Edgar Cayce material and, ultimately, to autogenic training, biofeedback, and past-life therapy. And, of course, the A.R.E. meeting in 1972 led to my meeting Henry Rucker and a commitment to medical intuition. When I first heard about biofeedback and autogenic training, I instantly saw the connection between these two. Basically, when intuition and the heart are united, even for a short period of time, miracles occur. At a deep, subconscious level, the greatest suppressed fear inside conventional medicine is that there might be something simple and safe that works! Suppose, just suppose, that all of these alternatives really work as well as or better than drugs or surgery and without potential side effects? Then the power of physicians would evaporate except for the management of acute illness.

Actually, in a sense, the greatest failure of the medical profession is not recognizing the value of alternative healing. Meanwhile, the science of medical discoveries has led the modern medical system to be the third leading cause of death in America! (*JAMA*, July 2000). Indeed Dr. Paul Rosch has argued that *American medicine is the number one cause of death!* To a great extent, all of the current interest in alternative, complementary, integrative, and holistic medicine is a long delayed recognition by the public that there are simple and safe alternatives. Conventional allopathic medicine has ignored the most important aspect of healing: The untapped miracle of the individual's personal will, intuition, and heart. When will, intuition, and the heart are united, even for a few moments, miracles occur.

The connection between synchronicity and intuition is perhaps best illustrated by the first major miracle in modern medicine: Alexander Fleming's discovery of penicillin, a simple mold. Frontiers of science were thrown open by this simple mold, which has saved many lives and given us what would now be called the scientific archetype. Unfortunately, wisdom does not always accomplish such discoveries. Just as nuclear energy was a great discovery, it carries the threat of total destruction of life unless we learn how to dispose of its waste. Similarly, antibiotics are now grossly overused and lead to countless allergic reactions and many other problems. They are used indiscriminately in our food chains in chickens, cows, and pigs, with unknown long-term outcomes.

The second great scientific miracle, Thorazine—the first major tranquilizer—has produced even broader societal problems, actually laying the foundation for many homeless individuals. A majority of psychotic patients, released from psychiatric institutions, will not take their medications. One hundred years ago such individuals were institutionalized. Today they are homeless. Overall, Thorazine and subsequent new generations of tranquilizers have led to serious complications:

• The foundation for the problem of homelessness. Patients who are seriously ill emotionally or mentally have been made placid enough (chemically lobotomized) to be turned out on the street without rehabilitation, and then they stop taking the medications.

• The tranquilization of America. Instead of dealing with stress and anxiety, physicians use tranquilizers to depress the symptoms until the patient has become addicted and depressed.

• Valium and its clones—Ativan and Xanax. The second major step in the evolution of tranquilizers has harmed many more Americans than marijuana or cocaine. They are major contributors to depression. They are a plague.

Folk remedies also belong here in our discussion of synchronicity and intuition. In an article in the *Southern Medical Journal*, Dr. Cheryl Cook and Denise Dabaisden reported that 72.9 percent of 170 individuals surveyed used at least one "folk" remedy in the preceding twelve months. Of those, seventy-six were from rural areas, and 70 percent of those from urban areas were using folk remedies. These ranged from salt to aloe vera, honey, alcohol, onions, and garlic, and at least 96 percent of the 170 people reported that they had used folk remedies at some time in their lives. All folk remedies were the result of some individual somewhere along the line "discovering" the use of these particular approaches.

I cannot overemphasize that every discovery is really the result of someone recognizing an intuitive hit. These often involve some degree of synchronicity turned into a creation. Sir Isaac Newton's discovery of gravity is said to have been the intuitive awareness that when an apple fell from a tree it had something of great importance to the world of physics. In fact, Lord John Maynard Keynes, speaking at the Tercenteanry of Newton in 1947, said that "his deepest instincts were occult, esoteric, semantic—with a profound shrinking from the world." *Science*, in 1984, called Dr. Albert Einstein the "Greatest Scientist of the 20th Century." The article indicated that he had been a high school dropout and had squeaked through college with a B average, but by 1905, without any of the usual academic mantle, he had written six epical papers that transformed the scientific landscape. Two of them created a new branch of physics—relativity. A third helped create quantum physics. Three others altered the course of atomic theory and statistical mechanics. All involved synchronistic intuition.

Search Magazine said of Thomas Edison, holder of more than one thousand patents, including the electric bulb, phonograph, and motion picture projector, "Much of what he put down on paper originated from a higher source, and that he was simply a vehicle or channel through which this information could flow freely." Interestingly, some people have felt, in looking at his original papers, that it resembles automatic writing. Nikola Tesla, whom some people considered an even greater genius than Einstein, acknowledged a "cosmic assist" in his work.

Thus, accurate medical intuition, especially by its very nature, challenges the laws of nature as defined by science. There is no law acceptable to conventional scientists that allows for the possibility of knowing something without any facts behind that knowledge. Quantum physicists, of course, are an exception. Rupert Sheldrake and David Bohm have little difficulty with the possibility of tuning into a morphogenic field of the collective unconscious described by Carl Jung. The terms *morphogenic field* and *collective unconscious* suggest the existence of a subtle electromagnetic framework, or pervasive background, of information. Just as television and radio signals go through us without our conscious awareness, we are surrounded by the "signals" of information, especially of great emotional common experiences. These signals, ignored by the conscious mind, are available to the intuitive mind. If your mind functions as a super receiver, it is able to tune into this information. J. B. Rhine, at Duke University, proved that some individuals can know intuitively which card is being drawn by another person, not 100 percent of the time but at a rate highly statistically greater than chance. One hundred years before Rhine, as we have already indicated, two of the fathers of hypnosis, John Elliotson and James Eisdale, demonstrated that some individuals enjoy an inherent clairvoyance great enough to make medical diagnoses without medical training. But, even in their day, "the Establishment" rejected the concept. Cayce's legacy, standing alone, provides more examples of miracles than the modern pharmacy. Dr. Irvin Page, the great Cleveland Clinic internist, wrote wisely three decades ago that intuition, for the most competent physician, is the key to diagnosis .

As we have indicated several times in other chapters, the greatest block to intuition, synchronicity, and the creation of miracles is unfinished emotional anguish, fear, anger, guilt, anxiety, or depression. I cannot overemphasize also that it is *critical* in most *acute* illnesses to use conventional medicine—that is, allopathic medicine that often requires drugs or surgery. It is important to recognize when one should use conventional medicine:

- Sudden acute pain, especially of the head, chest, or abdomen.
- Paralysis or numbness, partial or total, in any area of the body.
- Loss of consciousness.
- Seizures.
- Fever above 101 degrees.
- Difficulty in breathing.
- Confusion or significant personality change.
- Diastolic blood pressure above 100.
- Irregular or very rapid heartbeat or sudden drop in heart rate below 50 pulses per minute.
- Significant swelling or redness in any part of the body.
- Inability to urinate or defecate.
- Bleeding from wounds or unknown causes.
- Rapid weight loss, frequent urination, excessive stress.
- Any of the seven warning signs of cancer: a sore that won't heal;

any change in a wart or mole; indigestion more than occasionally or problems with swallowing; change in bowel or bladder habits; persistent cough or hoarseness; lump in the breast or elsewhere; any unusual bleeding or discharge.

- Any life-threatening illness.
- Psychosis.
- Severe dementia.
- Cognitive problems that require at least a CAT scan or MRI and neuropsychological testing.
- Fractures.
- Worrisome illness with uncertainty as to diagnosis.
- Heart attack.
- Acute stroke.
- Coma.
- Meningitis or encephalitis.
- Glomerulonephritis—severe kidney disease.
- Significant diarrhea in infants.

For illnesses that do not respond to conventional medicine or those for which physicians cannot find a cause or consider to be "all in your head," alternative approaches are far safer. Individuals with significant symptoms which cannot be diagnosed by a competent physician need a competent Medical Intuitive!

7

PRAYER, HEALING, AND MYSTICISM

To some extent, all aspects of religion, prayer, spirituality, and mysticism belong in the realm of intuition. Personally, I describe religion as the fight for God, because the hundreds of different religious divisions have been just that, divisions. Throughout at least the last five thousand years, the ups and downs of every religion, and those that are temporarily dominant, have generally led each to reject all except each sect's individual rigidity. I need not go into the various fractions within Protestantism and the continuing battle between Catholic and Protestants in Ireland or the eternal Middle East conflicts.

On the other hand, I describe mysticism as the search for God, and it is interesting that Edgar Cayce, of course, started the Search for God Study Groups. Among the most dominant religions in the world today, there are significant mystic groups. For instance, in Catholicism, some of the greatest mystics of all time have gotten the most attention, such as Theresa of Avila and St. John of the Cross. But Catholic mysticism insists that there has to be a prolonged and serious "dark night of the soul." On the other hand, the Kabbalah, which is the mystical arm of Judaism, does not go near the dark night of the soul. And in Islam, the really wonderful, peaceful mystical arm, the Sufis, certainly do not emphasize the dark night of the soul. In Hinduism, *The Yoga Sutras of*

Pantanjali are what Alice Bailey has called "The Light of the Soul."

To me, mysticism is one of the most fundamental human instincts. In relation to religion, my own belief is that the best book ever written was *The Varieties of Religious Experience* by William James. James covers religion beautifully but also defines four major aspects of mysticism:

1.   Ineffability. Virtually every mystic has described the ineffable nature of his or her experience. It is a feeling, not of intellect, and the greatest difficulty is expressing this feeling, especially to those who have never experienced it.

2.   A noetic quality. Despite the fact that these experiences are those of feeling, they convey to the individual experiencing them an absolute sense of "knowing." This includes revelation and illumination, which seem of utmost significance in importance to the individual, and certainly these are some of the peak intuitive experiences.

3.   Transience. The actual mystical state may last only a few minutes and rarely lasts more than an hour or two. Individuals who experience more than one such episode have a feeling of continuity between different episodes, but many mystics have a single great experience that changes their lives forever.

4.   Passivity. In the mystical state, the individual feels as if his or her will has been taken over by a higher power.

James examines the full breadth of mysticism from the simplest "ah ha" experience, with a profound sense of meaning and purpose, through such experiences as deja vous, including various and sundry "dreamy states." The ultimate higher states of mysticism often would be interpreted by psychologists and psychiatrists as actually pathological. Interestingly, these latter states are those that have been sought by indigenous people and Westerners through the use of such hallucinogenic drugs as marijuana, alcohol, and nitrous oxide. Working with nitrous oxide, James came to the conclusion that our waking, rational consciousness is one specialized form and that there is a much broader "potential" form of consciousness. He goes on to quote Dr. R.M. Bucke (*Cosmic Consciousness*): "The prime characteristic of cosmic consciousness is that consciousness of the cosmos is the life and order of the universe." This data is often associated with "Moral exaltation, an indescribable feeling of devotion, elation and joy, and a quickening of the moral sense, which is fully as striking, and more important, than is the enhanced intellectual power...." With this comes a "consciousness of eternal life." James further emphasizes that all major religions have "cultivated" mystical insights. In fact, the very nature of all aspects of Yoga, from simple Hatha Yoga to Raja Yoga, is the intent to get in touch with God. There are many, many interpretations of the Indian philosophical approach through *The Yoga Sutras of Pantanjali*. My favorite is by Charles Johnson, which is no longer in print. Currently in print that is the easiest to understand is the one by Daniel Condron.

When one reaches enlightenment, or samadhi, the individual comes out "a sage, a prophet or a saint, his whole character changes, his life changed, illumined." In Buddhism, there are four stages recognized. The first is concentration of the mind upon one point, excluding desire and being totally intellectual. In the second stage, the intellectual function is dropped off and the satisfied state of unity remains. In the third stage, satisfaction leads and indifference begins, along with memory and self-consciousness. In the final stage, the indifference, memory, and self-consciousness are perfected, and one then reaches into "the state in which there exists absolutely nothing." Especially in Sufism, the aim is "to detach the heart from all that is not God."

In many respects, Christian mysticism is very similar with the first aim—the mind's detachment from outer sensations with a goal of experiencing Christ and entering a state of rapture, which is described by St. John of the Cross as a "union of love." James goes on to say that there is "nothing objectively distinct about Catholic mysticism from that of other religions." I would disagree to some extent with James' statement on that, because true Catholics insist that the only way one can ultimately reach this state is to have gone through a dark night of the soul. In that dark night of the soul, the individual feels that God has abandoned or rejected the sinner, and those that experience this may go through many months or even years of such feelings. One of the reasons that Mother Theresa was considered a saint almost immediately after her death was that she had gone through fifty years in her private diaries essentially suffering the dark night of the soul.

But, on the other hand, in mystical states, individuals may have visions of the future, understanding of the universe, knowledge of distant events, and many of the other factors that are absolutely consistent with synchronicity and major psychic intuitive states. Many mystical writings are both poetic and mystical. Mystical states "tell the supremacy of the ideal, a vastness of unity, of safety, and of rest." Mystical experience cannot be upset by any amount of logical or rational "thinking." Carl Jung created the word *synchronicity* to describe a meaningful link between two events that cannot be explained by the concept of cause and effect. To some extent, this is the principle which David Boehm, the great quantum physicist, has linked to the universal connectedness of every event, namely, for instance, the difficult-to-understand concept that flapping of the wings of a butterfly can affect the weather on the other side of the earth. Jung emphasized that when we center ourselves in the Self, we obtain a type of inner harmony that is reflected back to us in the outer world. The concept of synchronicity is most easily understood through intuition. Jung described three types of synchronistic events:

The first involves the corresponsive meaning between an inner thought or feeling and an outer event. For instance, a woman in her therapeutic session was describing her distress over an earlier abortion. Just as she was in the midst of her narration, a sparrow flew into the window and was killed. Eugene Pascal mentions this case and says that the woman actually had the same thing happen in another therapeutic encounter when she was discussing her abortion.

The second kind of synchronicity is illustrated by a person waking from a dream who has a sudden intuitive insight that an event is happening far away exactly at that moment. This is later proved to have happened. Immanuel Kant, the great German philosopher, told of the equally famous Swedenborg, a Swedish clairvoyant and spiritual philosopher, having a vision of a fire raging in Stockholm, hundreds of miles away. It was later proved that the fire took place exactly as Swedenborg was recounting his vision.

The third type of synchronicity is precognition. That is, someone has a dream, an intuitive vision, or a premonition of something occurring at a later date. Abraham Lincoln is reported to have had a dream prior to his assassination in which he saw himself lying in state.

In describing synchronicity, Jung is validating intuition as equal to sensation, feeling, or thinking. Thoughts, visions, or premonitions that seem noncausally connected to an outer event are the substance of synchronicity. Pascal reports someone walking down the street and seeing an image of a student whom he had not seen for some three years. This happened just prior to his rounding a corner and encountering that student. The sudden image of the student and actual encounter are noncausal but represent synchronicity. The invisible connection is the Self. When we allow the energy of the transpersonal Self to flow through us, transcending pleasure, pain, love and hate, wisdom and ignorance, health and sickness, good or bad, we begin to see the Yin and the Yang, the Dark and the Light. Ultimately, connectedness with the Self leads to ecstasy, transcending polar opposites and ascending to a new transpersonal space, a divine state of consciousness beyond wisdom and compassion. In this state, we find ourselves standing outside all dualities and enjoying the bliss of universal Wisdom, Oneness, or God.

Thus, synchronicity is part of the path of mysticism and certainly is a striking instance of intuitive insight. William James defined mysticism as states of consciousness that range from the nonreligious to the most religiously profound. As indicated earlier, the simplest form of mystical experience, according to James, is a strong sense of significance and knowledge associated with the experience that it is "noetic." That is, a manifestation of the intellect. The experience is ineffable to the individual, meaning that it defies expression because of its subjective nature, and it is experienced much like a state of feeling. James calls these two qualities, noetic and ineffable, essential to the mystical state. The mystical experience is also generally transient: it fades quickly and the quality of the experience is difficult to recall. Some memory content always remains, however, and this memory content allows the individual to "modify the inner life of the subject during their times of recurrence." The experiences generally are interpreted to be past and happen without will. James suggests that these experiences increase in their frequency as one's "field of consciousness." Increases in this process are becoming more evolved toward the higher states of mysticism. I would also state that the more one detaches and resolves anger, guilt, anxiety, and sadness over anything that has happened in the past or present, the more one is moving toward this state. The sense of "Self, or the boundary between Self and the environment vanish." Then one has a feeling of unity with information formally defined as outside Self. Some refer to this as a loss of Self; to some who do not have a strong sense of Self to begin with, mystical experience can be frightening and confusing. James emphasizes the importance of keeping the definition of mystical states of consciousness as *value neutral.*

All mystical experiences, whether positive or negative, deserve recognition as part of our consciousness. According to James, mysticism may encompass truth and deception, pleasure and pain.

In summary, the mystical tradition includes the following concepts:

• The physical world of matter and individual personalities is only a small part of the whole.

• Human thought can know universal consciousness, or the Divine, by direct intuition, in which one feels united with the unknown becoming known.

• Human nature is dual. There are two cells: the personality, which most people regard as their true self, and the Self, or Soul, the inner person covering the spirit, the spark of divinity. With meditative practices, one can identify with the inner being, or the Self.

• The main purpose in the physical, earthly existence is to learn to identify with the Self. When one is in that state, one has universal intuitive knowledge, and in this state, individuals have concepts of eternal life, salvation, enlightenment, and bliss.

• *All individuals have the possibility of discerning spiritual truth, which is part of a sixth sense or intuition.*

• When one enters this transcendent state, one recognizes a connectedness between God and the Self. St. Augustine wrote: "Understanding is the reward of faith. Therefore, do not seek to understand an order that you may believe, but make the act of faith an order that you may understand; so unless you make an act of faith, you will not understand."

Even a modern physicist, Sir Edward Appleton, said: "The scientist for his part makes the assumption I mentioned as an act of faith; and he feels confirmed in that faith by his increasing ability to build up a consistent and satisfying picture of the universe and its behavior."

Or, Max Planck wrote: "When the pioneer in science sends forth the groping fingers of his thoughts, he must have a vivid, intuitive imagination for new ideas that are not generated by deduction but by an artistically creative imagination."

Lasson wrote: "The essence of mysticism is the assertion of an intuition that transcends the temporal categories of the understanding, relying on speculative reason. Rationalism cannot conduct us to the essence of things; we therefore need intellectual vision." He is calling intellectual vision here actually a form of intuition.

Evelyn Underhill, a great Christian mystic, wrote: "The mystic is a person who has attained that unit in a greater or lesser degree; or who aims at or believes in such attainment."

Even more important, Underhill went on to say, "Living the spiritual life is not living in a monastery or a nunnery. It is the attitude that you hold in your mind when you are down on your knees scrubbing the steps." Indeed, I say it is the attitude you hold in your mind when you are down on your knees scrubbing the toilet or looking at any of the stressful or negative aspects of life.

Thus, synchronistic events such as those described earlier as the three foundations of Jung are parts of the journey of mysticism. Mysticism is a particular and very specific form of spirituality, including experience, knowledge, and consciousness. There is an inherent urge in most humans to find the secret of the universe, to grasp it in its wholeness. To some extent, mysticism has a great similarity to synchronicity in that it is ineffable, and then both are ineffable; they both have a noetic quality because they seem to be remarkable new truths; they are usually very transient. Both mysticism and synchronicity give one a feeling of oneness in everything—OE—and they have a quality of passivity. You don't have to do anything to make it happen and they transcend time.

Shirley MacLaine has been reported to state that she became "psychic," or lucid, by acupuncture activations of a variety of points called Windows of the Sky. I know of no scientific study of the Window of the Sky acupuncture points being used in anyone other than Shirley MacLaine to open the intuitive process. The Window of the Sky points are these:

- Small Intestine 17 bilaterally
- Bladder 10 bilaterally
- Large Intestine 16 bilaterally

- Large Intestine 18 bilaterally
- Stomach 9 bilaterally
- Lung 3 bilaterally
- Triple Heater 16 bilaterally
- Gall Bladder 20 bilaterally
- Master of the Heart 1 bilaterally
- Governing Vessel 16; Conception Vessel 22

In Chinese cosmology, these are said to "open up movement of energy from body to head and vice versa." They are useful in poor memory, problems with concentration, insomnia, anxiety, and premature senility, and so on.

Over the last several years, I have worked with a series of personally intuitive perceived circuits within the body that appear to be pertinent. Our work with the Ring of Fire has demonstrated unequivocally that, by stimulating these 12 points, in a significant majority of people, we can raise DHEA; control and decrease the frequency and severity of migraine headaches in at least 75 percent of people; markedly improve pain sensation in diabetic neuropathy; markedly improve the well-being in patients with chronic rheumatoid arthritis; and help 70 percent of patients who have failed antidepressants to come out of depression.

More recently, I have also intuitively discovered the "Ring of Air." I believe it to be related to synchronicity of thought or lucidity, or to activate intuition. Stimulation of these points leads to "holographic thinking," mental creativity, symbolic thinking, and mystical insight. We have stimulated these points in some several hundred students now, with a number of them reporting transcendent experiences. These are the points of the Ring of Air:

- Spleen 1A bilaterally
- Liver 3 bilaterally
- Stomach 36 bilaterally
- Lung 1 bilaterally
- Gall Bladder 20 bilaterally
- Governing Vessel 1; Governing Vessel 16; Governing Vessel 20

Interestingly, the Ring of Air strikingly increases neurotensin, a neurochemical considered a neuroleptic, which helps body/mind disassociation.

As we will describe later in some greater detail, it is suggested that, as there are many paths to Rome, there are many paths to the mystical state. There are a number of adjuncts that assist this process and, of course, all of these assist the intuitive process:

- Music
- Meditation
- Physical Meditation (Tai Chi, Qi Gong, vapassana walking, Sufi dancing)
- Aromas
- Photostimulation
- Hallucinatory drugs and herbs
- Drumming
- Chanting
- Guided imagery
- Prayer

As Ambrose Worrall stated so elegantly in his marvelous little booklet, *Essay on Prayer,* "Every thought is a prayer. We all lead prayerful lives, whether we go to church or not, whether we are believers or nonbelievers." Ambrose Worrall emphasizes that prayer is not requesting and urging God to "give" something but does involve visualization to "create" the desired effect. Thus, properly done guided imagery is a positive prayer. As with all thinking, it is critical to create and desire only positive outcomes, never negative ones.

Ambrose Worrall further states in *Essay on Prayer:* "It is evident, for instance, that a man must *think,* for he *is* what he thinks. The thinking is what sets in motion the spiritual forces to bring about the changes in his environment, his body, his companions, his language, his desires, his hopes, his despairs."

Vision, of course, is one of the great "knowings" of intuition. Many artists, scientists, poets, musicians, architects, and the like, have had spontaneous images that they then move on to create. In fact, I suspect that most of the great contributions to the world have come through intuitive vision. Just as there are certain individuals whose intuition focuses in the field of science or poetry, or what not, there are some who focus in the field of medical intuition. Caroline Myss; Robert Leichtman, M.D.; Henry Rucker; Cay Randall–May; and Deena Spear are among those who have had the best expression of medical intuition in the last several decades. None have quite yet reached the depth and breadth of Edgar Cayce, but sooner or later, it is highly likely that others will become medical–intuitive geniuses.

Ultimately, as stated earlier, intuition is the foundation for creativity, science, mysticism, and health.

BIBLIOGRAPHY

1. Happold, F.C. *Mysticism: A Study and an Anthology.* Penguin Books: 1990, New York, NY.

2. Harvey, Andrew. *The Essential Mystic.* Harper and Rowe: 1996, San Francisco, CA.

3. Muses, Charles and Arthur M. Young. *Consciousness and Reality.* Outerbridgenlazard Inc.: 1972, New York, NY.

4. Muto, Susan. *John of the Cross for Today: The Dark Night.* Ave Maria Press: 1994, Notre Dame, IN.

5. Underhill, Evelyn. *The Spiritual Life.* One World: 1993, Oxford.

6. Roads, Michael J. *Journey Into Nature.* H. J. Kramer, Inc.: 1999, Tiburon, CA.

7. Pascal, Eugene. *Jung to Live By.* Warner Books: 1992, New York, NY.

8. Johnston, Charles. *The Yoga Sutras of Patanjali.* Brotherhood of Life: 1983, Albuquerque, NM.

9. James, William. *The Varieties of Religious Experience: A Study of Human Nature.* Modern Library: 1929, New York, NY.

10. Borysenko, Joan. *The Ways of the Mystic.* Hays House: 1997, Carlsbad, CA.

8

STRESS MANAGEMENT—
ANTIDOTES TO ILLNESS

Ultimately, stress is the total pressure experienced from physical, chemical, emotional, and electromagnetic energy. Some stress is essential to development of psychological, emotional, and even physical hardiness. Individuals who have reasonable self-esteem tolerate a moderate amount of stress, but one's ability to handle stress is genetic, karmic, and acquired. That is, we carry with us into each life a specific memory of previous incarnations of strengths and weaknesses. In today's society, the two most prevalent stressors are physical inactivity and unhealthy nutrition. Certainly, up until at least 1940, most people had a reasonably physically active life just to function. Even such modern conveniences as electric washing machines and dryers were not common, and there was no television. Both children and adults tended to be more physically active just to survive.

Roughly at the same time, essentially the beginning of World War II, nutrition began to change radically. Up until that time, approximately 90 percent of all food consumed was grown within fifty miles of the individual eating it. Interestingly, Edgar Cayce emphasized the need for the earth's magnetic imprint upon one's food and felt that it should be grown near where you live. In addition to the gradually increasing distribution of food grown around the world, more critical changes were

taking place in the commercialization of food. Over the next two decades, margarine began to be more commonly used than butter. This
was one of the first major transformations of fat, and although we have
known for fifty years that trans fats are not healthy, they have been
incorporated into a huge percentage of all packaged food. Preparation
of bread began to change, so that we went from truly whole-grain
breads almost exclusively to "white bread." And, I have to say, I have not
seen a commercial white bread that is fit to eat. Fortunately, my grandfather called all store-bought white bread "wasp nests," and I have never
learned to like it. So the staff of life, or bread, is filled with chemicals
that have nothing to do with whole grain itself. So-called bleached,
enriched bread is among the most unhealthy and stress-inducing foods
of all kinds. Indeed, the bleaching is done with bromine, and there is
some evidence that people who eat a great deal of bleached wheat bread
can become bromide toxic.

Then in the late '50s or early '60s, "fast foods" came into vogue, and
today 45 percent of all food consumed in this country is from fast-food
restaurants. Personally, I do not go to them. I went to a McDonald's in
1962, took one bite, spit it into my napkin, threw the whole thing away,
and I will never go back. The restaurants not only have a variety of
unsavory and chemically stressful ways of preparing their food, which
are almost always associated with junk white bread, they also add
monosodium glutamate, or MSG, which is a brain toxin. So today in
grocery stores at least 60 percent of the food sold is "processed." In
general, if it has more than one ingredient, it is processed. Thus, when
we compare the 60 percent in grocery stores and the 45 percent of all
junk from fast-food restaurants, some 80 percent is not real food. That
is taking its toll because, in the last ten years, as this has become the
dominant nutritional status of our country, obesity has doubled. Today
one-third of all Americans are overweight, which means a body mass
index between 25 and 29; and one third are truly obese, which means a
body index of 30 or above. The higher the body mass index, the greater
the stress of the individual. Heart disease, diabetes, stroke, and cancer
are illnesses resulting, to a huge extent, from our own natural and stressful nutritional patterns.

To manage stress, then, one of the basics is to eat real food (Appendix

B). Real food is food that has not been processed to alter its basic nature from the farm nature. Nonreal is all those packaged "foods" that contain sugar, monosodium glutamate, trans fats, artificial anything, and so on!

An approximate minimum of 75 percent of all that one eats should be natural fruits and vegetables—those raised without poisons, such as herbicides and pesticides. In general, although grains are vegetables, the most common grain eaten in this country is wheat, and one-third of Americans have mild to severe allergies to gluten. If in doubt, you should have at least a stool gluten sensitivity test available from Entero Labs, www.enterolabs.com. Peanut butter should be old-fashioned, in which the oil separates from the peanuts and should not include sugar or trans fats. Pumpkin seeds are marvelous and almost all nuts are among the best of foods, as are most legumes. Of course, peanuts are a legume, as are cashew nuts. Some people, of course, have problems with many members of the bean family. The ones that are least likely to cause gaseousness and other associated symptoms are chickpeas, lima beans, and plain-old green sweet peas, as well as peanut butter and cashews. Eggs, in my opinion, are one of the finest of all foods, and two eggs a day will often help you have a lower cholesterol, not a higher one. Some dairy products are good. I prefer Bulgarian-style buttermilk and drink about two glasses a day. I also like plain yogurt sweetened with fruits and a tiny bit of honey.

Then there is the question of water. Coronary artery disease was virtually unknown prior to chlorination of water. Within ten years of chlorination of water, it began to be the epidemic it is today. Now, chlorination of water alone is not the only thing that is stressful, but chlorine is a weapon of mass destruction, and if you happen to live in a city with chlorinated water, I strongly recommend that you reduce that stress by at least getting a filter to remove the chlorine from all water that you drink and eat. Indeed, if I lived with such water, I would get the whole house or whole apartment dechlorinated, because there is some evidence that you absorb it through the skin when you bathe or shower in it. So, the beginning of stress management is to eat right and drink right.

Perhaps the next most important factor in stress management is physical activity. In general, you need a minimum of thirty minutes of moderate exercise daily, and an hour a day is optimal for both health and stress management. It does not have to be physically extreme. Yoga, tai chi, walking, and active swimming are all excellent exercises. If you aren't going to do anything else, then I suggest you build up to bouncing in place three minutes, ten times a day. Go to www.youtube.com. Type in "Norm Shealy" and click on "Bounce for Health."

Beyond physical exercise and nutrition, adequate sleep and relaxation are critical. There is a reason for a forty–hour workweek. Lack of sleep itself is one of the greatest stressors possible. Individuals who do not sleep a minimum average of seven hours each night have increasing illnesses of all kinds. Of course, those individuals who work night shifts or evening shifts, and especially those who have different shifts every month or so, are among the most disease–prone individuals. Thus, working approximately 8 a.m. to 5 p.m., with time out for lunch, is the ideal, from a stress management point of view. And I would only recommend doing any other shifts if it is absolutely essential for your financial well–being. If you need help with sleep, I would start by avoiding caffeine after 3:00 p.m., taking a hot soak about three hours before going to bed, and be certain that there is no light in the room, especially of a green, yellow, or white type. Even night lights can disturb the production of melatonin. Timed–release melatonin is one of the safest and most effective aids for adequate sleep. In general, I would say to start with 1 mg. and build up to a maximum of 3 mg. If that is inadequate, you might add taurine and build up to about 3,000 mg. at bedtime. Since most people are deficient in magnesium, you could also add magnesium lotion, two teaspoons twice a day, to build up your intracellular levels of magnesium. Finally, adequate sleep may be assisted by using something like the Shealy RelaxMate, a photostimulator that provides the rhythm that the brain seeks for deep relaxation.

Relaxation is the ultimate stress reducer. Two major developments in the early part of the 20th century laid the foundation for the most successful antidotes to stress. Edmond Jacobson in 1929 published his magnificent book *Progressive Relaxation*. He had measured everything physiologically measurable and discovered that his technique reduced what was called, at that time, psychosomatic diseases by 80 percent. Today I would call them stress diseases. His technique consisted of a systematic and slow, thirty-minute exercise in which one selectively tenses individual muscle groups and then relaxes them. It is at least as good as any other technique and still works today, eighty years after his first publication.

At the same time, starting in 1912 and publishing his first book in 1932, Johann II. Schultz discovered autogenic training, a very successful self-regulating and self-hypnosis technique. By 1969, there were six volumes on autogenic therapy and over twenty-six hundred scientific references. Interestingly, only two hundred of them are in English. Autogenic training, by that time, was widely used by Olympic teams throughout Europe and Japan, and as a single mental tool, I still consider autogenic training to be the best. Again, 80 percent of stress illnesses can be brought under control with simple autogenic training. These are the phrases used:

- My arms and legs are heavy and warm
- My heartbeat is calm and regular
- My breathing is free and easy
- My abdomen is warm
- My forehead is cool
- My mind is quiet and still
- I am at peace

Blood pressure and pulse both decrease about 10 percent the first time one practices this. Doing this at least once daily is one of the greatest stress relievers that I know. There have been two doctoral dissertations using the most simplified version of this, an eighteen-minute tape or CD. One doctoral student found it highly statistically significant in patients with fibromyalgia who listened to the CD just once a day. Fibromyalgia is one of the most difficult diseases to manage, and yet, just doing autogenic training can have a striking improvement. Another doctoral student used autogenic training in caregivers for chronically ill individuals. The caregivers often actually have greater stress than the ill individuals! Again, there was a marked reduction in the stress reaction when they practiced autogenic training daily.

There are a number of other tools somewhat modified from these. Of course, in the 1970s, Herb Benson began his work on the "Relaxation Response" and found that individuals who would do twenty minutes of deep relaxation twice a day lowered their insulin requirement and their adrenaline production by 50 percent for the entire twenty-four hours. He emphasized simple things like just repeating a single positive word and many other similar ones. My own work involved the creation of what I call the software for biofeedback, because it is the mental exercises and not the electrical measuring devices that are really ultimately responsible for reducing stress. The most critical factors are the following:

• Be in present time. "Be here now." Focusing on the past or the future of one's problems creates distress.

• Belief in self. If you don't have that adequate belief that you can do it, then you may well need a clinical experience of biofeedback. I find temperature biofeedback to be adequate for most people. You can buy a simple, little finger thermometer, tape it loosely to one of your fingers, and just keep repeating "my finger is warm" while imagining the sun beaming down upon your finger. Measure the temperature before you begin and then not again until five or ten minutes later. Once you gain control over blood flow and temperature in one area of the body, it is possible to transfer it to other parts of the body, and you begin to realize that you really do have self-control.

• Sensory biofeedback, or balancing physical sensation. You can actually learn to turn off, turn on, and control every sensation in the body. I have developed a series of exercises for this that includes talking to the body; variations on autogenic training; tensing and releasing muscles; the progressive relaxation tool; feeling the pulse in individual parts of your body in all except the head (that could produce a migraine headache); collecting tension systematically, from the feet up through the entire body, and blowing it away as you breathe out, collecting tension as you breathe in, then blowing it away.

• Circulating the electrical energy in your body. Everything in your body is electrical, and you can imagine the electrical current gently and pleasantly moving up the back of your legs and the entire back of your body to the top of your head as you breath in and down the front, back through the tops of the feet, into the soles of the feet as you breath out. Expanding the electromagnetic energy around your body, you can create a sense of an electromagnetic aura, or capsule, one inch in diameter, gradually moving around from the feet up to the top of the head and then expanding the aura to twelve inches. This is an especially deep relaxing tool and one of the best for opening yourself to your own intuition.

• The next big step is balancing emotions. Essentially, there are a number of tools for learning to resolve all of your unfinished anger, guilt, anxiety, or depression. I have a wide variety of these exercises, which can be simply done by yourself and are outlined throughout my book *90 Days to Stress Free Living.*

• The final stage in mental self-regulation is spiritual attunement. Indeed, Schultz stated that one should not practice meditation until one has first practiced autogenic training or self-regulation for at least six months, because that would balance all of the unfinished business and then allow one to be ready for meditation. He also stated that those who practiced autogenic training daily for six months began to have spontaneous spiritual imagery, moving into a state of true spiritual meditation and imagery.

John Knowles wrote, back in the '70s, that 99 percent of people are born healthy and made ill by human misbehavior. That human misbehavior involves nutritional, physical, and psychological emotions, the stressors that we have discussed. There is adequate evidence that a minimum of 85 percent of illnesses could both be prevented and treated if one practiced a full stress-management lifestyle.

ZUNG TEST FOR DEPRESSION

Name _____

Age ____ Sex ____ Date _____

	None OR a Little of the Time	Some of the Time	Good Part of the Time	Most OR All of the Time
1. I FEEL DOWN-HEARTED, BLUE, AND SAD				
2. MORNING IS WHEN I FEEL THE BEST				
3. I HAVE CRYING SPELLS OR FEEL LIKE IT				
4. I HAVE TROUBLE SLEEPING THROUGH THE NIGHT				
5. I EAT AS MUCH AS I USED TO				
6. I ENJOY LOOKING AT, TALKING TO, AND BEING WITH ATTRACTIVE WOMEN/MEN				
7. I NOTICE THAT I AM LOSING WEIGHT				
8. 1 HAVE TROUBLE WITH CONSTIPATION				
9. MY HEART BEATS FASTER THAN USUAL				
10. I GET TIRED FOR NO REASON				
11. MY MIND IS AS CLEAR AS IT USED TO BE				
12. I FIND IT EASY TO DO THE THINGS I USED TO				
13. I AM RESTLESS AND CAN'T KEEP STILL				
14. 1 FEEL HOPEFUL ABOUT THE FUTURE				
15. I AM MORE IRRITABLE THAN USUAL				
16. I FIND IT **EASY** TO MAKE DECISIONS				
17. I FEEL THAT I AM USEFUL AND NEEDED				
18. MY LIFE IS PRETTY FULL				
19. I FEEL THAT OTHERS WOULD BE BETTER OFF IF I WERE DEAD				
20. I STILL ENJOY THE THINGS I USED TO DO				

SDS RAW SCORE ____

SDS INDEX ____

ZUNG TEST FOR DEPRESSION

Name _____

Age _____ Sex _____ Date _____

	None OR a Little of the Time	Some of the Time	Good Part of the Time	Most OR All of the Time	
1. I FEEL DOWN-HEARTED, BLUE, AND SAD	1	2	3	4	
2. MORNING IS WHEN I FEEL THE BEST	4	3	2	1	
3. I HAVE CRYING SPELLS OR FEEL LIKE IT	1	2	3	4	
4. I HAVE TROUBLE SLEEPING THROUGH THE NIGHT	1	2	3	4	
5. I EAT AS MUCH AS I USED TO	4	3	2	1	
6. I ENJOY LOOKING AT, TALKING TO, AND BEING WITH ATTRACTIVE WOMEN/MEN	4	3	2	1	
7. I NOTICE THAT I AM LOSING WEIGHT	1	2	3	4	
8. 1 HAVE TROUBLE WITH CONSTIPATION	1	2	3	4	
9. MY HEART BEATS FASTER THAN USUAL	1	2	3	4	
10. I GET TIRED FOR NO REASON	1	2	3	4	
11. MY MIND IS AS CLEAR AS IT USED TO BE	4	3	2	1	
12. I FIND IT EASY TO DO THE THINGS I USED TO	4	3	2	1	
13. I AM RESTLESS AND CAN'T KEEP STILL	1	2	3	4	
14. 1 FEEL HOPEFUL ABOUT THE FUTURE	4	3	2	1	
15. I AM MORE IRRITABLE THAN USUAL	1	2	3	4	
16. I FIND IT **EASY** TO MAKE DECISIONS	4	3	2	1	
17. I FEEL THAT I AM USEFUL AND NEEDED	4	3	2	1	
18. MY LIFE IS PRETTY FULL	4	3	2	1	
19. I FEEL THAT OTHERS WOULD BE BETTER OFF IF I WERE DEAD	1	2	3	4	
20. I STILL ENJOY THE THINGS I USED TO DO	4	3	2	1	
			SDS RAW SCORE		
			SDS INDEX		

ZUNG TEST FOR DEPRESSION

TABLE 1. Conversion of Raw Scores to the SDS Index

(Index = Raw Score Total _____ x100)
Maximum Score of 80

Raw Score	SDS Index	Raw Score	SDS Index	Raw Score	SDS Index
20	25	40	50	60	75
21	26	41	51	61	76
22	28	42	53	62	78
23	29	43	54	63	79
24	30	44	55	64	80
25	31	45	56	65	81
26	33	46	58	66	83
27	34	47	59	67	84
28	35	48	60	68	85
29	36	49	61	69	86
30	38	50	63	70	88
31	39	51	64	71	89
32	40	52	65	72	90
33	41	53	66	73	91
34	43	54	68	74	92
35	44	55	69	75	94
36	45	56	70	76	95
37	46	57	71	77	96
38	48	58	73	78	98
39	49	59	74	79	99
				80	100

SDS INDEX	EQUIVALENT CLINICAL GLOBAL IMPRESSION
Below 50	Within normal range, no psychopathology
50 - 59	Presence of minimal to mild depression
60 - 69	Presence of moderate to marked depression
70 & over	Presence of severe to most extremely depressed

If your final score is 50 or above, you are clinically depressed. If it is 40 to 49, you have what I call a subclinical depressive miasma and need to find a way to deal with unfinished business!

Symptom Index

Name: _____Date_____

When people are chronically ill, they often have other symptoms. Do you have any of the following?

PLEASE CHECK ONLY THOSE THAT YOU HAVE NOW OR HAVE HAD WITH YOUR CURRENT ILLNESS.

____ Depressed mood.

____ Loss of interest or pleasure in things you used to enjoy.

____ Significant weight change (loss or gain).

____ Frequent eating between meals.

____ Insomnia.

____ Snoring.

____ Sleep walking.

____ Hypersomnia.

____ Agitation.

____ Sluggishness; slow to function.

____ Fatigue, low energy, feeling tired all of the time.

____ Feelings of worthlessness or guilt.

____ Difficulty concentrating, thinking, and remembering.

____ Indecisiveness.

____ Recurrent thoughts of death or suicide.

____ Suicide attempts.

____ Nervous exhaustion.

____ Worrying excessively or being anxious.

____ Frequent crying.

____ Being extremely shy or sensitive.

____ Lumps or swelling in your neck.

____ Blurring of vision.

____ Seeing double.

____ Seeing colored halos around lights.

____ Pains or itching around the eyes.

___ Excess blinking or watering of the eyes.

___ Loss of vision.

___ Difficulty hearing.

___ Earache.

___ Running ear.

___ Buzzing or other noises in the ears.

___ Motion sickness.

___ Teeth or gum problems.

___ Sore or sensitive tongue.

___ Change in sense of taste.

___ Nose stuffed up.

___ Runny nose.

___ Sneezing spells.

___ Frequent head colds.

___ Bleeding from the nose.

___ Sore throat even without a cold.

___ Enlarged tonsils.

___ Hoarse voice even without a cold.

___ Difficulty or pain in swallowing.

___ Wheezing or difficulty breathing.

___ Coughing spells.

___ Coughing up a lot of phlegm.

___ Coughing up blood.

___ Chest colds more than once a month.

___ High blood pressure.

___ Low blood pressure.

___ Heart trouble.

___ Thumping or racing heart.

___ Pain or tightness in the chest.

___ Shortness of breath.

___ Heartburn.

___ Feeling bloated.

___ Excess belching.

___ Discomfort in the pit of your stomach.

___ Nausea.

___ Vomiting blood.

___ Peptic ulcer.

___ Change in appetite.

___ Digestive problems.

___ Excess hunger.

___ Getting up frequently at night to urinate.

___ Urinating more than 5-6 times a day.

___ Unable to control your urine.

___ Burning or pains when you urinate.

___ Black, brown, or bloody urine.

___ Difficulty starting your urine.

___ Constant urge to urinate.

___ Constipation.

___ Diarrhea.

___ Black or bloody bowel movement.

___ Grey bowel movement.

___ Pain when you move your bowels.

___ Bleeding from your rectum.

___ Stomach pains which double you up.

___ Frequent stomach trouble.

___ Intestinal worms.

___ Hemorrhoids.

___ Yellow jaundice.

___ Biting your nails.

___ Stuttering or stammering.

___ Any kind of problem with your genital or sexual organs.

___ Sexual problems.

___ Hernia or rupture.

___ Kidney or bladder disease.

___ Stiff or painful muscles or joints.

___ Swelling joints.

___ Pain in your back or shoulders.

___ Painful feet.

___ Swelling in your armpits or groin.

___ Trouble with swollen feet or ankles.

___ Cramps in your legs at night or with walking.

___ Itching or burning skin.

___ Rash or pimples.

___ Excess bleeding from a small cut.

___ Easy burning skin.

___ Dizziness or lightheadedness.

___ Feeling faint or fainting.

___ Numbness in any part of your body.

___ Cold hands or feet even in hot weather.

___ Paralysis.

___ Blacking out.

___ Fits, convulsions, or epilepsy.

___ Change in your handwriting.

___ Tendency to shake or tremble.

___ Tendency to be too hot or too cold.

___ Sweating more than usual.

___ Hot flashes.

___ Being short of breath with minimal effort.

___ Failure to get adequate exercise.

___ Being overweight.

___ Being underweight.

___ Having lost more than half of your teeth.

___ Bleeding gums.

___ Badly coated tongue.

___ A lot of small accidents or injuries.

___ Varicose veins.

___ Headaches.

___ Other aches and pains.

___ Feeling pessimistic or hopeless.

___ Have had any kind of surgery within the past year.

___ Being upset easily by criticism.

___ Having little annoyances get on your nerves and make you angry.

___ Getting angry easily.

___ Getting nervous around strangers.

___ Feeling lonely.

___ Having difficulty relaxing.

___ Being troubled by frightening dreams or thoughts.

___ Being disturbed by work or family problems.

___ Wishing that you could get psychological or psychiatric help.

___ Being tense or jittery.

___ Being easily upset.

___ Being in low spirits.

___ Being in *very* low spirits.

___ Believing that your life is out of your hands and controlled by external forces.

___ Feeling that life is empty, filled with despair.

___ Having no goals or aims at all.

___ Having failed to make progress towards your life goals.

___ Feeling that you are completely bound by factors outside yourself.

___ Feeling sad, blue, or down in the dumps.

___ Feeling slowed down or restless and unable to sit still.

___ Frequent illness.

___ Being confined to bed by illness.

For men only:

___ Having a urine stream that's very weak or very slow.

___ Having prostate trouble.

___ Having unusual burning or discharge from your penis.

___ Having swelling or lumps in your testicles.

___ Having your testicles painful.

___ Having trouble getting erections (getting hard).

For women only:

___ Having trouble with your menstrual period.

___ Bleeding between your periods.

___ Having heavy bleeding with your periods.

___ Getting bloated or irritable before your periods.

___ Taking birth control pills (in the last year).

___ Having lumps in your breasts.

___ Having excess discharge from your vagina.

___ Feeling weak or sick with your periods.

___ Having to lie down when your periods start.

___ Feeling tense and jumpy with your periods.

___ Having constant hot flashes and sweats.

___ Have had a hysterectomy or are on hormonal replacement.

If your total symptoms are greater than 20, the more your total stress is affecting your physiology and the more your unfinished business is likely to block your intuition.

Ultimately, your number one key to optimizing your intuition is reducing all your stress and symptoms! Once you are mentally, physically, and emotionally balanced, you are ready to move into developing your Medical Intuition.

PERSONAL STRESS ASSESSMENT
Total Life Stress Test

NAME _____ DATE _____

Record your stress points on the lines in the right-hand margin, and indicate subtotals in the boxes at the end of each section. Then add your subtotals (on page 4) to determine your total score.

A. DIETARY STRESS
Average Daily Sugar Consumption

Sugar added to food or drink	1 point per 5 teaspoons
Sweet roll, piece of pie/cake, brownie, other dessert	1 point each
Coke or can of pop; candy bar	2 points each
Banana split, commercial milk shake, sundae, etc.	5 points each
White flour (white bread, spaghetti, etc.)	5 points

Average Daily Salt consumption

Little or no "added" salt	0 points
Few salty foods (pretzels, potato chips, etc.)	0 points
Moderate "added" salt and/or salty foods at least once per day	3 points
Heavy salt user, regularly (use of "table salt" and/or salty foods at least twice per day)	10 points

Average Daily Caffeine Consumption

Coffee	½ point each cup
Tea	½ point each cup
Cola drink or Mountain Dew	1 point each cup
2 Anacin or APC tabs	½ point per dose
Caffeine Benzoate tablets (NoDoz, Vivarin, etc.)	2 points each

Average Weekly Eating Out

2-4 times per week	3 points
5-10 times per week	6 points
More than 10 times per week	10 points

DIETARY SUBTOTAL [ ] **A**

B. ENVIRONMENTAL STRESS

Drinking Water

Chlorinated only	1 point
Chlorinated and fluoridated	2 points

Soil and Air Pollution

Live within 10 miles of city of 500,000 or more	10 points
Live within 10 miles of city of 250,000 or more	5 points
Live within 10 miles of city of 50,000 or more	2 points
Live in the country but use pesticides, herbicides, and/or chemical fertilizer	10 points
Exposed to cigarette smoke of someone else more than 1 hour per day	5 points

Television Watched

For each hour over 1 per day	½ point

ENVIRONMENTAL
SUBTOTAL [   ] B

C. CHEMICAL STRESS

Drugs (any amount of usage)

Antidepressants	1 point
Tranquilizers	3 points
Sleeping pills	3 points
Narcotics	5 points
Other pain relievers	3 points

Nicotine

3-10 cigarettes per day	5 points
11-20 cigarettes per day	15 points
21-30 cigarettes per day	20 points
31-40 cigarettes per day	35 points
Over 40 cigarettes per day	40 points
Cigar(s) per day	1 point each
Pipeful(s) of tobacco per day	1 point each
Chewing tobacco -"chews" per day	1 point each

Average Daily Alcohol Consumption

1 oz. whiskey, gin, vodka, etc.	2 points each
8 oz. beer	2 points each
4-6 oz. glass of wine	2 points each

CHEMICAL SUBTOTAL [   ] C

D. PHYSICAL STRESS
Weight

Underweight more than 10 lbs.	5 points
10 to 15 lbs. overweight	5 points
16 to 25 lbs. overweight	10 points
26 to 40 lbs. overweight	25 points
More than 40 lbs. overweight	40 points

Activity

Adequate exercise*, 3 days or more per week	0 points
Some physical exercise, 1 or 2 days per week	15 points
No regular exercise	40 points

Work Stress

Sit most of the day	3 points
Industrial/factory worker	3 points
Overnight travel more than once a week	5 points
Work more than 50 hours per week	2 points per hour over 50
Work varying shifts	10 points
Work night shift	5 points

PHYSICAL SUBTOTAL [_____] D

*Adequate means doubling heartbeat and/or sweating minimum of 30 minutes per time.

E. Holmes-Rahe Social Readjustment Rating*

(Circle the mean values that correspond with life events listed below which you have experienced during the past 12 months.)

Death of spouse	100
Divorce	73
Marital separation	65
Jail term	63
Death of close family member	63
Personal injury or illness	53
Marriage	50
Fired at work	47
Marital reconciliation	45
Retirement	45
Change in health of family member	44
Pregnancy	40
Sexual difficulties	39
Gain of new family member	39
Business readjustment	39
Change in financial state	38
Death of close friend	37
Change to different line of work	36
Change in number of arguments with spouse	35
Mortgage over $20,000	31
Foreclosure of mortgage or loan	30
Change in responsibilities at work	29
Son or daughter leaving home	29
Trouble with in-laws	29
Outstanding personal achievement	28
Spouse begins or stops work	26
Begin or end school	25
Change in living conditions	24
Revision of personal habits	23
Trouble with boss	20

Change in work hours or conditions	20
Change in residence	20
Change in schools	19
Change in recreation	19
Change in church activities	18
Change in social activities	17
Mortgage or loan less than $20,000	16
Change in sleeping habits	15
Change in eating habits	15
Vacation, especially if away from home	13
Christmas or other major holiday stress	12
Minor violations of the law	11

(Add the mean values to get the Holmes-Rahe total. Then refer to the conversion table to determine your number of points.)

Conversion Table

Holmes-Rahe less than	60	110	160	170	180	190	200	210	220	230	240	250	260	265	270	275	280	285	290	295	300	305	310	315	320	325	330	335	340	345	350	Anything over 351=40+
Your number of points:	0	1	2	3	4	5	6	7	8	9	10	11	12	13	14	15	16	17	18	19	20	21	22	23	24	25	26	27	28	29	30	

Holmes-Rahe Social Readjustment Rating (Converted) [   ]   E

*The Social Readjustment Rating Scale: See Holmes. T. H. and Rahe, R.H.: The social readjustment raring scale. *journal of Psychosomatic Research.* 11:213218, 1967, for complete wording; of these items. Reproduced with permission of the authors and publisher.

EMOTIONAL STRESS
Sleep

Less than 7 hours per night	3 points
Usually 7 or 8 hours per night	0 points
More than 8 hours per night	2 points

Relaxation

Relax only during sleep	10 points
Relax or meditate at least 20 minutes per day	0 points

Frustration at work

Enjoy work	0 points
Mildly frustrated by job	1 point
Moderately frustrated by job	3 points
Very frustrated by job	5 points

Marital Status

Married, happily	0 points
Married, moderately unhappy	2 points
Married, very unhappy	5 points
Unmarried man over 30	5 points
Unmarried woman over 30	2 points

Usual Mood

Happy, well adjusted	0 points
Moderately angry, depressed, or frustrated	10 points
Very angry, depressed, or frustrated	20 points

Any Other Major Stress Not Mentioned Above—
You Judge Intensity (Specify):

_____ (10 to 40 points)

                              EMOTIONAL
                              SUBTOTAL   [   ] F

Add A_____+B_____ +C_____

+D_____+E_____ +F_____

YOUR PERSONAL STRESS ASSESSMENT SCORE

If your score exceeds 25 points, you probably will feel better if you reduce your stress; greater than 50 points, you definitely need to eliminate stress in your life.

Circle your stressor with the highest number of points and work first to eliminate it; then circle your next greatest stressor, overcome it; and so on.

SELF-HEALTH SYSTEMS OF BRINDABELLA FARMS
5607 South 222nd Rd. • Fair Grove, Missouri 65648
Phone: 417-267-2900 • Fax: 417-267-3102

9

TOOLS FOR OPTIMIZING INTUITION

As I will emphasize perhaps more often than you would like, the greatest blocks to intuition are anger, guilt, anxiety, or depression over anything. As one of my patients said, "I now realize that I cannot afford the luxury of depression." From both a health point of view and an intuitive point of view, we cannot afford the luxury of any of these, because virtually all negative emotional states are synonyms for them. Thus, the number-one tool for optimizing intuition is working toward personal self-actualization, as Maslow would describe it, or autonomy, as Hans Eysenck would describe it. Remember, as Eysenck said, essentially 99 percent of people who die from heart disease or cancer, the two leading causes of death, are primarily depressed, angry, or both. So the first tool is detachment. How do you detach? As emphasized in "Stress Management," chapter eight, it is accomplished by focusing on something positive. It can be simple. It can be amusing. It can be watching a scene in nature but, again, if you don't already have a tool, I strongly suggest that you practice autogenic training a minimum of six months. Of course, once you have done it for that long, let us hope that it will have become such a habit that you will never give it up.

Meditation, of course, is another major tool. To me, meditation is not rare, and it is not necessarily guided imagery, although spontaneous imagery can occur. Imagery happens frequently in individuals who practice autogenic training for at least six months. Meditation is essentially very much the same as mysticism. It is a *focus* on unity with soul, God, or the Divine. Now to get to true meditation, you need to practice deep relaxation, balancing physical feelings and emotions, and then staying in that state of detachment and attunement. There are, on the other hand, a number of tools that can assist in optimizing intuition. My favorite of these is music—great classical music particularly. My own two favorites are Mozart's *Requiem* and Rachmaninoff's *Isle of the Dead*. Personally, I think *Isle of the Dead* should be called Isle of Life, as I consider it one of the most transcendent pieces of music I have ever experienced. The vibratory part is quite easy, and there is good scientific evidence that feeling, as well as hearing, music is physiologically and psychologically more intense than just hearing music. To build your own vibratory music bed, go to an Army surplus store and buy at least a four-inch piece of polyurethane foam, and then go to Best Buy or one of the stores that has a whole room full of speakers. Go around the room and feel the output of various speakers. Choose a pair that provides the greatest vibratory sensation. Cut holes in the foam adequate to fit these two speakers longitudinally, with one at the top of your head and one a few inches below the top speaker, so that it covers essentially the rest of your spine down to the base of the spine. Purchase an air mattress, fill it with air, and put it on top of the foam. You may need to build a frame around the air mattress so that it won't slide off. Connect the speakers to a good quality but very inexpensive audio system. Play and experience different vibratory feelings. Again, my most favorites on vibratory music are Mozart's *Requiem* and *Rachmaninoff's Isle of the Dead* as well as *The Best of Kitaro*. Do not use such types of music as jazz or rock. Listening and feeling music, especially the ones that I have mentioned, have been very helpful to people in detaching and entering at least the foothills of mysticism.

Learning to use feedback from your own body, some form of kinesiology is also another excellent adjunct for expressing intuition. There are three forms that I have found particularly useful.

• The "O Ring." The O Ring is very simple. You make a circle with the thumb and the long finger with each hand, place one of these circles inside the other (I generally use my right hand as the active hand and pull it through the long finger of the left hand), and play, asking obvious questions and reinforcing what you know to be the answer. Always ask questions only in a yes–or–no fashion, such as: My birthday is? Today is? As you reinforce to your ever conscious/subconscious mind what positive and negative really are, then you can begin to ask other questions in this way. For me, yes leads to much greater resistance with the left hand, whereas, when the answer is no, there is no resistance at all, and the right O Ring comes directly through.

• A pendulum. Small pendulums are easily available at many metaphysical stores. They can be made of anything. I rather like crystal ones, but even brass or silver ones can be used. In general, holding the pendulum in your dominant hand, with your elbow resting on your knee or a table, is the best way to use a pendulum. For most people, a clockwise movement is positive and a counter clockwise is negative. Do not allow your subconscious ego id/ib to give you an "I don't know." It is of no value. So, again, practice many times with answers that you know to be correct, and direct your subconscious to what is positive and what is negative. We will come back to the use of this and the O Ring in the next chapter.

• Radionics. Although the original radionic device of Abramson was very complex, with all kinds of dials and numbers that had no wires connecting them, Francis K. Farralty taught me back in the early 70s that one can use any smooth surface, even a piece of paper, and you just rub a finger. Using my right index finger, a "yes" causes the finger to stick as one rubs across a smooth surface, and a "no" allows the finger to keep moving without any resistance. Practice. Practice. Practice. You should find that one of these three tools will give you increasingly accurate answers, but if you don't practice it, it can't be of much use.

• For many people, just quietly walking, focusing on each step, and slow deep breathing can allow one to detach from the kafuffle of idle thoughts. My own best intuitive insights come when I am jogging, walking, or even working in my garden.

• Aromas. For more than thirty years, I have used rose oil fragrance to assist me, because of my intent that it repel negativity. I learned this from Torkom Saraydarian in his wonderful little booklet, *Irritation—The*

Destructive Fire. But, some two decades ago, Caroline Myss and I created a combination of essential oils, grounding them in musk to make it a true perfume, and we called this In–Tu–It. It gives me much the same feeling that I get with other states of detached meditation, especially the Ring of Air. I have also created one that I call Bliss, which creates a similar but clearly different psychological mental effect. You might want to play with either of these.

• Photostimulation. There is no question that people who are in a state of spontaneous, creative imagery generally have a dominant brain activity that is in the theta range, 4 to 7 cycles/second or hertz. The use of the Shealy RelaxMate II is of great assistance in reaching this state, and we have proved that use of these frequencies, in nondepressed people at least, significantly increases theta activity in the computerized EEG, or brain map. Photostimulation also aids relaxation and helps people sleep deeper and dream more. I do not like or recommend any hallucinogenic drugs or herbs.

• Drumming. Drumming is undoubtedly one of the most primitive and basic methods of major entrainment or trance induction. Just simple drumming is well worth exploring and practicing, because almost all individuals enter some type of trance or light hypnotic state during drumming experiences.

• Chanting. Many of the great religions include chants. I have to admit that my own favorites are Gregorian chants. I must have at least twenty different CDs with various Gregorian chants. I have often said that if I reach a state in which I can't take care of myself, I want to go into a room, lock the door, and turn on the Gregorian chants until I am gone. Of course, chanting Ohm is another of the well-known tools for altering consciousness, and all of these tools can be helpful in optimizing intuition.

• The Ring of Air. Finally, the Ring of Air, when the acupuncture points are stimulated with human DNA frequency of 54–78 billion cycles/sec. or gigahertz (GHz), the brain output of neurotensin increases naturally. Neurotensin is a neurotrophic drug that puts one into an altered state of consciousness and allows one to feel pleasantly "spacey." As I mentioned earlier, the points are: Spleen 1A bilaterally; Liver 3 bilaterally; Stomach 36 bilaterally; Lung 1 bilaterally; Gall Bladder 20 bilaterally; Governing Vessel 1; Governing Vessel 16; Governing Vessel 20. Note: Photos of the Ring of Air points are in Appendix C.

I have found, both with individuals and when I am doing group workshops, that doing brief massage and vigorous tapping of each of these points, always starting at the foot and moving up to the top of the head, can assist one in moving into a delightful and very pleasant detached state of bliss. You can sometimes enhance this by using a drop of In-Tu-It on the points while tapping them. In addition, you can do visualizations of this particular acupuncture circuit. I have made a CD of the Ring of Air, which assists some people in doing the creative visualization to optimize Ring of Air stimulation.

10

CONTACTING GUIDES AND ANGELS

Angels are recognized in Christianity, Judaism, and Islam. The Old Testament actually mentions three: Michael, Gabriel and Raphael. Michael is actually the only one in the scriptures called an archangel, although the Catholic Church has added to these Gabriel and Raphael. Michael is essentially the great warrior archangel, sometimes also called the Angel of God. The archangel Gabriel is the one associated with the angel who said to Mary, "Hail, Mary full of grace, the Lord is with thee." The archangel Raphael is a great healer and is an example of an angel reported to have assumed a human form. There are a number of sacred shrines throughout the Christian world dedicated to St. Raphael where reported miraculous cures have taken place.

Other than these three archangels, there are numerous other angels who have been identified in various texts. It is essential to remember that Edgar Cayce's channeling reveals all the elements that suggest that he was constantly inspired by or channeling an angel. It is also important to remember Cayce's essential principles that have much to do with the whole field of intuition. For instance, in the *Edgar Cayce Handbook for Creating Your Future* by Mark Thurston and Christopher Fazel, the principles for creating the future are listed as these:

- Mind is the builder of what you think you have become.

- Changing anything starts with motives and ideals.
- God is *living*—active and responsive.
- All is one—everything is connected.
- Live with a purpose greater than yourself.
- Truth is a growing thing.
- Evil is just good gone wrong.
- Personal alchemy: Sometimes a weakness can become a strength.
- Anger, used correctly, serves a good purpose.
- The good you see in others is also in yourself.
- Every crisis is an opportunity for a breakthrough.
- Life is a pattern of cycles.
- Everything happens for a reason: you have a purpose in life.
- God wants us to learn how to make decisions.
- In every moment we are either helping or hurting.
- Love means honoring the other person's free will.
- Compassion is a way of seeing and knowing.
- There is power in groups.
- Take the initiative: it is best to be doing *something*.
- Give if you want to receive: only what you give away do you own.
- Why worry when you can pray?
- There is power in a person's name.
- Health comes from balancing body, mind, and heart.
- Grace is yours for the asking.

Focusing on all of these characteristics is, of course, the outline for A Life Well Lived.

The word *angel* means messenger, and nothing is more appropriate since angels are generally given credit for unusual information, such as instant knowing or even words that may save one's life in a crisis. Angels are mentioned 108 times in the Old Testament and 165 times in the New Testament. It appears that all angels were created simultaneously with the creation of Heaven itself. Angels are not subject to death, and it is almost certain that there are at least as many angels as there are human beings, since each of us has a "Guardian Angel." Angels do not appear to bi-locate. That is, they appear at only one location at a time, and although they can take the appearance of human beings they do not ordinarily incarnate. They are Spirits, rather than physical beings, and apparently there are "Fallen Angels," like Lucifer or Satan, so that there can be some angels who are voices that speak to us from a negative point of view. As always, the fruit is in the eating.

I can assume from many things that have happened over the years that I have been "inspired" by at least my own personal angels and perhaps angelic guides throughout life. I have already discussed some of my earlier intuitive hits. The first time that I was consciously aware of an angelic guide was in December 1983. I had a bout of flu, and I started taking Symmetrel, an antiflu medication that I used to take, but I noticed on several occasions that I became very spacey when taking it. The first night in 1983, after I had taken two Symmetrel, I awoke at midnight and could not go back to sleep. I suddenly began having conversations with fourteen distinct voices. I sat busily at my desk, attempting to take notes and to distinguish between the voices that certainly sounded different from one another, and I recognized one of those who identified herself as Muriel. I had no further open conversation with her until some years later. On that occasion I was in Holland on a late afternoon walk, and I suddenly "demanded" that my guardian angel come and speak with me. Suddenly the voice that I recognized as Muriel appeared, and we had a wonderful conversation for about an hour and a half about a number of simple aspects of the meaning of life. I got somewhat lost, even though I had been in those woods with their wide paths many times, and I wound up about three miles away from where I was staying. Since that time, I have had a number of such conversations and have many more "knowings." Among other things, my major teacher guide, who was different from my personal guide, has told me that, although angels do not actually have a sex, in the human sense of the form, and do not reproduce themselves, they essentially take on masculine or feminine energies. One of the most interesting comments that my teacher guide has stated is, "In the eyes of the Universe, the only sin is murder." All our other problems are just lessons in life! I sometimes see images, I sometimes have abstract knowing, and sometimes I hear voices. All of these seem somewhat distinct, and yet I have no way of totally distinguishing them.

I have been told by a number of excellent intuitives that I also have "guides" who are non-angels, and I am not aware of any direct verbal communication with any of them. I presume that they are also most often responsible for assisting me in receiving intuition.

Hence the question arises, how can individuals begin the process of communicating with their guides? As with all aspects of intuition, the most important prerequisite for communicating with your angels is to be at peace. Don't try to do it when you are in a rushed or upset state of mind. Now that does not necessarily mean that you have to be sitting quietly in a meditative state. For some of us, clearing the mind of idle chatter, or chitta, is the most important thing; and it may occur while you are sleeping, walking, jogging, gardening, and so on, but it is being present in the "as of now" state of mind. As with the other tools that assist in receiving intuition, music may be of great assistance. Once you have cleared your mind and are in present time, simply ask first, especially your guardian angel, to come and talk with you—and then wait. You may receive a sense, a knowing; you may hear a voice; and you may begin to get images. The most important thing is not to become frustrated if you don't have a materialization of your angel! Such materializations are exquisitely rare.

Another way of encouraging a "visit" by your angels or other guides is to prepare yourself as you go to sleep at night. Quiet your mind and repeat a small mantra, such as, "I encourage my angel to visit in my dreams," or words that are particularly meaningful to you. Don't become discouraged if it doesn't happen the first night. Try it nightly for one month, and if it hasn't happened by then, just let it go and say something like, "When the time is right, I would like to meet you."

Furthermore, any time you receive an obvious intuitive insight, you might ask, "Is this from my angelic guide?" Amazon.com has at least fifty different listings under "Angel Cards." Several of these include such topics as "Connecting With Your Angels Kit," "The Angel Insight Pack: Oracle Cards for Inspiration, Guidance and Wisdom," and "Angel Cards and Book—Expanded Edition," or the original "Angel Cards."

11

BECOMING A MEDICAL INTUITIVE

As Edgar Cayce often mentioned, all of us are intuitive. Cayce happened to have a broad ability to use his intuition. He also emphasized that we can develop our intuitive ability. To a significant extent, intuition is just an expansion of our imagination in which images that we "receive" or create become increasingly more accurate. From a quantum physics point of view, there is no time and everything is connected. Ultimately, optimal intuition is the experience of spontaneously "knowing" some aspect of the work without having direct physical knowledge of it. *Medical intuition* is, of course, a more specific term because, to be useful from a medical point of view, it requires that you know the physical location of a ·medically diagnosable problem as well as at least the physiological (electrical/chemical) "cause" of the problem. As you will see at the end of this chapter, this requires very specific intuition.

Over the past twenty years, I have received numerous letters from individuals who write, "I am another Caroline Myss." Well, I haven't met one yet. In years gone by, I occasionally would write back to such a person and say that I would give them three names, and if they were at least 50 percent accurate on those three, I would examine them further. Not having found even one who was close to 50 percent accurate, I gave up that practice long ago. Perhaps the most ridiculous such person wrote that she actually worked as a "Medical Intuitive." So I gave her my name and birth date and asked her to do a reading. She responded with three pages of nonsense. Not one sentence was actually correct, and on the last page, she wrote, "And on your left calf there is an area the size of a dime that is weeping." She apparently thought that was from the loss of a sibling when I was about nine years of age. First of all, I didn't lose a sibling at age nine, and secondly, I looked down to make sure I had not wet myself. I then wrote back and said, "Please take down your shingle, burn, it and bury the ashes, because you are a danger to the human race." Obviously, I never heard from her again. Eventually, Caroline Myss and I established over ten years ago a training course for individuals interested in becoming medically intuitive and then established the American Board of Scientific Medical Intuition, to provide board certification to those individuals who were capable of passing the exam. The exam consists of forty patient names, with ages or birth dates, and to be board certified, an individual has to have an accuracy score of 75 percent. Very few people put the work in to become that. On the other hand, with adequate training, almost anyone can become a counseling intuitive, and there are dozens of techniques that assist individuals in using this particular skill. I have actually often said that almost everyone is a phenomenal counselor to anyone except themselves.

Obviously, the foundation for becoming a Medical Intuitive is developing intuition itself. The single most important requirement for optimizing your own intuition is to resolve all your own unfinished business related to anger, guilt, anxiety, or depression. These festering emotional problems will bleed through and color almost everything you do in life, not only with intuition but in your relationships with other individuals. In order to do this, most people need some form of training, and if you really need to do that aspect of the work, I suggest you do the 90-day program in my book *90 Days to Stress Free Living* (Element Books, Inc., Boston, MA, 1999)

The basic need for optimizing intuition is relaxation, because it allows you to detach from all the conflicting chitta (chatter) of the mind. There are, of course, probably as many methods of relaxation as there are people, but the following are those that are most useful for most people:

- Slow, deep breathing.
- Assuming a comfortable position that most often should not be reclining, as it is much easier to fall asleep. Sitting straight up, with the arms and legs uncrossed and the spine erect, is an ideal place because it helps prevent you from going to sleep. Just paying attention to the breathing, observing and moving air in and out of your nostrils, is one way of doing it. Interestingly, in Yoga, it is believed that when you breathe through the left nostril, you are activating the right brain, and when you breathe through the right nostril you are activating the left brain. Most of us move back and forth between those two every twenty to thirty minutes, and there is a brief time in between when you breathe through both nostrils. You can practice this by using your fingers to block airflow in one nostril, allowing you to breathe through only one nostril for several minutes, then switch to the other. Eventually, you learn to do it without holding the other nostril. There is good evidence physiologically that this does have quite striking effects on reducing overactivity in the sympathetic nervous system or stress. For some people, movement is better than sitting still, so Yoga, walking without thinking about what is happening, and listening to calming music may also be helpful. With Vapassana walking, you keep your attention focused upon breathing and each step one at a time without allowing yourself to get involved with chasing in your imagination all of the sidetracks you could take as you walk about. In other words, you detach from the environment but not so thoroughly that you walk into something or walk into the path of an oncoming car!
- The next step is learning to balance sensations and emotions. There are nine techniques that allow this to happen:

1. Talking to the Body. This is based upon Johan H. Schultz's technique of autogenic training. *My arms and legs are heavy and warm. My heartbeat is calm and regular. My breathing is free and easy. My abdomen is warm and cool. My mind is quiet and still. I am at peace.* Individuals who practice this simple tool reduce stress illnesses by 80 percent and, after about six months of daily practice, begin to have spontaneous spiritual images. This is entering the foothills of intuition and mysticism.

2. Progressive Relaxation. Edmond Jacobson demonstrated beautifully in his 1929 book, *Progressive Relaxation*, that individuals who go

through the body systematically, slowly tensing a muscle group, focusing upon the tension, taking a deep breath and releasing the tension,
enter a state of very deep, balanced relaxation. Again, stress illnesses are
reduced by 80 percent.

3. Circulating the Electrical Energy. Everything in the body, of course,
is electrical. You can imagine, as you breathe in, that you are circulating
the electrical energy from the back of your heels, up the back of your
thighs, buttocks, low back, chest, arms, neck, back of your head, back of
your hands and fingers. Then, as you breathe out, imagine that you are
moving the electrical energy down the front of your head, over your
hands and forearms, down the front of your neck, down the front of
your upper arms and over the chest, abdomen, pelvis, thighs, calves,
and feet into the soles of your feet. This produces a state of excellent
deep relaxation and physiological balance.

4. A Native American technique for producing or preparing for
meditation is to collect tension and breathe it away. You start at the feet,
take a deep breath, collect it in your feet, and blow it away. Do this for
two breaths in each body area, moving up to and through the calves
and thighs, the lower body and pelvis, and upper abdomen. Then do
the upper abdomen, chest, arms, neck, and face, and then sweep the
whole body. Again, this accomplishes a very deep state of relaxation.

5. One other superb technique is to imagine that you are expanding
your electromagnetic energy field, or aura, one inch in diameter, starting with the feet and moving up, allowing this to spread up around the
calves, thighs, groin, lower abdomen and back, upper abdomen and
back, around the chest in all directions, around each part of the arms,
up around the neck, and around the face and head so that you feel and
sense or see the entire body surrounded by this one inch of expanded
energy. Then you do the same thing with twelve inches of expanded
energy. This was described many years ago as the "Christos Effect" and
is an excellent tool for entering a deep state of relaxation, as well as
spontaneous imagery, as well as traveling in time and space.

And, of course, there are all kinds of other imagery that one might
use to enter deeper states of relaxation. But, once in that state, it is
important to balance emotion, to make choices of less irritating or an-
noying reactions to past events. Here there are a number of tools that

one can use, such as one that I call the Zen Exercise. Once you have entered the state of deep relaxation, you re-create in your memory, attempting to re-create the most painful physical or emotional experience of your life, only for a maximum of thirty seconds. Then you take a deep breath, collect all of the feelings that have come with it and blow it away several times. Then you repeat this with the second most painful experience of your life and the third most painful experience of your life, and then you begin to ask such questions as these: How much energy am I wasting every day of my life reliving the pains of my past? Does it make me feel good to relive these experiences? Is it ever going to make me feel good to keep reliving them. Am I ready to release them and let them go? Then you bring all three of those memories back up one more time and scream loudly "pain" half a dozen times, taking a deep breath at the end, and then truly letting them go. Finally, you re-create the most happy, loving, joyous experience of your life, sense and feel that in every part of your body, and repeat silently to yourself with every breath, love, love, love. There are many other such exercises that are outlined in a way that you can do them on your own in *90 Days to Stress Free Living*.

Once you have balanced emotions, as well as balanced the physical feelings of the body, you are ready for true spiritual attunement—connection with Soul, God, and the Divine. You can create all types of imagery to assist this process. It is in this state, ideally, that one truly has connection with what I prefer to call the ever-conscious mind, or the soul, and there you are much more capable of intuitive impression. Now for some people, running, riding a bicycle, or twirling, as in the Sufi Dervish tradition, can assist one in this ultimate detachment.

Some individuals do not easily create images. You can practice this by looking at a rose intensely for a couple of minutes, closing your eyes and moving back and forth while opening and closing your eyes until you really do see the image with your eyes closed. You can also do such things as imagining yourself taking a big, juicy lemon out of the refrigerator, rolling it in your hands and feeling the juice in it, placing it on the kitchen counter, slicing it, and seeing the juice ooze out, cutting yourself a slice, squeezing the juice into your mouth, tasting it, and then squeezing the peel and smelling the lemon aroma. You can do the same type of preemptive knowing every time you pick up a letter or a book and intuiting what the letter is about or what the content of the book is. For many people, metaphors or symbols are the images that they most easily receive. The problem with that is only that you have to learn what the image means.

Finally, there are a number of assistants in developing intuitive ability. One of these is using a pair of goggles with flashing lights. The Shealy RelaxMate is the one that I have worked with and developed over the past thirty-five years. You can choose between red, blue, or mixtures of red and blue at frequencies of one to seven cycles/second and varying degrees of brightness; you use this with your eyes closed. Ninety percent of people go into a deep state of relaxation within five minutes of applying this, and the deeper you can go into relaxation, the easier it is to have your intuition flow. Some years ago, Caroline Myss and I created a perfume, In-Tu-It, a blend of aroma oils stabilized with musk, and we feel that a tiny bit of this does significantly help one enter that altered state of consciousness and detachment where intuition flows. And then there is the Ring of Air. The Ring of Air consists of thirteen specific acupuncture points, starting at the lowest point on the body and moving up to the top of the body. You can activate these extremely easily by massaging the points for fifteen to thirty seconds and then tapping vigorously on each point or pair of points as you move from the tip of the inside of the big toenails up to the top of the head. We have demonstrated that when these are stimulated electrically with human DNA frequency of 54–78 billion cycles/second, it strikingly increases neurotensin, a neuroleptic, which is a chemical produced in the brain that actually does allow one to enter that state that I call spacey or detached. In doing this with many hundreds of individuals mostly in group workshops, most individuals do achieve exactly that same state just by massaging and tapping the points. I always also accompany it with a guided imagery that is available on a CD, *Ring of Air*.

Ultimately, most individuals seem to express a desire to "see" auras of the human energy field. I have been aware of auras all of my life, and I was forty years of age before I realized that most people are not aware of them. However, you can train yourself to see the energy coming off of the body in the same way you look at a distant star, not directly but out of your side vision, or what some people call "soft eyes." This is best done in very low light, having the person you are observing stand in front of a very light wall, and you just stare in a nonstrained way at the space, particularly around the head and shoulders. It also can be enhanced in equally bright light with the individual against a black background. At first, you may see what I describe as energy that looks similar to heat waves rising off the hood of a car or off the pavement, and eventually, as you look at these, you may begin to see flashes of color. These colors will vary from person to person, and several highly intuitive individuals may see different colors or different shades of those colors looking at the same individual. You have to learn what these mean to you because, again, these may well be metaphors for you. On the other hand, I find that brown, black, or smudgy energy means there is a problem in that area.

One other technique worth mentioning is *Super Brain Yoga* (Master Choa Kok Sui. Published by Institute for Inner Studies Publishing Foundation, Inc., Metro Manila Philippines, copyright 2005). The essential technique is first to place the left arm across your body in order to grab the lower lobe of your right ear with the thumb in the front and the index finger behind the ear. Then you do the same thing with the right arm, crossing your right arm over the left arm to grasp the lobe of the left ear with the thumb on the front and the index finger on the back. You then face east if you are up through age fifty to sixty, and face north if you are more than sixty years of age. You place the tip of the tongue on the top of your palate, behind the upper teeth, and breathe slowly and deeply. Gradually you do full knee squats, breathing in as you squat down and breathing out as you stand up. You repeat this, building up to at least twenty-one times. The feet should be about shoulder width apart.

Incidentally, it is my impression that when you are not talking or eating but just being, if the tip of your tongue tends to rest against that upper palate behind the upper teeth, you are much more likely to be relaxed and possibly having good interaction between the left and right brain.

Other techniques that you might want to explore are emotional freedom techniques. Just basically tapping above each eye, on the side of each eye, below each eye and then just below the collarbone on both sides in a straight line down from each eye can remarkably assist you in reaching a balanced state of body, mind, and emotion.

Now you might want to test yourself for your own intuitive potential with a little test that I created some years ago. Score yourself on a *preference* with a score of 0 to 5, 5 being the strongest possible and 0 being not all.

Intuitive Potential

_____1. Exploring every possible solution to a problem.

_____2. Being given specific details as to the solution of a problem.

_____3. People who are logical and realistic.

_____4. People who are imaginative and creative.

_____5. Friends who are serious and hard working.

_____6. Friends who are exciting and strongly emotional.

_____7. Having others support my basic assumptions.

_____8. Having others question my assumptions, pushing me to be more specific.

_____9. Having and following a daily schedule.

_____10. Letting each day flow as it goes.

_____11. Examining every figure in a table of numbers.

_____12. Just looking at the bottom-line summary of reports.

_____13. Enjoying daydreaming.

_____14. Avoiding daydreaming.

_____15. Finding ways around or shortcuts to rules and instructions.

_____16. Having and following rules and instructions.

_____17. Seeing a picture of a completed project.

_____18. Having step-by-step instructions to a project.

_____19. People who are happy-go-lucky.

_____20. People who are well organized.

_____21. In a crisis are you most likely to feel excited but be calm and focused.

_____22. In a crisis you are more likely to be anxious and worried.

_____23. Feelings, values.   _____24. Logic, Reason, Purpose.
_____25. Art, Music.   _____26. Math, Language.
_____27. Going by the "seat of my   _____28. Analyze the situation
        pants."   before choosing.
_____29. Feeling an answer.   _____30. Seeing the answer.
_____31. Following my heart.   _____32. Following my gut feelings.
_____33. Feelings.   _____34. Details.
_____35. Fantasy.   _____36. Precision.
_____37. Images.   _____38. Reason.
_____39. Possibilities.   _____40. Plans.
_____41. Design.   _____42. Consistency.
_____43. Dreams.   _____44. Reality.
_____45. Symbols.   _____46. Facts.
_____47. Metaphor.   _____48. Logic.
_____49. Patterns.   _____50. Analysis.

Total for the Right Brain—even numbers   _____
Total for the Left Brain—odd numbers   _____

Now that you have the totals for the right and left brain, subtract the right brain numbers from the left brain numbers. This is your intuition potential. The maximum score would be 125. The least possible is 0. Either of those might actually mean that you are highly intuitive, because a 0 would mean that the right and left brain are working absolutely equally together and the 125 would mean that your right brain is working almost exclusively without interference from the left. There is no right or wrong; this is just a fun way to explore that aspect.

It is far easier to intuit emotional factors in an individual because those energies tend to be much more powerful, especially when you are dealing with anger, guilt, anxiety, or depression, or any of their synonyms. Many intuitives are very excellent at sensing these emotions and the foundation for them. Although that can be remarkably useful in working with a client or doing counseling with someone, if the patient has cancer of the pancreas, the medical diagnosis is cancer of the pancreas. It is not depression because something happened at age five or six. Yes, it may well be related also to how much red meat the individual has eaten and other such things, but again, from a medical diagnostic point of view, the diagnosis would be cancer of the pancreas. Similarly, heart disease from hardening of the arteries is exactly that. From a medical point of view, sensing that the individual has unresolved anger over something in the past is not of any use. In counseling of the individual, however, it could be of great use. In our chapter "Who's The Matter With Me?" we discuss some of these emotional backgrounds for various problems. Another excellent book is *Permanent Healing* by Daniel R. Condron (SOM Publishing, Windyville, Missouri, 1995). For instance, Dr. Condron lists for the heart "misuse or misunderstanding of responsibility" and trying to compete with others in life when they have desires different from your own. Or for heart attack, "stubbornness and refusal to admit that circumstances or conditions do not match one's thoughts and ideas about the situation." Now if you really want to practice being a Medical Intuitive, I have provided you with the Medical Intuition Diagnostic Checklist. You can use this with friends and eventually with others, but remember: *You must not intuit emotions or physical ailments in any other individuals without their permission!* It is psychic voyeurism and psychic malpractice to do so without permission.

CRITERIA FOR MEDICAL DIAGNOSES
C. Norman Shealy, M.D., Ph.D.

DO EITHER A & B or B, C, & D
If you feel comfortable that you know the specific disease, *just* do A & B. Otherwise, give the location and the cause of the problem.

A. Specific Disease

B. Patient is DEAD_____ or ALIVE_____

C. Physical Location of significant disorder:
1. Brain
2. Head: eyes, ears, nose, mouth, tongue, teeth, sinuses
3. Neck: thyroid, parathyroid, esophagus, bronchi

4. Chest: heart, lungs, esophagus, aorta, ribs, breasts
5. Abdomen: stomach, liver, spleen, pancreas, small intestine, large intestine, kidneys, adrenals
6. Spine: cervical, thoracic, lumbar, sacral
7. Pelvis: bladder, rectum, pelvic bones
8. Reproductive organs: uterus, ovaries, fallopian tubes, vagina, external genitalia or
   prostate, testes, penis
9. Legs: thighs, calves, feet
10. Arms: shoulders, upper arms, hands
11. Skin
12. Immune system: deficient, allergies, acute or chronic infection, cancer, autoimmune, white blood cells, antibodies, lymph system
13. Chemical system: electrolytes, general chemistry, neurochemistry, neurochemical, hormonal
14. Electrical system: epilepsy, hyperactive, imbalanced
15. Spinal cord
16. Peripheral nerves
17. Autonomic nervous system
18. Blood vessels: veins, arteries, capillaries
19. Systemic: nonspecific, high blood pressure, generalized biochemical
20. Skeletal: spine, skull, pelvis, arm, leg, ribs
21. Muscular: specific muscles, generalized muscular
22. Obesity
23. Other—Describe

D. Type of disorder:
1. Addiction
2. Autoimmune
3. Benign tumor
4. Biochemical, metabolic
5. Degenerative
6. Electrical
7. Endocrine
8. Hematologic
9. Hereditary/congenital

10. Immunological
11. Infectious: bacterial, viral, fungal, protozoan, amoebic
12. Inflammatory
13. Psychological/emotional/spiritual
    (experiences, traumas, personal issues)
14. Malignant tumor
15. Surgical
16. Traumatic
17. Vascular

CONCLUSIONS TO BECOMING A MEDICAL INTUITIVE:

MEDICAL INTUITION—OPENING TO WHOLENESS

Medical intuition is the ability to make a physical, mental, or emotional diagnosis of medically diagnosable disorders, diseases, or illnesses. The categories of diagnosis include the following:
  • Specific disease, such as diabetes, hypertension, depression, etc., or *at least*:
  • Physical location of diagnosable problems *and*:
  • Type of disorder—17 different categories, as on the "Criteria for Medical Diagnoses."
Remember that most physical diseases begin with emotional or spiritual issues that fester for long periods before they create physical difficulties. *However*, these underlying issues are not medically diagnosable! Those are the realm of emotional intuition. And emotional energy is far easier to "feel" than physical disorders. But emotional issues are also easy to misinterpret because of our own unfinished business.

MEDICAL AND EMOTIONAL DIAGNOSIS
BEGINS AT HOME!

All of us have our individual unfinished business. This colors everything we think or do. All intuitives must first learn to discern their own imbalances so that their problems are not projected onto others! Therefore, the most important foundation for medical intuition is to *know thyself.* You have a Symptom Index, Total Life Stress, and Zung test for depression. If your Total Life Stress, score is above 25, you will be far less accurate and less productive in all aspects of your life until you reduce your stress. If you have 20 or more symptoms, those are the result of personal, unresolved stress! If your total score on the Zung is 40 to 49, you have subclinical or potential depression. If your Zung score is 50 or above, you are clinically depressed.

First and foremost you need to be able to admit, sense, and potentially reduce your own anger, depression, anxiety, and guilt in order to *know yourself* and to begin to intuit whether what you sense is yours or comes from someone else!

Thus, your initial journey into medical intuition is to learn your own psychological, physiological, and physical problems so that they do not sap your life energy and prevent you from sensing the problems in others. These are the keys to *self* knowledge:

- Relaxation
- Sensing imbalances in feeling and muscle tension in your own body
- Learning to balance tension and discomfort in your own body awareness
- Balancing/resolving your own anger, guilt, anxiety, and depression
- Spiritual Attunement

Once you know and balance yourself and can detach from your own unfinished business, you will also be less influenced by the emotional kafuffle from others. If you want to develop accurate medical intuition to work with others, the key is to be *whole* yourself.

As I have indicated several times, the field of medical intuition is one that seems to have attracted undoubtedly a few good people, and yet the vast majority of them have no documentation or proof of efficacy. Several years ago, when one put *medical intuition* into Google, it came up with over 12 million listings. Today there are just 900,000+, but if you enter *medical intuitives*, there are over 5 million listings. Some of these I know, and some of them are true frauds; but unfortunately, it is inappropriate in a book such as this to mention such names. It is appropriate, however, to discuss those people who are good, and valuable to mention a few of the best. Apparently, there are only five that I consider adequate from my own testing to be called Medical Intuitives.

Caroline Myss—Caroline Myss and I began working together in 1984. In 1988 we collaborated on two books, *AIDS—Passageway to Transformation* and *The Creation of Health*. Since then, Caroline has gone on to have a number of bestseller books. She does workshops, both in her hometown of Greater Chicago as well as around the world. When I tested Caroline with fifty specific cases of which I knew the diagnoses, she was 93 percent accurate on making either a physical diagnosis or a psychological diagnosis. I also learned at that time that Caroline could accurately do no more than eight such "readings" in a given day. As we went beyond that, her accuracy rapidly fell off. Caroline used to do frequent readings in her workshops. Today she rarely does so, and I think a great reason for that is the heightened risk of burnout in a room of two hundred or more people. And, unfortunately, for those interested, Caroline does no private readings today.
www.myss.com

Robert Leichtman—Bob has been a friend since 1974, when we first corresponded. When I tested him, he was 96 percent accurate on making a psychological diagnosis and only 80 percent accurate in physical diagnosis. He said that this is because he trained himself to "visit the mind." This physical diagnosis can be very simple and extremely accurate. However, his psychological diagnoses, which are also extremely accurate, tend to be the best understanding of a given personality that I have personally read. He may write as much as three to five pages describing in great detail the individual personality quirks, both good and not so good.

Cay Randall-May—I have known Cay Randall-May for almost thirty years. Cay has a Ph.D., so she understands science extremely well. She is at least 75 percent accurate in giving a physical diagnosis and often gives very constructive advice about further evaluation and possible treatments. She does medical intuitive readings, general intuitive consultations, office personnel mentoring, and teaches classes on how to begin and grow as an intuitive or healer. She has written several books and is an accomplished artist. Her Web sites: www.praynow.net and www.cayrandallmaysart.com. She can be contacted at caysart@aol.com or 602-404-8646.

Deena Spear—Although Deena would not call herself a Medical Intuitive, and I have not actually tested her in the organized way in which I have tested others, she is remarkably accurate. She tends to concentrate very intensely on unfinished psychological problems as the root cause. Sometimes they are cumulative from this life, as are many illnesses, or the result of trauma carried into this life from a previous one. She works only by e-mail, and once a client agrees to work with her, she does her absent healing sessions for a week. Deena can tune a violin from a thousand miles or more away. She trained originally at the Barbara Brennan School of Spiritual Healing, and she teaches her own unique form of healing. www.singingwoods.org.

In the broader field of healing and intuition, there are a number of individuals that I appreciate and who give good advice, and so on. One of the best of these is Barbara Rasor. Barbara calls herself an *emotional intuitive*, and I know no one with whom I have personally worked who is better as a one-on-one counselor by phone or in person. She approaches the root, emotional trauma virtually instantly in every case I have observed while working with her. Contact Information: www.emotionalintuitive.com.

Finally, I encourage you to review the information about the American Board of Scientific Medical Intuition:

President: Caroline M. Myss, Ph.D.
Secretary-Treasurer: C. Norman Shealy, M.D., Ph.D.
Larry Burk, M.D.
Sally Rhine Feather, Ph.D.
Cay Randall-May, Ph.D.
Patricia A. Norris, Ph.D.
Christine Page, M.D.
Kevin Todeschi, M.A.

ABSMI certifies students who have achieved established proficiency in Medical Intuition or Counseling Intuition. These standards represent specific educational criteria for this aspect of Complementary and Alternative Medicine. Diplomats are expected to adhere to health–professional ethical, moral, and legal standards.

Medical Intuition is the science of intuitively assisting clients in cooperation with their primary health care professional, in Intuitive Analysis of physical, emotional, mental, and spiritual stress reactions.

Counseling Intuition is the science of intuitively assisting clients in identifying and resolving physical, emotional, mental, and spiritual stress patterns, including the following:

- Career decisions
- Creative expression
- Family
- Life Transitions
- Parenting
- Partnerships
- Relationships
- Sexuality
- Spiritual direction

Counseling Intuitives work with a variety of Complementary and Alternative skills, including but not limited to

- Inner Counselor
- Past–life regression
- Sacred Contracts/Archetypal Analysis

ABSMI is a 501–C–6 not–for–profit organization dedicated to the development of Medical Intuition and Counseling Intuition. The only activity of ABSMI is to provide examination in these fields. www.absmi.com

12

REINCARNATION AND PAST-LIFE THERAPY

In chapter one I mentioned my first experience of sensing, seeing, and feeling a past life as a physician in Egypt. I was still relatively neutral about the whole concept of reincarnation, not having strong "beliefs" and certainly not doubting it. Four months later, I was at a meeting of the Neuroelectric Society in Snowmass Aspen. Dr. William Kroger, OB/GYN physician, who was also an expert hypnotist, was giving his lecture just before mine, and he was trying to convince the audience that acupuncture was hypnosis. Having done acupuncture since 1967, I was sitting there saying to myself, "Bull—." Suddenly Bill said, "And, in the last century, there was a British physician who demonstrated that you could operate upon mesmerized patients. His name was John Elliotson." When he said that, I felt as if an iceberg had been thrown against my spine, and I said to myself, "My God. I was John Elliotson." I went up to Bill after his talk and asked for more information. He could not provide it. I called our medical librarian, and she could find nothing on John Elliotson. So I planned a trip to London to look up John Elliotson, assuming that he might have been a surgeon, since he demonstrated that you could operate upon mesmerized patients. I asked the cab driver to take me to the Royal College of Surgeons. Rushing through London traffic, he turned to the right. I was sitting in the back seat of the cab and felt the iceberg down my spine. I was literally physically picked up by some force and turned in the opposite direction. I therefore asked the cab driver to take me down in the opposite direction despite his knowing the route to the Royal College of Surgeons. About two blocks in the opposite direction, we encountered a large, circular brick build-ing. I went in and truly felt totally at home. I sensed that I knew every room. I went on to the Royal College of Surgeons, where I learned that, actually, John Elliotson was an internist, not a surgeon. So I went to the Royal College of Physicians, where I was able to find two photographs of John Elliotson and a great deal of history about him. His father was a pharmacist. Growing up, John had some problems that left him with a limp. After medical school, he studied in Paris and brought home to England both the use of the stethoscope and the use of opioids for pain relief.

John Elliotson was the first physician in London to give up the wear-ing of knickers with high socks. When I was nine years of age, all the boys in my class wore knickers. My mother bought me knickers—I liter-ally tore them apart and had a temper tantrum, refusing to wear them. John had striking, black, curly hair; I had blond hair and, as a child, craved having black hair. In fact, when I was about five, I went up to an aunt of mine who had black, curly hair and cut off a lock of her hair. When I was sixteen, I asked my mother to dye my hair black before I went off to college. I did it only once and settled for blond hair, which gradually became sandy colored and then, fifty years later, began to turn blond again as my hair would bleach in the sun.

John was a Latin scholar. In high school I was a Latin scholar and won the Latin medal two years in a row. Remember, I was going into neurosurgery and needed a year of surgery before I could do neurosur-gery, but instead I interned in internal medicine. He introduced opioids into London. I have spent much of this life trying to wean patients from opioids, as I think they are of no value except in acute pain.

John's reputation as an internist was made because of his giving public lectures, which attracted large numbers of followers. Finally, when the new medical school, University College Hospital—London, opened, John was appointed the first chairman of the Department of Medicine. Shortly thereafter, he began to do mesmerism and carried on

public demonstrations of mesmerism in the amphitheater of the hospital. Both Charles Dickens and William Thackery became friends of his
through that circumstance, and in fact, he taught Dickens to do mesmerism on his wife, who had a lot of psychosomatic problems. William
Thackery wrote a book, *Pendennis*, which was dedicated to John Elliotson,
and in the novel, Dr. Goodenough is reported to have been patterned
after Elliotson. (Ref.: John Elliotson, "William Makepeace Thackery and
Dr. Goodenough." *International Journal of Clinical and Experimental Hypnosis*,
Vol. 11, April 1963, pg. 122–130). As a teenager, my favorite author was
Charles Dickens.

One of Elliotson's most unique contributions, other than the introduction of the stethoscope and opioids, was to demonstrate in mesmerized patients that they could make a medical diagnosis. This was further
documented in Eisdale's book, *Natural and Mesmeric Clairvoyance*. After
some years of demonstrating and practicing mesmerism, as well as his
busy medical practice and teaching, the Board of Trustees of the University College Hospital—London told Elliotson that he would have to
give up practicing mesmerism in the hospital amphitheater. Elliotson
resigned, went into private practice, and for some twelve years wrote *der
Zoist*, in which he largely wrote about experiences with mesmerism. It
was during that period that he demonstrated, with the help of surgeons, that he could put patients into a mesmeric trance and allow
surgery to be carried out. This was also continued in India by his friend
who wrote the book on natural and mesmeric clairvoyance.

Over the next year, seventy five "psychics" confirmed that I had been
John Elliotson, and eventually, Kevin Ryerson also confirmed that I was
John Elliotson. This was reported in Dr. Walter Semkiw's book, *Return of
the Revolutionaries.*

I have gone into great deal about this particular past life because of
the remarkable number of synchronicities between Elliotson's life and
my own. Since that time, I have had a number of spontaneous recalls of
past lives, as well as ones that have been revealed to me during past–life
therapy with a number of talented past–life therapists. Overall, I "know"
about thirty of my previous lives:

- A Jewish, small tribal leader more than 3,500 years ago.
- A Greek physician 3,500 years ago.

- Egyptian physician 3,000 years ago.
- A Roman senator at the time of Christ, confirmed by several intuitives.
- Executioner, approximately the ninth century, for "The" Church, confirmed by one intuitive.
- A priest with St. Francis in the 13th century, confirmed by a number of intuitives as well as by the current reincarnation of St. Francis himself.
- A priest in France in 1600.
- Peter III. I mention this because it is certainly *not a grandiose claim*. Peter was a phenomenal, unbelievably weak wimp. I have no respect whatsoever for wimps! More importantly, for many, many years, I had nightmares in which I would feel myself being closed in and choked to death, and I would awaken screaming. As soon as I knew about Peter III, the nightmares ceased. Peter was married to Catherine the Great, who had him imprisoned in a very small room and choked to death by her lover, Orlov. Fascinatingly, I personally figured out who Catherine the Great is in this life, as well as who Orlov is in this life, and all of this has been confirmed by two excellent intuitives.
- Mathew Thornton, a signer of the Declaration of Independence from New Hampshire.
- There is one other of whom I am certainly not proud but who has great relevance to the whole field of intuition and synchronicity. In 1995 I awoke about 75 percent paralyzed as the result of that physician who had visited me to show me his "hot hands." Having seen many healers who have really hot, red hands, I asked him to show them to me. He put his hands on my head and jerked my head 180 degrees in both directions. It dislocated my spine and I wound up developing, over subsequent years, over 50 percent compression of the spinal cord at C7 T1, leading to a fusion of my spine from the fifth cervical vertebra through the first thoracic vertebra. It took me many months to recover, and I still have some residual weakness and spasticity in the legs. However, from the moment this happened, I knew it was karmic. Thus, I never "blamed" the individual who jerked my neck. I would often say that it was probably someone whose head I had cut off in a previous life. Some years later, I suddenly knew, and had confirmed, a life several

hundred years ago in which I really was quite a brute and had my own son murdered in order to prevent him from taking over my position. The man who jerked my neck was indeed my son in that life.

As I have often said, going from the brute I was several hundred years ago to what I am today isn't bad, as well as understanding that each of us has the potential, perhaps currently or in the future, as well as in the past, to have done brutal things. To me, it becomes much more important to work out, as much as possible, any unfinished business from those previous lives. That is the value of past-life therapy. For instance, in the Peter III life, even though the nightmares stopped as soon as I knew the details, I wanted to go through the death process, which I did with Dr. Morris Netherton, whom I consider the world's best living past-life therapist. Of the roughly thirty past lives that I have gone through, being choked to death was the most painful!

I have listed in some detail some of my past-life experiences because I think it is important to recognize that all of us have a long history of incarnation and reincarnation. Ultimately, the purpose of existence in this apparent universe is to work only to do good to self and others. Once we learn that, it is my impression that we then are able to move into a higher dimension. As I have indicated, I have had a number of past-life therapy sessions with such talented past-life therapists as Morris Netherton, Dr. Denys Kelsey, and Kay Ortmans. Kay was one of the more unique past-life therapists. She never said a word, never asked you to say a word, and said that if you had any images that you wished to share, please share them. She would then set to work with her talented hands, finding areas of muscle tension, and she might work on one area for an hour or even two hours while playing relatively loud classical music. I once invited her to come to my clinic, and I took four of my patients who had chronic pain and just told them she was a superb masseuse, which is really what she did. Each of them came out of the room having experienced vivid imagery of a past life. One of the patients said, "What did that woman do?" I said, "Well, the woman didn't do anything. You did it because you released memories from your past." After a couple of sessions with Kay, all she would have to do is lay her hands on me and turn on Mozart's *Requiem*, and I would suddenly be in a past life. One of the most vivid was an instance in 1975. She had been working on me for two hours, I had had no imagery, and all of a sudden I had the most vivid image of seeing myself hanged as a priest. I burst out laughing, not from being hanged, but because my image then slipped backward so that the incident that led to my hanging was that I was caught having sex with the bishop's daughter. And, although it was okay for the bishop to have a daughter, it was not okay for a lowly priest!

In 1988, the last session I ever had with Kay, she had come to our clinic to do a training program for ten individuals, and we each worked on one another. On the last day, Kay said, "I want to work on you." She put her hands on my abdomen, began Mozart's *Requiem*, and instantly I saw a path that divided into two branches. I knew that if I went up one of the paths, I would enter another past life, but I chose to go to the left, which really was a requiem for the priest who had been hanged without proper last rites. It was indeed a requiem for the priest who was hanged.

One can argue whatever one wishes about images, memories, beliefs, and feelings, but experiences like this have powerful potential for healing. I will mention just two such examples in my own experience with patients:

A woman came in to see me with intractable pain. The history she gave was that she had shot herself accidentally while cleaning her husband's gun. The shot went through her abdomen, severing her spinal cord, and she was paralyzed and had intractable pain. I took her through a past-life experience, and she gave an absolutely perfect account of being Anne Boleyn, right up to the rolling of her head after the guillotine. When I brought her back out of a very, very light trance, I asked her what the meaning of this experience was. She said she had no memory whatsoever of anything. Fortunately, I had taped the experience, and I played it back for her. Again, I asked, What does this mean? She started to cry and said, "I don't know." I replied, "I know. You think your husband shot you, because you just gave me the story of a martyred wife." She then told me that when she awoke after surgery, she was told that she had shot her husband while cleaning his gun. He was a policeman. All she remembers as the last thing before she passed out was that they were having an argument. As a result of this experience, she divorced her husband, her pain went away, and she went back to work as a counselor. Does this mean that that patient was indeed Anne Boleyn? I doubt it, and I think that sometimes what we perceive, even in our spontaneous memories, as well as those evoked during past-life therapy, are allegories for something that happened. In her case, the metaphor may have been at some subconscious level and perhaps the only way that she could come near the idea of her husband damaging her. So it is not important whether a past life really happened, but it is important to clear any emotions associated with metaphorical images.

Another man, who had very intractable pain and had had two unsuccessful neck operations, had his pain disappear instantly when I did a past-life therapy session in which he saw himself killed in a very primitive time by an opponent who knocked him to the ground with a club and broke his neck. In this life, he had his neck injured when he was working as a veterinarian, doing artificial insemination on a cow, and the cow kicked him. The allegory in this case was that his wife had taken up a lover after he had become disabled. Again, did it happen as he saw it, or was it only an allegory? Over and over again I would say that I don't think it matters. Past-life therapy is the single most powerful tool one can use in reaching deep into the subconscious or even conscious mind for "meaning." To me, the past lives that I have experienced, both in past-life therapy sessions and in spontaneous recall, lead me not to "believe" in past-life therapy but to "know" that that is the way it is. When one or more excellent intuitives can confirm what the client has brought up in a session, then it seems to me to be as real as anything else that we experience. I do think that for those who have not had a past-life experience, it is advisable to seek a session with someone who has been certified by Dr. Morris Netherton. I have made one CD—"Multilevel Awareness"—which is the basic technique that I use in past-life therapy.

In summary, past-life therapy is a prominent tool for evoking intuitive memories that are absolutely real or allegorical/metaphorical. As such, it may be the most useful medical intuitive tool of all.

As far as I can tell, perhaps the most difficult problem Edgar Cayce had in accepting his remarkable talent was the concept of reincarnation. But, as it appeared so many times in his readings, he eventually did accept it. He not infrequently gave reasons for a patient's problems as coming from a past life and gave some readings of his own past lives as well as that of a number of individuals. Perhaps my own favorite of all of Cayce's commentaries is that he often said, especially in a disease like multiple sclerosis, "This is a case of the entity meeting self." Multiple sclerosis is a disease that we now know to be an autoimmune disease, in which the body is attacking itself. Certainly, that is a case of the entity meeting itself better than anything else I can imagine, but the implication in Cayce's readings was that the disease was the result of the entity coping with some problem from the past. Whether it was a past life or this life is not always clear. My friend Marianne Woodward, who wrote the *Edgar Cayce Story of Karma* and *Scars of the Soul*, discussed problems that we develop in this life as a result of some misbehavior, or "cash karma."

What is most important in understanding karma is not *blame*. There is no reason to believe that God or even the soul punishes someone for past behavior. It is just the simple fact that when you do something that is harmful to another individual, it is creating an energy in the collective unconscious. Just as negative thinking attracts other people with negative thinking, it is as if one has a magnet in one's personal energy bank that is attracting something to clean up whatever needs to be purified. It would be interesting if we could foresee what will happen to all of the corporate leaders of the past couple of decades who have been greedy and created great harm to other individuals.

I often say to a patient, "Have you ever murdered anyone, raped anyone, robbed anyone or purposely harmed anyone?" If you have not had any of those behaviors, then you have nothing about which to feel guilty. Actually, my own guide once said, "The only sin in the eyes of the Universe is murder." I have had a number of discussions with this guide, and it appears that God, whom he calls the Universe, does not consider some of these other behaviors sin, although most of us consider them bad behavior at the very least. Whether or not it is a sin, it is a negative effect on someone. Thus, we need to dissolve the magnetic attraction that we may have set in motion in some previous life. Obviously, helping others is one of the ways of washing one's slate clean.

13

RECOMMENDED BOOKS, COURSES, AND PROGRAMS FOR BUILDING INTUITION

▶The only course I know for professional training in Medical Intuition is the one I teach. The essentials follow:

You can take this as an independent course, Medical Intuition. Contact 888-242-6105 for more information.

A formal Certificate Program in Medical Intuition is available through www.holosuniversity.org, along with other courses.

The Board Certification in Medical Intuition or Counseling Intuition is available through www.absmi.com.

President: Caroline M. Myss, Ph.D.
Secretary–Treasurer: C. Norman Shealy, M.D., Ph.D.
Larry Burk, M.D.
Sally Rhine Feather, Ph.D.
Cay Randall–May, Ph.D.
Patricia A. Norris, Ph.D.
Christine Page, M.D.
Kevin Todeschi, M.A.

ABSMI certifies students who have achieved established proficiency in Medical Intuition or Counseling Intuition. These standards represent specific educational criteria for this aspect of Complementary and Alternative Medicine. Diplomats are expected to adhere to health–professional ethical, moral, and legal standards.

Medical Intuition is the science of intuitively assisting clients in cooperation with their primary health care professional, in Intuitive Analysis of physical, emotional, mental, and spiritual stress reactions.

Counseling Intuition is the science of intuitively assisting clients in identifying and resolving physical, emotional, mental, and spiritual stress patterns, including the following:

- Career decisions
- Creative expression
- Family
- Life Transitions
- Parenting
- Partnerships
- Relationships
- Sexuality
- Spiritual direction

Counseling Intuitives work with a variety of Complementary and Alternative skills, including but not limited to:

- Inner Counselor
- Past–life regression
- Sacred Contracts/Archetypal Analysis

ABSMI is a 501–C–6 not–for–profit organization dedicated to the development of Medical Intuition and Counseling Intuition. The only activity of ABSMI is to provide examination in these fields. www.absmi.com

RECOMMENDED BOOKS:

1. Bailey, A. *Esoteric Healing*. NY: Lucis Publishing, 1970.
2. Baraff, C. *The Edgar Cayce Remedies—Thirty-five Years of Research*. Virginia Beach, VA: Heritage Publications.

3. Condron, D.R. *Dreams of the Soul: The Yoga Sutras of Patanjali.* Windyville, MO: SCM Publishing, 1991.

4. Emery, M. *Intuition Workbook: An Expert's Guide to Unlocking the Wisdom of Your Subconscious Mind.* Upper Saddle River, NJ: Prentice Hall, 1994.

5. Emery, M. *PowerHunch!—Living an Intuitive Life.* Hillsboro, OR: Beyond Words Publishing, 2001.

6. Mishlove, J., and G. Zukav. *The Intuitive Factor: Genius or Chance?* Seattle: Zoie Films, 2007.

7. Myss, C., and C.N. Shealy. *The Creation of Health.* London: Bantam Books, 1999.

8. Myss C. *Anatomy of the Spirit.* NY: Crown, Random House, 1997.

9. Sontag, A. *Illness as a Metaphor and AIDS and Its Metaphors.* NY: Doubleday, Anchor Books, 2001.

Appendix A

PERSPECTIVES ON PSYCHIC DIAGNOSIS
by C. Norman Shealy, M.D.

The interest in clairvoyant diagnosis–or psychic diagnosis, if you pre-fer–almost certainly goes back to the days of Hippocrates. Many famous physicians throughout the history of the world seem to have been in-volved in things which we today would call parapsychology, and many of them were probably psychic themselves. Paracelsus is one example of such an individual; Mesmer, who some 200 years ago laid the foun-dations of psychiatry and psychology, is another. To my knowledge, however, the first formal study of clairvoyant diagnosis occurred about 130 years ago, when a British physician, John Elliotson, began to work with mesmerism. Dr. Elliotson had introduced to England the stetho-scope, the use of narcotics, and a variety of other medical advances. He was the leading internist in London and a professor of medicine at Uni-versity Hospital, University College, London. But suddenly he became bored with what was going on in medicine and got involved in mes-merism. He then learned that patients who were mesmerized could properly diagnose difficult medical cases. He would carry one of his mesmerized patients through the wards and have him diagnose pa-

tients whose illnesses had confounded the faculty. He even staged public demonstrations in the hospital amphitheater. Among the people who
attended these demonstrations were Charles Dickens and William
Thackeray. (Thackeray later dedicated one of his books to Elliotson, who
in the book is called Dr. Goodenough.)

As anyone acquainted with the history of medicine might expect,
such innovative ideas were not well received among his conservative
colleagues. They finally suggested that if Elliotson wished to continue to
practice medicine, he should give up that nonsense. His reaction was:
"Gentlemen, I resign." He then went out and continued to practice mesmerism, demonstrating, among other things, that mesmerized patients
could be successfully operated on, apparently without feeling any pain.
Elliotson, because of his tilting at the windmill of traditional medicine,
is not well known today, and no serious scientific study of clairvoyant
diagnosis has been done since his time.

In 1951, as an undergraduate student at Duke University, I was invited by the Duke Players, of which I was a member, to write a radio skit
on parapsychology. I spent three-and-a-half months working with Dr.
J.B. Rhine, not as one of his subjects, but observing what he was doing
and conducting an investigation of his work. I was totally convinced
that clairvoyance, telepathy, and psychokinesis were very real phenomena, and I wondered why, after almost 30 years of experimentation, we
were still playing with cards and dice and not using these techniques in
a practical way. Then the rigors of medical school caused me to put
aside my interest in parapsychology until about five years ago, when I
became intensely interested in it again after reading *Psychic Discoveries
Behind the Iron Curtain* and *Breakthrough to Creativity*.

I tried to obtain an introduction to clairvoyance through Dr.
Karagulla, author of *Breakthrough to Creativity*, but she would not divulge
any of her secret connections. Finally, thanks to Dr. Paul Dudley White,
I was asked to speak at a meeting of the Academy of Parapsychology
and Medicine at Stanford just three years ago. This immediately put me
in contact with individuals who eventually led me to meet my first
known psychic, the Reverend Henry Rucker of Chicago. I was so intrigued by Henry's analysis of me, whom he had never met before, that
I invited him and his colleagues to come to La Crosse so that I might see

how good they would be at doing psychic diagnoses.

During that first weekend we saw 17 patients. Each patient was brought into a room for about 10 minutes. The patient was then escorted out of the room, and each of the sensitives was asked a variety of questions concerning the patient's personality and physical condition. We then pooled the results; only when a clear majority of the sensitives agreed on a given diagnosis was it considered the proper answer. Pooling the results of the eight psychics and considering their responses to eight individual questions, we found this group to be 98% accurate in making personality diagnoses and 80% accurate in diagnosing physical conditions. For instance, they clearly distinguished between three totally separate cases of paraplegia–paralysis from the waist down–one traumatic, one infectious, and one degenerative in nature.

A more formal research project was then done with 54 different questions. Each patient to be studied was known to me, had been examined by me, and had taken an elaborate personality test, the Minnesota Multi-Phasic Personality Inventory. A color Polaroid photograph of each patient was taken by my research assistant, and the patient's name and birth date were written on the back of the photograph. Handwriting samples, using a standard request, were obtained from each patient, and palm prints were taken.

All six clairvoyants were supplied with the photographs, names and birth dates. A numerologist used only the patients' names and birth dates. The graphologist was given the handwriting sample, and the palmist evaluated the palm prints. Each sensitive was asked to fill out the same questionnaire, having had no other contact with the patient. (Seethe *Research Data Form* at the end of this article.)

Controls consisted of my filling out the same questionnaire to serve as the "correct" answer sheet. In addition, random choices were made by two psychology students who filled out questionnaires. A professor of psychology, with no known psychic ability, did his own "guessing" of the answers, using the patients' photographs.

Unfortunately, I could not be certain of a number of the answers on the personality test, and so the master sheet had to be shortened. We settled on retaining two categories of questions: (1) Where does the patient have difficulty or pain? and (2) What is the major and primary cause of the patient's illness? In answering these questions the sensitives showed significant positive results, as determined by computerized evaluation of the various answer sheets.

We had complete data on some 78 patients and at least one or more clairvoyant diagnoses carried out on almost 200. Two of the clairvoyants were 75% accurate and a third was 70% accurate in locating the site of the pain. (Numerology was 60% accurate, astrology 35%, and palmistry and graphology 25%–the same as chance.) In determining the cause of the pain, the clairvoyants ranged from 65% accuracy down to 30%. Here there was only a 10% probability of obtaining the correct diagnosis by chance.

In a separate study of personality, one outstanding psychic, Dr. Robert Leichtman, an internist and probably one of the most talented clairvoyants in this country today, was 96% accurate in giving very lengthy and elaborate descriptions of the patients' personalities. He used only photographs and the patients' names and birth data to do his psychic tune-in.

These statistics clearly show that clairvoyant diagnosis not only is possible but can be highly successful. The real question is where it fits into the scheme of healing and medicine today.

Although physicians are at least 80% accurate in their primary diagnostic attempts, we are frustrated in determining the exact diagnoses for a variety of illnesses. Furthermore, many of the diagnostic tests carry a significant risk of damage to the patient. In instances such as these, it seems most obvious that the opinion of two or three talented clairvoyants could help us avoid risky diagnostic tests and help both physician and patient rest more comfortably in the knowledge that everything reasonable has been done to make the proper diagnosis.

Although not a formal part of this paper, it seems necessary that I also mention some experiences I have had with healers. I have visited, talked with, and had readings by approximately 60 clairvoyants in the past several years. I consider half a dozen of these to be outstanding individuals; most of them do healing through the laying on of hands. I have seen two patients with breast cancer apparently be cured or have "spontaneous remissions" following the laying on of hands by Dr. Olga Worrall of Baltimore. I know of other cases in which healing seems to have occurred. Again, these cases need more careful scientific study. In addition, we need to do a study in which 100 patients with a known physical illness, such as cancer, are treated by a given healer, to see exactly what percentage of such patients are helped in this way. On the other hand, when medicine fails to cure a patient and we have nothing else to offer, it seems quite reasonable that healers may be used to benefit patients for whom no alternative therapy is possible.

Author's note:
One of the most difficult problems facing physicians is the collection of data concerning the results of treatment. What criteria satisfy scientific requirements for success of any treatment? The big question is that of psychosomatic influence. I should be most interested in soliciting physician reports concerning:
1. "spontaneous" cures in diseases otherwise thought incurable;
2. documented cases where such cures seem to be the result of faith or spiritual healing.

I am particularly interested in cancer cases where tissue diagnosis is available and the physician is willing to certify the "cure" beyond any reasonable doubt. Obviously, physicians' names will be confidential.

C. Norman Shealy, M.D., Fellow, American College of Surgeons, received his medical degree from Duke University in 1956. He is Clinical Associate, Department of Psychology, University of Wisconsin, and Associate Clinical Professor, Universities of Wisconsin and Minnesota. As Director of the Pain Rehabilitation Center at LaCrosse, Wisconsin, he has had broad experience in alternative, therapeutic modalities.

Research Data Form

Sex: Male _____ Female _____

Personality Inventory
Is the patient:
1. Depressed—Avg.   (50-60) ( );
   Slight (60-70) ( );
   Marked (70-80) ( );
   Severe (80 +) ().
2. Hostile—Avg. (50-60) ( );
   Slight (60-70) ( );
   Marked (70-80) ( );
   Severe (80 + ( ).
3. Hypochondriacal—Avg.   (50-60) ( );
   Slight (60-70) ( );
   Marked (70-80) ( );
   Severe (80 +) ().
4. Hysterical—Avg. (50-60) ( );
   Slight (60-70) ( );
   Marked (70-80) ( );
   Severe (80 + ( ).

PSYCHIC DIAGNOSIS

5. Sexual adjustment-Poor ( ); Good ( ); Avg. ( ).

6. Hetero drive—Avg.   ( ); Decreased ( ); Increased ( ).
   Homo drive—Avg. ( ); Decreased ( ); Increased ( ).
   Adjustment: Poor ( ); Fair ( ); Good ( ).

7. Hetero interest: Avg. ( ); Decreased ( ); Increased ( ).
   Homo interest: Avg. ( ); Decreased ( ); Increased ( ).
   Adjustment: Poor ( ); Fair ( ); Good ( ).

8. Is the patient: Passive ( ); Aggressive ( ); Balanced ( ). (60 and up good).

9. Paranoia—Mild ( ); Moderate ( ); Extreme ( ).

10. Conflicts with:
    a. father—yes ( ); no ( )
    b. mother—yes ( ); no ( )
    c. siblings—yes ( ); no ( )
    d. offspring—yes ( ); no ( )
    e. authorities (teachers, civil, physicians)—yes ( ); no ( )
    f. spouse—yes ( ); no ( )

   g. lover—yes ( ); no ( )
   h. everybody—yes ( ); no ( ).

11. Is the patient mentally:
   a. clear—yes ( ); no ( )
   b. confused—yes ( ); no ( )
      1. from physical problems—yes ( ); no ( )
      2. from emotional instability—yes ( ); no ( )
      3. from drugs—yes ( ); no ( ).

12. Is the patient's pain perpetuated by some emotional conflicts? yes( ); no( )

13. Does the patient really desire pain relief? yes ( ); no ( )

14. If freed of pain, will the patient return to normal activity?
    25% ( ); 50% ( ); 75% ( ); 100% ( )

15. Is the patient likely to have a "nervous breakdown"? yes ( ); no( )

16. Does the patient contemplate suicide? Yes ( ); no ( )

17. Is he likely to try to commit suicide? yes ( ); no ( )

18. Extent of drug dependency—mild ( ); strong ( ); addicted ( ).

19. Does the patient have insight into his illness? Yes ( ); no( )

Physical Inventory
Pain Problems
1. Location of pain. Circle the description or shade the numbered area(s):
   a. trigeminal nerve
   b. occipital nerve
   c. neck
   d. bilateral upper extremities
   e. right upper extremity
   f. left upper extremity
   g. bilateral anterior thorax
   h. bilateral posterior thorax
   i. right hemithorax
   j. left hemithorax
   k. bilateral lower back
   l. right lower back
   m. left lower back
   n. bilateral abdomen
   o. right abdomen
   p. left abdomen

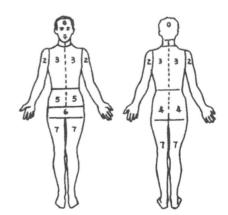

q. pelvis
   left
   right
r. perineal
   genitalia
   rectum
s. bilateral lower extremities
t. right lower extremity
u. left lower extremity
v. viscera (specify) _
w. other (specify) _
Comments:

Cause of Pain
1. Cancer
2. Amputation
3. Arthritis
4. Scar
5. Trauma
6. Infection
7. Birth
8. Multiple sclerosis
9. Other degenerative diseases
10. Stroke
11. Spine problems
    a. neck
    b. chest
    c. lumbar
12. Spinal cord difficulty
    a. congenital
    b. infectious
    c. traumatic
    d. degenerative
    e. tumor
    f. vascular
13. Shingles
14. Compensation injury

Other Physical Problems

		Remote	Current
1.	Eyes		
2.	Ears		
3.	Nose		
4.	Mouth-throat		
5.	Arms		
6.	Chest or trunk		

	Remote	**Current**
7. Abdomen		
8. Pelvic		
a. bladder		
b. prostate		
c. uterus		
d. rectum		
9. Legs		
10. Brain		
11. Hands		
12. Feet		
13. Blood pressure		
14. Heart		
15. Lungs		
16. Liver		
17. Kidney		
18. Stomach		
19. Intestine		
a. small		
b. large		
20. Gall bladder		
21. Bone		
22. Muscle-tendon		
23. Nerve		
24. Skin		
25. Genitalia		
26. Thyroid		
27. Adrenals		
28. Appendix		
29. Spleen		
30. Hair		
31. Blood chemistries		
32. Endocrine		
33. Pancreas		

Intensity of Pain

	Most of time	**Occasional**	**Intermittent**	**Time of Pain**
1. Severe				
2. Moderate				
3. Slight				
4. None				

Recent Physical Activity
1. Unrestricted
2. Slightly restricted
3. Moderately restricted
4. Inactive

Patient's Job
1. Housewife
2. Farmer
3. Laborer
4. Executive
5. Physician, nurse, medical field
6. Secretary
7. Teacher
8. Lawyer
9. Civil worker or military
10. Retired
11. Clerk
12. Recreation
13. Entertainment
14. Religious
15. Other

Recommended Treatment (1 or more)
1. Operant conditioning
2. Psychiatric
3. Psychic
4. Electrical stimulation across skin
5. Electrical stimulation of peripheral nerve
6. Electrical stimulation of dorsal columns
7. Electrical stimulation of brain
8. Facet rhizotomy
9. Cordotomy
10. Cingulumotomy
11. Disc surgery, laminectomy
12. Removal of tumor
13. Nerve destruction
14. Drugs (specify)
15. Magnetic
16. Diet (specify)
17. Vitamins
18. Massage
19. Herbs (specify)
20. X-ray
21. Autogenic training and/or biofeedback

Prognosis
1. For pain relief
   a. good
   b. fair
   c. poor
   d. uncertain
   e. timing

2. For physical activity
   a. good
   b. fair
   c. poor
   d. uncertain
   e. timing

3. For drug withdrawal
   a. good
   b. fair
   c. poor
   d. uncertain
   e. timing

4. For life expectancy next 5 years
   a. good
   b. fair
   c. poor
   d. uncertain
   e. timing

5. General health
   a. good
   b. fair
   c. poor
   d. uncertain
   e. timing

6. Emotional stability
   a. good
   b. fair
   c. poor
   d. uncertain
   e. timing

1. Physician's Name:_____

2. Astrological and Numerological:_____

3. Palmistry: _____

4. Handwriting:_____

5. Psychic:_____

6. Rev. Jack Schwarz:_____

APPENDIX B

EAT LOW GLYCEMIC ©

C. Norman Shealy, M.D., Ph.D.

The higher the Glycemic Index, the greater the metabolic stress. The greater the metabolic stress, the greater the insulin requirement and the more likely you are to gain weight with all the accompanying problems! Below are the major foods with a GI 55 or below. That appears to be the healthy way to eat!

Apple, medium	38
Apple juice, 8 oz	40
Almonds	0
Apricots, 5 halves, dried	31
Banana, medium	55
Baked beans, 4 oz	48
Barley, pearl, boiled, ½ cup	25
Black beans, ¾ cup	30
Black-eyed peas, ½ cup	42
Rice bran, 1 tbl	19

Butter beans, ½ cup	31
Carrots, cooked, ½ cup	49
Bulgar, cooked, ½ cup	48
Brown rice, 1 cup, cooked	5
Cherries, 10 large	22
Chick peas, cooked, ½ cup	42
I oz dark chocolate	32
Milk, 2%, 1 cup	30
Yogurt, non-fat, fruit	33
Fettucini, 1 cup, cooked	32
Grapes, green, 1 cup	46
Mango, small	55
Orange, medium	44
Orange juice, 8 oz	46
Peach, medium	42
Peanuts	14
Cashews	22
Pecans	0
Pear, medium	38
Pineapple juice, 8 oz	46
Plums, medium	39
Grapefruit, ½ medium	25
Grapefruit juice, 8 oz	48
Honey, 1 tsp	20
Kidney beans, ½ cup	37
Lentils, ½ cup	30
Lima beans, ½ cup	32
Macaroni, cooked, 1 cup	5
Navy beans, ½ cup	38
Oatmeal, old type, 1 cup	49
Spaghetti, 1 cup, cooked	41
Peanuts, ½ cup, roasted	14
Peas, ½ cup	48
Pinto beans, ½ cup	45
Sweet potato, ½ cup	54
Pumpernickel bread, 1 slice	51

Semolina, ⅔ cup, cooked   55
Tomato soup, 1 cup   38
Sourdough bread, 1 slice   52
Artichokes, asparagus, broccoli, cauliflower, celery, cucumber, eggplant, green beans, lettuce, peppers, spinach, tomatoes, zucchini–all have a GI of around 15!

Note that meats, fish, fowl, and eggs have no carbohydrate, so they have a zero GI. In general, raw, non-starchy vegetables have very low GI. Olive oil and butter, or coconut oil, are the only added fats I recommend. They have no measurable GI. At least 90% to 100% of all the food eaten should be from the foods listed above and in this paragraph! Most cheeses have low GI. Although some boxed cereals have GI within the 55 or lower range I think is ideal, virtually all are really semi-junk!

EATING FOR HEALTH ©

C. Norman Shealy, M.D., Ph.D.

Food should taste good and should be good for you. Unfortunately, in the past 60 years nutrition has changed more than in the previous 10,000 years! Until World War II, the vast majority of food was grown within 50 miles of consumption. Now the vast majority of food is grown all over the world, with little control over quality. Thirty years ago, Ross Hume Hall noted in *Food for Nought* that even the produce sold in grocery stores was often not truly ripe and was often deficient in vitamins and minerals.

More critically, even the majority of food sold in grocery stores is highly processed, further depleting its nutrient value. And a striking 40% or more of all food eaten is at "fast food" restaurants, which puts it at the top of the junk category.

What you should NOT eat:

• White flour, bread, pastries, crackers
• Sugar
• High fructose sweeteners
• Aspartame

- Splenda
- Olestra
- Margarine
- MSG
- Any artificial sweetener
- Instant pastry and bread mixes
- Colas and all pop
- All commercial candies, except 70 to 75% cocoa dark chocolate (and then only an ounce daily)
- Processed cheese
- Canned fruits in light or heavy syrup
- Snack crackers and cookies
- All the highly sweetened coffees, etc.
- 90+% of all packaged cereals
- "Luncheon meats"
- Fast food restaurant food
- Almost all boxed cereals
- Most "trail mixes"

What you should eat in moderation:
- Range fed beef—not more than 8 ounces per week
- Organically raised lamb or pork—not more than 8 ounces per week
- Skimmed or 2% milk from non BHG cows—not more than 16 ounces per day
- Buttermilk, up to 16 oz per day, instead of milk
- Bacon, sausage, and ham—as a rare treat
- 100% whole grain or sour dough or semolina bread, up to 2 slices daily
- Tuna fish, not more than once a week
- Irish potatoes, baked or boiled, once or twice a week
- Sauerkraut
- Pickles or beets
- Honey, up to several teaspoons daily
- Coffee, up to 2 cups daily
- Quality dark chocolate, 70 to 75% cocoa, one ounce daily
- Commercial ice cream—as a rare treat

- Dried fruits—sparingly. Be sure they are not "sweetened."
- Wine, 4 to 6 ounces daily, if not overweight
- Beer instead of wine, occasionally, not more than 12 ounces

What you should eat freely, as long as your Body Mass Index is between 19 and 24:
- Fresh vegetables, organically raised if possible
- Fresh fruits, organic when possible
- Eggs, especially from range chickens, up to 2 daily
- Range fed chicken or turkey—up to 4 ounces daily
- Alaskan salmon, even canned
- Fresh fish
- Old-fashioned peanut butter or almond butter
- Cooked dried beans, peas, or lentils
- Homemade soups—virtually all the canned soups have MSG!
- Chia seeds—I'll be doing another newsletter on these
- Raw or roasted almonds, walnuts, cashews, peanuts, sunflower seeds, sesame seeds
- Plain yogurt, can be sweetened with honey and fruit
- Non-processed cheese, up to an ounce daily
- Butter, up to an ounce daily
- Olive oil, up to an ounce daily
- You may substitute coconut oil or flax seed oil for olive oil
- Sweet potatoes
- Brown rice
- Old-fashioned oatmeal
- Yellow grits, buckwheat, millet, quinoa
- Black or green tea, up to 2 or 3 cups daily
- Non-caffeinated herb teas
- Non-chlorinated, non-fluoridated water

Real food, fast:
- A handful of nuts or peanuts, and fresh fruit
- Fresh fruit and cheese
- Canned sardines or salmon on real bread, as listed above
- Old-fashioned peanut butter, good right out of the spoon

• A fruit smoothie—one banana, plus a handful of any other fruit, 2 tablespoons of peanut butter or chia seeds and water, blenderized

FOOD ADDICTION ©

C. Norman Shealy, M.D., Ph.D.

It is highly unlikely that anyone has ever become a food addict from eating real food—vegetables, fruits, nuts and seeds, and modest amounts of natural meat—fish, range-fed fowl or beef. **What makes food addicting?**

• Fat
• Sugar
• All sugar substitutes—aspartame, Sucralose, etc. They fool the brain, aggravate addiction to sweets, and lead to obesity.
• Corn syrup and fructose
• Salt
• Monosodium glutamate (MSG)

Fast food restaurants and the big food manufacturers—isn't that an oxymoron? Manufacturing food!! **If it was not there on the farm, it is not natural!** White flour was one of the original MANUFACTURED artificial foods. The loss of fiber and vitamins makes white flour products potentially addicting. That includes most pasta. The fast food chains lace their so-called foods with salt, MSG, and fat, as well as sugar and sugar substitutes. All of their bread is junk. The food manufacturers do the same. Just read the labels. Many popular canned soups may be advertised as being good for you, but none of them can be good if they contain MSG. They are loaded with MSG. Potato chips and almost all snack foods are loaded with fat and MSG, as well as trans fats and other junk, including sugar. ALL POP is junk. Virtually all store-bought bread is junk. Incidentally, fruit juices without the pulp of the fruit are loaded with natural sugar, but they lack the fiber to moderate that sugar! At home we make our juice from whole fruits. Virtually all peanut butter is junk—loaded with sugar, more salt than necessary to enhance natural flavor, and most have trans fats. There is NO margarine that I would eat. Approximately 80% of everything you eat should be fresh or frozen fruits, vegetables, nuts, and seeds. For most people grains other than brown rice and old-fashioned oatmeal should be minimized. Meats (all flesh foods) and cheeses should be treated as condiments—four ounces daily. Two eggs a day are super for most people. If you are eating foods according to this recommendation, you will need little salt and little oil, mostly olive oil and a little butter. *The single best way to avoid food addiction is to eat this way.*

IODINE—THE SILENT DEFICIT

C. Norman Shealy, M.D., Ph.D.

Iodine deficiency was first recognized almost 80 years ago, as a cause of goiter. During the 1920s it was determined that the MINIMUM daily requirement for adults was 150 micrograms daily. Deficiencies led not only to goiter but, when iodine-deficient pregnant women delivered babies, the brain of the newborn was severely damaged, leading to cretinism. Salt was iodized in order to supply this essential nutrient. However, only half the salt in the U.S. is iodized, and for 50 years physicians have recommended minimizing salt intake. In the past 15 years average intake in this country has fallen from 300 to 150 micrograms daily.

Meanwhile, many factors that affect thyroid function have changed. Chlorinated water is the standard in all cities, but chlorine interferes with iodine absorption. High protein intake interferes with iodine absorption. Much higher consumption of cruciferous vegetables blocks iodine uptake by the thyroid. While beneficial to the colon, and high in antioxidants, cabbage, broccoli, cauliflower, Brussels sprouts all block thyroid uptake of iodine. Finally, over the past 50 years everyone in the world has been nuked. It seems obvious to me that thyroid size, to palpation, is much smaller than it was 50 years ago. Despite the general medical dependence upon special hormone tests, such as TSH, etc., temperature appears to be much more accurate for assessing thyroid function. During the past decade, I have noticed that 90% of individuals have a temperature BELOW normal. The oral temperature before get-ting out of bed in the morning should be 97.6 degrees Fahrenheit or higher. Mid-afternoon the temperature should be 98.6. Temperature is the simplest measure of basal metabolic rate, the key function of the thyroid gland.

Interestingly, hypothyroidism can cause virtually every symptom: high blood pressure, low blood pressure, obesity, fatigue, depression, hair loss, infertility, poor memory, cold intolerance, nervousness and anxi-ety, muscle cramps, muscle weakness, menstrual irregularities, poor in-tellect, fibrocystic breast disease, immune deficiency, and even low gastric acid production, etc. There is increasing evidence that breast cancer and prostate cancer are increased in those deficient in iodine. The thyroid gland also produces Calcitonin, the hormone responsible for maintaining the calcium in bone. Low Calcitonin leads to osteoporo-sis. Hypothyroidism greatly aggravates osteoporosis!

The single best way to restore thyroid function is to take adequate io-dine. Start with 1500 to 2000 micrograms daily. This is best done with Liquid Iodine by Biotics. If your temperature does not come up to 98.6 within 4 to 6 weeks, it may help to stimulate the Ring of Fire with the SheLI TENS. Restoration of thyroid function is one of the most critical essentials for optimal health. The only contraindication to high dosages is a nodule in the thyroid gland. This can easily be determined by a competent physical examination. If there is a nodule, special tests such as a thyroid scan should be done to rule out a malignancy of the gland.

Once your temperature returns to normal, you may need 450 to 750 micrograms of iodine daily to maintain normal thyroid function. Your body will be grateful for your attention to this essential nutrient!

Shealy, C.N., Borgmeyer, V. and Jones, C. (2002). "Correction of low body temperature with iodine supplementation." *Frontier Perspectives*, Vol. 11, No. 1, pp. 6-8.

MONOSODIUM GLUTAMATE POISONING AND FATTENING AMERICA

C. Norman Shealy, M.D., Ph.D.

MSG is implicated in:

- Addiction
- Alcoholism
- Allergies
- A.L.S.
- Alzheimer's
- Asthma
- Atrial Fibrillation
- Attention Deficit Disorder/ADHD
- Autism
- Blindness
- Celiac Sprue
- Depression
- Dizziness
- Diabetes
- Epilepsy
- Fibromyalgia
- Headache
- Heat Stroke
- Hypertension
- Hypothyroidism
- Insomnia
- Irritable Bowel Syndrome
- Inflammation
- Migraine
- Multiple Sclerosis
- Myopia
- Obesity
- Panic Disorders
- Pituitary Tumors
- Rage

- Rosacea
- Tinnitus—hearing loss
- Sleeplessness

There may be no other additive in food that has so many harmful effects! And it is in virtually every processed food. If a package has a label with more than one ingredient, it is likely to have MSG!! From soups to "snacks," and of course in all junk "fast " foods (more poison from McDonald's and its clones), MSG may be more prevalent than any other molecule! MSG may even push you to the couch to be less active!!

The bottom line:

AVOID MSG LIKE THE POISON THAT IT IS!! That means DO NOT BUY OR EAT PACKAGED FOODS, SOUPS, CRACKERS, SNACKS, FAST FOOD!!

For more information on this widespread POISON. see:

www.**msg**truth.org/**obesity**.htmMSG and ADD

http://www.newstarget.com/009379.html

Am J Physiol Endocrinol Metab **234: E532-E534, 1978; 0193-1849/78 $5.00**AJP: Endocrinology and Metabolism, Vol 234, Issue 5, E532-E534
Copyright © 1978 by American Physiological Society

NUTRITION FOR OPTIMAL WEIGHT

C. Norman Shealy, M.D., Ph.D.

Nothing is more important than optimal nutrition for health and optimal weight. Of course, attitude and exercise are equally important, but not one of these is ultimately better than the other two!

All individuals will do well to take Vitamin D 3, 50,000 units, and K 2, 100 micrograms, each once a week; 8 Essentials daily; and use Magnesium Lotion, 2 teaspoons on the skin, twice daily.

TOTAL AVOIDS
Pop of all kinds
Fast food of all kinds
Packaged foods with more than one ingredient (except that one ounce of 70% dark chocolate)
MSG
Aspartame
Sugar
Fructose
Corn syrup
Other artificial sweeteners
Alcohol
Most bread!!!!!!!

CHOOSE ONE OF THE FOLLOWING:

1. THE INSTANT BLISS DIET
If you want to lose weight quickly, up to 10 pounds a month, this is the best approach.

Breakfast
One fresh orange or small apple
Three eggs, plus cheese if desired

(Or three eggs beaten with 3 tablespoons of half and half plus 2 teaspoons of cinnamon scrambled into a pan with hot olive oil)

Tea or coffee—no sweetener
2 tablespoons of chia seeds
One slice of sourdough toast

For lunch and/or dinner, Bliss Cream Shake:
One egg
One cup of whipping cream
1 teaspoon of cinnamon
1 teaspoon of unsweetened coconut
¼ teaspoon of vanilla extract
One tablespoon of chia seeds

If you use the cream shake for only one meal, the other will be:
A serving of range fed chicken, turkey, or Alaskan salmon or halibut

Unlimited non-starchy vegetables with two tablespoons of olive oil

You may have one more slice of any sourdough bread, but it is not necessary! Actually, two tablespoons of chia seeds will provide a much healthier alternative to any bread. And you may have NOT MORE THAN one ounce of 70% excellent dark chocolate daily.

OR . . .

You may have two meals of brown rice with range fed chicken or Alaskan salmon (including canned pink salmon) or halibut and non-starchy veggies. In general, the Bliss Cream Shake provides the fastest weight loss. At least 90% of people will lower cholesterol on this diet!

2. MODIFIED RICE DIET

Unlimited brown rice
Unlimited fresh fruit, except bananas
2 scoops of WHEY Protein Isolate
8 Dr Shealy's Essentials
2 GRAMS Omega 3 fatty acid

3. MODIFIED MACROBIOTIC DIET
Brown rice
Steamed, non-starchy veggies

Broiled, baked, or poached fish or range-fed chicken
For breakfast, consider brown rice with one tablespoon of Smuckers
Old-Fashioned peanut butter and an apple

SEASONINGS:
Sea salt
Pepper
Smoked Spanish Paprika
Rosemary
Turmeric
Cumin
Coriander
Cinnamon
Non-chlorinated, non-fluoridated water—at least 2 quarts daily!!!!
Stevia

If your oral temperature is consistently less than 98.6 Fahrenheit after
you have been out of bed several hours, take Iodoral, one daily, for at
least 6 weeks and then one a week forever.

MIX AND MATCH
Have one meal of macrobiotic, one of modified rice, and one of Bliss
shake!

EXERCISE
Ideally, bounce one minute, 3 times a day, and add one minute every
day, building to a minimum of 10 times a day. Then add one minute
each day until you are at 2 minutes, 10 times a day. Then add one
minute every day until you are at 3 minutes, 10 times daily!!!!
www.youtube.com/watch?v=WtMVJ6yJaBs

ATTITUDE
You must have an attitude that you are OK. Unless you have murdered
or raped someone, you have nothing about which to feel inferior or
guilty! You may wish to use my Weight Balance or Enhancing Self-
Esteem CD once or twice daily.

158   *Medical Intuition*

NUTRITION—THE CROWN JEWEL OF CAM

C. Norman Shealy, M.D., Ph.D.

Two critical works influenced my interest in safe "alternatives" to drugs and surgery for most chronic diseases. *The Role of Medicine* by Dr. Thomas McKeown (The Nuffield Trust, 1976) emphasized the fact that 92% of advances in longevity were the result of sanitation, chlorination of water, pasteurization of milk, and adequate protein. Dr. John Knowles, late president of the Rockefeller Foundation, stated that 80% of illnesses are the result of unhealthy behavior ("The Responsibility of the Individual," *Daedalus*, Winter, 1977). The current epidemic of obesity is clearly the result of poor nutritional choices, and nutrition is a major contributor to stroke; coronary artery disease; cataracts; macular degeneration and cancer of the colon, breast, and prostate, to name a few. I have room in this brief article for only a few references, but there are more scientific articles supporting nutrition than there are for all drugs in the PDR. I have reviewed over 10,000 journal articles and created an annotated bibliography to give me rapid access to important published data. The most important findings seem to be those affecting cholesterol, cardiovascular disease, mental health, cancer, and degenerative diseases, especially cataracts and macular degeneration. Here are just a few of the important topics.

CHOLESTEROL—Perhaps there is no more medically attacked nutrient than cholesterol. People who eat the most cholesterol and saturated fat, including the French, Okinawanese, Yemen Jews, Northern Indians, and African Masai, have half the death rate from heart disease as do Americans. More importantly, cholesterol can be remarkably lowered to safer levels with lecithin, arginine, taurine, saw palmetto extract, and even Red Rice yeast. (Rosch, Paul J. "Ignore the experts and eat more meat and fat?" *Health and Stress*, American Institute of Stress, N.Y., # 11, 2003). And of course homocysteine is far more important than cholesterol!!

HOMOCYSTEINE levels even in the "normal" mid-range and above are associated with marked increases in hypertension, stroke, coronary artery disease, and Alzheimer's, not to mention spina bifida with meningoceles. This is perhaps the most treatable of all nutritional problems, although the levels of B 12 and especially folate may need to be much higher than the measly 400 micrograms recommended.

IODINE—Subclinical hypothyroidism has been a major controversy for over three-quarters of a century. My own studies have shown that at least 80% of individuals have a body temperature below normal and low levels of iodine, many of the symptoms of low thyroid function, etc. Average iodine intake has fallen in the past two decades to only 150 micrograms per day, the supposed minimal daily requirement. Meanwhile a variety of factors have increased our need for iodine—marked increased intake of cruciferous vegetables, chlorination of water, higher intake of protein, and nuclear contamination over the past 50 years. Additionally, only half the salt in the U.S. is iodized, and physicians have recommended low salt intake for decades. At least 60% of individuals have body temperature return to normal within one month of adding iodine to their diet.

MAGNESIUM—Magnesium deficiency is rampant throughout the world. At least 80% of women and 70% of men do not eat the recommended minimal daily requirement of magnesium. There are over 350 enzymes that require magnesium. Magnesium is the major determinant of cellular membrane potential. Magnesium deficiency has been reported in virtually every major disease—hypertension, eclampsia, diabetes, asthma, cancer, allergies, migraine, coronary artery disease, etc. Magnesium is notoriously difficult to absorb orally, as its salts are laxatives. If magnesium goes through the intestines in less than 12 hours, absorption is seriously impaired. In my experience, even the best of the oral preparations, Magnesium Taurate, requires oral supplementation for 6 to 12 months to restore intracellular levels. Incidentally, only two tests for magnesium are accurate—the magnesium load test and the intracellular spectrometric exam. Blood levels are notoriously inaccurate, with true serum deficiencies found primarily in starvation and acute alcoholism. Transdermally applied, magnesium lotion, with 25% magnesium chloride, restores intracellular levels within 4 to 6 weeks.

TAURINE—Taurine, the most abundant amino acid in the body, is found only in animal protein and is synergistic with magnesium in maintaining cell membrane potential. Taurine is deficient in 86% of depressed individuals. 100% of depressed patients have deficiencies of one to seven essential amino acids, the building blocks of neurochemicals such as serotonin, norepinephrine, etc. Taurine is one of several essentials for preventing macular degeneration and is almost equally important in heart muscle.

OMEGA-3 FATTY ACIDS—Omega-3s are the most essential fats and are remarkably low in the American diet. Depression, atherosclerosis, arthritis, and many degenerative diseases are helped by increased intake of the critical fish-oil omega-3's found in salmon, sardines, mackerel, cod liver, etc.

VITAMIN D—There is increasing evidence that a minimum of 1000 units of vitamin D is required. Skin and colon cancer and many immune disorders, including autoimmune diseases such as multiple sclerosis, are strongly influenced by D deficiency.

BORON—To name just a few important correlations—bone strength, testosterone, and estrogen are dependent upon adequate levels of boron.

LITHIUM—Tryptophan cannot be converted into serotonin without lithium, B 3, and B 6.

B COMPLEX—80% of smokers and 35% of non-smokers are deficient in B 6, even when they are taking an RDA multivitamin.

ANTIOXIDANTS—Free radicals are major determinants of inflammation, degenerative diseases, cancer, and death. Inflammatory reactions are major contributors to virtually every disease. There are several herbal preparations that are superior to NSAIDS, without the "side effects." These include bromelain, ginger, curcumin, licorice, and frankincense (Boswellia). Of course, adequate levels of vitamins C, E, and beta-carotene are also essential. The primary antioxidants are vitamins C, E, and beta-carotene. Only one very flawed study has been done with moderate dosages of beta-carotene. In Finland they gave 25,000 units of beta-carotene to men and found an increase in lung cancer in smokers. Increased amounts of beta-carotene must be matched with increased C and E, as they work synergistically. Large dosages of C given intravenously are quite safe if balanced with B 6, calcium, and magnesium. In metastatic bone pain, nothing works better than IV vitamin C –25 grams in 500 cc IV fluid over 8 hours. There is excellent evidence for significant benefit of mega dosages of C in hepatitis and acute viral infections. Large dosages of vitamin A are toxic, but beta-carotene is safe up to several hundred thousand units daily.

ZINC—Another of the essential minerals. Zinc deficiency leads to significant defects in immunity. Specific diseases that may respond to zinc are macular degeneration, tinnitus, and benign prostatic hypertrophy. Zinc excesses occur in some welders and can lead to polyneuropathy. Two cases of this seen by me responded well to chelation.

CHROMIUM—1000 micrograms of chromium daily has been reported to assist significantly in Type II diabetes. Gymnema sylvestra and gugulipid are also of benefit. These herbs, plus deep relaxation, proper nutrition, and exercise, are far better methods of management of adult onset diabetes than oral antidiabetics.

IRON—Deficiencies of iron are less common today but can of course lead to anemia. Jim Blaine has addressed well the problems of excess iron.

PEANUT BUTTER—NECTAR OF THE GODS ®

C. Norman Shealy, M.D., Ph.D.

Peanut butter has always been one of my favorite foods, any time of day or night. Whenever a meal is just not satisfying, I finish with a spoonful of Smucker's peanut butter. Now, I want to assure you that I have no financial interest in Smuckers—not even any stock. But having tasted all the *natural* peanut butters I can find, Smuckers is absolutely tops.

Incidentally, I hasten to mention that most of the peanut butter brands on the market usually have sugar as well as artificially hydrogenated fat—DO NOT EAT THEM!!

This Christmas a friend gave me the ultimate gourmet delight for a natural, old-fashioned peanut butter fan—a peanut butter stirrer!! For years I have stored the jar upside down in the cupboard to help move the oil into the peanut butter and stirred it as well as I could with a spoon before putting it into the refrigerator. Inevitably the oil did not mix well and some of the peanut butter became rather more chewy and not as smooth. Not now! The stirrer is super. Once stirred, the refrigerated peanut butter remains creamy to the last drop. You can purchase the stirrers on Amazon but they are a dollar cheaper at Lehman's! Lehman's is one of the best sources for a wide variety of unusual items— widely used by the Amish. And the Smucker's Web site also has the stirrer.

Of further interest, Smucker's organic peanut butter is not nearly as tasty! They also put out a brand, Adams· which is not as good.

Now for the really good news about peanut butter. Peanuts themselves are an excellent nutritional value, especially if taken with a tiny bit of milk. The amino acid content is not perfect, but the quality of the fat makes up for that. Even more importantly, the glycemic index is low! They are digested slowly so they have a long appetite satisfaction index. Indeed, with a bit of milk or cottage cheese, you could live quite well long term with these as the main protein sources. And peanuts are an excellent source of minerals as well as antioxidants.

Some people are concerned about aflatoxins in peanuts. Certainly poor quality peanuts may have them. So do almonds, pistachios, and hazelnuts! Somehow, the quality of Smucker's peanut butter seems too good for me to worry about aflatoxins. A day without Smucker's peanut butter is a day of lost pleasure! It is the ultimate, healthy fast food. A heaping tablespoon of peanut butter with a banana or an apple makes one of the best quick meals, far better than most other quick meals! When I travel, I often just have peanuts and fruit for at least one meal a day.

Personally, I think peanut butter is ruined when combined with jelly! But in soups, muffins, biscuits, and bread (gluten free for at least the third of us who are sensitive to gluten) it adds a succulent flavor unequaled by any other food. Of course, you can also make peanut butter cookies with the basic gluten-free recipe and a touch of honey!

PEANUT BUTTER GRANOLA
    Melt in a double boiler:
    12 oz old-fashioned peanut butter (Smucker's is best!)
    4 oz butter
    ⅓ cup honey
    1 teaspoon vanilla
    3 teaspoons cinnamon
Stir the liquid into 6 cups of old-fashioned GLUTEN-FREE (from Bob's Red Mill) rolled oats and spread into a flat pan. Place into the oven at 375 degrees. Stir every 5 minutes. It is done in 20 minutes. Add, then, 1 cup raisins and 1 cup of any nut desired.

Serve with milk or half and half and any fruit or yogurt.

PROBIOTICS ©

C. Norman Shealy, M.D., Ph.D.

Some 56 years ago, I learned in medical school that individuals on even those early day antibiotics needed Probiotics. The commercially available one then was Lactinex, containing lactobacillus acidophilus. I have routinely recommended it to all patients taking antibiotics. It needs to be taken at least two hours away from taking an oral antibiotic. And this old standard is still available.

The intestines contain over 400 useful bacteria, and the balance between them is critically important. These GOOD bacteria are one of the
most important factors in a healthy immune system. Because of the
rather frequent use of antibiotics and many other factors, normal gut
flora are frequently upset. Indeed, low-grade intestinal inflammation
from inadequate gut flora may be a "cause" of many diseases—ranging
from peptic ulcer, where Helicobacter pylori takes over. H. Pylori is even
one of the contributors to atherosclerosis.

Yogurt, especially unsweetened yogurt, is one of the best foods for many
individuals, as it has largely had digested all the lactose. Most people
who cannot drink milk tolerate yogurt well. Yogurt can be used vagi-
nally to treat yeast infections. More importantly, there are benefits for
those who regularly eat fermented milk products:

Reduced harmful bacteria in the bowel
Reduced number of cancer-producing substances in urine and stool
Decreased yeast infections, including Candidiasis
Lower LDL cholesterol
Reduced incidence of traveler's diarrhea
Reduced inflammatory cytokines and inflammation

Failure to drink milk, especially in the two-thirds of individuals who
lack lactase, is another potential cause of inadequate gut flora. Although
lactobacillus acidophilus is perhaps the best known, there are a variety
of friendly bacteria. The most common Probiotics used today include
the following:

Lactobacillus acidophilus
Lactobacillus casei
Lactobacillus rhamnosus
Lactobacillus salivarius
Staphylococcus thermophilus
Bifidobacterium bifidum
Bifidobacterium longum
Bifidobacterium lactis

It is most important, if you take probiotic capsules, that you use one that is stable at room temperature! Personally I take Gr8-Dophilus, available at www.selfhealthsystems.com, 888-242-6105

PROTEINS—THE FOUNDATION OF LIFE ©

C. Norman Shealy, M.D., Ph.D.

Although not an ideal diet, proteins are the most essential of all foods. You cannot make DNA without them! You can make carbohydrates and fats from them, and of course most protein foods also contain some fat. In order of quality, the following is a good start

- Eggs
- Fish
- Cheese, especially goat cheese
- Fowl
- Beef, venison, rabbit, buffalo, etc
- Pork
- Yeast, especially saccromyces cervicae
- Chia seeds—no taurine
- Legumes—the critical missing amino acid is taurine!
- Nuts—no taurine
- Seeds—no taurine

As I have indicated in earlier newsletters, you should eat the following each day
- One super salad
- Two other veggie vegetables
- Two fruits
- One or two servings of the good starches, not essential, but OK
- One serving of the first 6 highest-quality proteins, AT LEAST 3 or 4 times each week—essential for B 12
- Up to one serving of the lower 4 high-protein foods, especially any day without the higher quality ones. If you skip the top 6, you should add yeast on these days!

Added fats, up to two tablespoons daily, especially with no-starch meals:

- Butter
- Olive oil
- Coconut oil

Condiments and herbs:
Scores of these marvelous taste treats, most of which are loaded with antioxidants and great minerals. My favorites:
- Cinnamon
- Turmeric
- Coriander
- Cumin
- Ginger
- Rosemary
- Thyme
- Mint
- Pimenton—smoked Spanish paprika
- Oregano
- Onions and garlic may be eaten as a serving of vegetables or used as seasonings

Obviously, various seaweed products can be used, if you like them. With this as a guide for nutrition, there is no need for desserts. However, if you are not overweight and are otherwise healthy, then a dessert treat once a week is fine!

PRIMARY SALAD VEGGIES ©

C. Norman Shealy, M.D., Ph.D.

You think a salad is lettuce and maybe spinach with a few minor additions?? Then see how many of these you know.
- Amaranth
- Arugula
- Beet greens
- Bitterleaf
- Catsear

- Celtuce
- Ceylon spinach
- Chicory
- Chinese mallow
- Chrysanthemum
- Corn salad
- Cress
- Dandelion
- Endive
- Epazote
- Fat hen
- Fiddlehead
- Fluted pumpkin
- Golden samphire
- Good King Henry
- Iceplant
- Kuka
- Lagos bologi
- Land cress
- Lettuce—scores of varieties!
- Lizard's tail
- Melokhia
- Mustard
- New Zealand Spinach
- Orache
- Parsley
- Radicchio
- Salad rape
- Samphire
- Sea Beet
- Sea kale
- Sierra Leone bologi
- Soko
- Sorrel
- Spinach—scores of varieties
- Summer purslane

- Swiss chard
- Watercress
- Water spinach
- Winter purslane

Perhaps half of these may not be available, and many of these have various varieties, each of which has different nutritional value. The more variety, the better. At the bottom of the list in value is iceberg lettuce. Skip it in favor of leafy (especially red) or romaine lettuce. And of course add lots of other great salad enhancers, such as cabbage, celery, peppers, artichokes, marigolds, nasturtiums, grapes and other fruits—not to mention nuts and cheeses. Your diet should include at least one great salad a day!

SUGAR BLUES—THE DARK SIDE OF SWEET

C. Norman Shealy, M.D., Ph.D.

Frank Dufty's book *Sugar Blues* should have been the death knell to the exorbitant use of sugar (sucrose). Of course, half a century earlier, Price and Pottenger (*Nutrition and Physical Degeneration*) had scientifically documented the role of sugar and white flour as major contributors to DIS-EASE, ranging from dental decay to atherosclerosis and cancer, especially of the colon. Much of this took place before the plague of McDonalds and its fast-food clones, the increased processing of food, and the maddening array of artificial additives, such as Equal, Splenda, MSG, Olestra, and other food mafia addicting and deadening approaches. And sugar certainly contributes to the epidemic of depression.

There are only 4 primary tastes: sweet, sour, bitter, and salty. Most of the overtones to these tastes come from the wide array of aromas that are part of food's enticement. It is hard to fathom why such artificial and unhealthy practices as additions of sugar, white flour, and white rice became staples. None of these is NATURAL. All are much inferior to the original products. All are deficient in fiber, minerals, and vitamins, all of which are essential for health and life. White flour has NO fiber and is oxymoronically "enriched" with one-seventh the normal content of B 6.

Sugar has ZERO, ZIP, NO nutrient VALUE. Indeed, it sucks vital nutrients from whatever other sources you have.

ARTIFICIAL sweeteners are chemical slop at best and toxins at worst. These and saccharin are not food and should be abandoned by anyone with an IQ of 90 and above. And for those with lower IQ, these nonsense chemicals may be even worse! Aspartame at least significantly worsens obesity, migraine, epilepsy, and hypertension. And constantly stimulating your sweet tooth is a major assistant to developing insulin malfunctions.

Are there any good, healthy sweets? Yes, of course. Fruits and honey. For almost all people these are healthier and more desirable than any other sweet-tasting foods. Honey is sweeter than sugar, tastes better, and is an excellent antioxidant. Incidentally, xylitol has been touted as a great substitute, and it may be minimally better that sugar. However, it does raise blood sugar, cause release of insulin, and has led to serious complications even in dogs! Its only use might be as a nasal spray in children with frequent ear infections, where regular use does appear to be helpful. Fructose is also not healthier, although it is twice as sweet as sugar, so that less is needed to satisfy sweetness. Stevia MAY be a relatively less harmful substitute, but my big question is why? There has been an occasional resultant hypertension, and it still feeds the sweet addiction craze. Now, if you are really healthy and eat an otherwise good diet, etc., I do not feel a need to be a total nihilist. For healthy people, an occasional dose of sugar may be fine. Especially if it is in dark chocolate!

REFERENCES:
Forster, H., et al. "Metabolic tolerance to high doses of oral xylitol inhuman volunteers not previously adapted to xylitol," *Int. J. Vitam Nutr Res Suppl.* 1982; 22: 67–88, 1982

Huttunen, JK, et al. "Turku sugar studies XL. Effects of sucrose, fructose and xylitol diets on glucose, lipid and urate metabolism," *Acta Odontol Scand*, 34: 341–351, 1976.

Makinen, KK. "Long-term tolerance of healthy human subjects to high amounts of xylitol and fructose: general and biochemical findings," *Int Z Vitam Ernahrungsforsch Beih*, 15: 92–104, 1976

TO EAT OR NOT TO EAT ©

C. Norman Shealy, M.D., Ph.D.

There is no greater controversy than that over nutrition. Some claim that virtually every food is harmful, and a remarkable variety of fad diets exist, from all raw to vegan. I consider vegan one of the WORST. Interestingly, vegans eat yeast, a member of the animal kingdom; and most wear later shoes and belts. So much for their purity. Meanwhile, all vegans eventually suffer B 12 deficiency and usually are deficient in one or more essential amino acids.

Other extremes are the Rice Diet of Walter Kempner, a several-decade fad at Duke University—white rice, unlimited canned fruits, and a one-a-day vitamin supplement. It is remarkably successful in controlling Type II diabetes, malignant hypertension, and obesity. It contains about 10% protein (and is deficient in some essential amino acids); ZERO fat; and 90% carbohydrate. The secret is no fat and low protein. It is also the most esthetically obnoxious diet I know.

At the opposite end of the scale is the Atkins Diet, a relatively recent fad: roughly 60% fat, 20% protein, and 20% or less carbohydrate. Basically, it consists of unlimited meat, cheese, fats, and non-starchy vegetables. It tastes great and is excellent for obesity as well as lowering cholesterol.

Slightly more palatable long term is the Broda Barnes diet, which allows two pieces of bread and two small fruit servings daily; otherwise it consists of virtually unlimited meat, eggs, cheese, and non-starchy vegetables. It long preceded the Atkins diet and has all the benefits.

Interestingly, the Macrobiotic diet is also an excellent alternative—brown rice, steamed vegetables, and broiled, baked, or poached fish, with occasional chicken.

Of all the modern fads, Dr. Mercola's NO-GRAIN DIET is perhaps the most ludicrous. While I respect much of Mercola's material, he misses the boat almost totally on this one. Admittedly, white, "enriched" wheat is an oxymoron and is definitely a junk food. And wheat is one of the most common allergens. But rice is a terrific food. In fact, it is the single greatest contribution to the diet of the Okinawans, the world's longest-lived and healthiest people.

It is essential for most of us to add vitamin and mineral supplements, and these will be covered in a later article.

Here are my recommendations for an optimally healthy diet, adjusting your servings to keep your weight ideal (Body Mass Index 19-24; see BMI below):

Brown rice, one to three cups of cooked rice daily; you may substitute
    other grains as below
Corn, millet, quinoa, oatmeal, barley, buckwheat, one to seven times per
    week
Sweet potatoes, 3 to 7 servings per week
Irish potatoes (never fried), once or twice a week
Sourdough or 100% whole grain bread, one serving per day
Tofu, chickpeas, soybeans, navy beans, garbanzos, or old-fashioned pea-
    nut butter: one or two servings daily
Eggs, one or two daily
Low- or no-fat yogurt, 8 oz per day
Buttermilk, up to 8 oz per day
Cheese, one oz per day
Fish, range chicken, or range beef, 4 oz per day
Non-starchy vegetables, unlimited
Fresh fruits, two to four servings daily
Olive oil, one to two tablespoons daily
Butter, one tablespoon daily

Nuts, up to 2 tablespoons daily
Honey, two to six teaspoons daily
Black, green, or jasmine tea, 3 to 6 cups daily
Turmeric, cinnamon, and most herbs, freely

As much as I like the idea of "organic" foods, in general, the cost and low availability in most locations makes me hesitate to recommend them. If you raise your own, without poisons, GREAT. If they are easily available and you can afford them, go for it. Otherwise, it is more important to eat a wide variety of real food and enjoy it.

BMI (kg/m²)	19	20	21	22	23	24	25	26	27	28	29	30	35	40
Height (in.)	Weight (lb.)													
58	91	96	100	105	110	115	119	124	129	134	138	143	167	191
59	94	99	104	109	114	119	124	128	133	138	143	148	173	198
60	97	102	107	112	118	123	128	133	138	143	148	153	179	204
61	100	106	111	116	122	127	132	137	143	148	153	158	185	211
62	104	109	115	120	126	131	136	142	147	153	158	164	191	218
63	107	113	118	124	130	135	141	146	152	158	163	169	197	225
64	110	116	122	128	134	140	145	151	157	163	169	174	204	232
65	114	120	126	132	138	144	150	156	162	168	174	180	210	240
66	118	124	130	136	142	148	155	161	167	173	179	186	216	247
67	121	127	134	140	146	153	159	166	172	178	185	191	223	255
68	125	131	138	144	151	158	164	171	177	184	190	197	230	262
69	128	135	142	149	155	162	169	176	182	189	196	203	236	270
70	132	139	146	153	160	167	174	181	188	195	202	207	243	278
71	136	143	150	157	165	172	179	186	193	200	208	215	250	286
72	140	147	154	162	169	177	184	191	199	206	213	221	258	294
73	144	151	159	166	174	182	189	197	204	212	219	227	265	302
74	148	155	163	171	179	186	194	202	210	218	225	233	272	311
75	152	160	168	176	184	192	200	208	216	224	232	240	279	319
76	156	164	172	180	189	197	205	213	221	230	238	246	287	328

APPENDIX C

PHOTOS OF THE
RING OF AIR PLACEMENT
FOR TAPPING

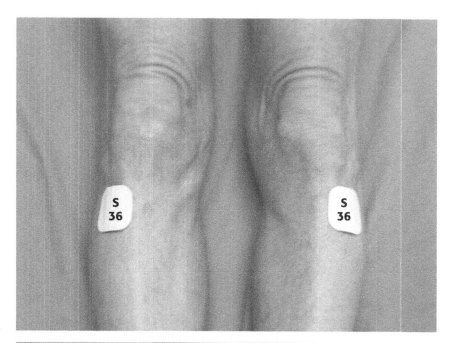

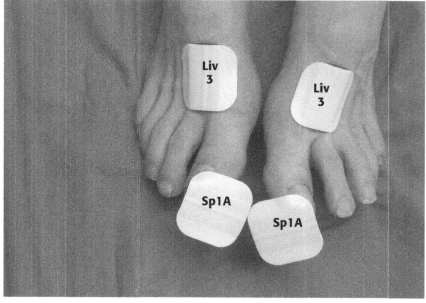

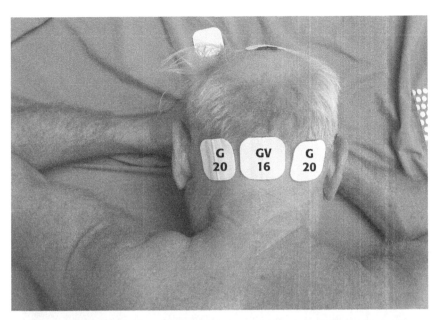

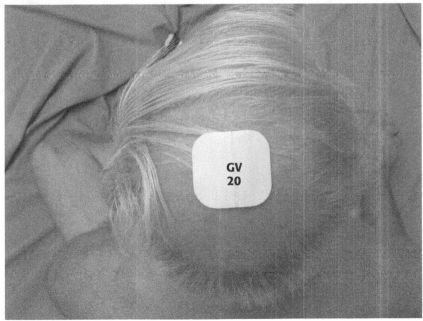

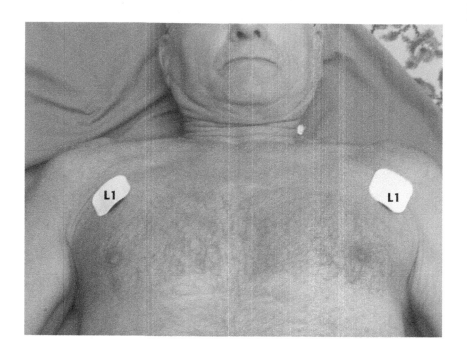

GV 1 is not shown but is the bottom of the spine.

APPENDIX D

THE EDGAR CAYCE PERSPECTIVE OF AUTISM

▶Edgar Cayce gave several readings for individuals exhibiting autistic features. Because Edgar Cayce was more interested in the uniqueness of each individual than in diagnostic labels, we cannot be certain as to whether these cases are representative of autism. The word *autism* was never used in any reading or correspondence. However, descriptions of behaviors and functioning do suggest that certain persons who received readings may have suffered from autism.

Notably, three readings given for an eight–year–old girl (2253), are indicative of autism.

(Q) Why does she not talk?
(A) This reaction, or refractory reaction in system, prevents the contraction in the muscular forces that have to do with the plexus from the secondary cardiac to the central nerve system. This is directly to the vocal box. In the corrections in the 3rd and 4th dorsal, and the 2nd and 3rd cervical, this will be stimulated, see? as will necessary later to stimulate along the eustachian tube for the reaction there, see? This *not* in the beginning. The manipulations we would make at least three times each week, and *one* of the treat-

ments and *adjustment* treatment—the other the drainages set up
and the muscular forces and tendons so relaxed as to make for the
feeding out or building up of nerve impulses as between the sympathetic and cerebro-spinal system.

(Q) Why does she wring her hands?

(A) Nervous reaction. When these come, there is some form of expression—and in the attempt to find an outlet for that *innately*
felt, the lack of knowing *what* to do—see?

(Q) Will she ever be able to understand and carry out a spoken
suggestion?

(A) She will, if these [treatments] are carried out as has been outlined.

(Q) Where will the first improvement be noticed?

(A) The gradual relaxation, and *not* so nervous.

(Q) Is her brain alright, or just dormant?

(A) Just dormant.   2253-1

Edgar Cayce traced the cause of the condition to pressures along the
spine where nerve plexus coordinate the functioning of the system.
Nervous system incoordination resulted, producing a disturbance to
the "imaginative nerve forces of the body," causing the child to be "over
sensitive."

The pressures, as we find, exist principally in those of the sacral,
the lower dorsal, and the *whole* of the cervical areas. These are especially seen in the 4th *lumbar* plexus, that prevents coordination in
the sympathetic and cerebro-spinal impulses; while those of the
central or lower dorsal, sympathetically with the upper or 4th and
5th dorsal, prevent those impulses to the central nerve force as to
cause any reaction in this direction, and little or no response is seen
in that of a refractory reaction, save as comes through impulses in
the imaginative nerve forces of the body. Hence those tendencies of
the body to be over sensitive to certain vibrations that may be set
up, without the proper coordinating even to *brain* impulses as to
what the reaction *should* be. Hence often the body responds in a
manner as apparently directly opposite from that as would be, or

should be, expected from voluntary or involuntary refractory, or refraction. 2253-1

Osteopathic manipulations to relieve the pressure were recommended. A mild, natural herbal formula (containing may blossom and ginseng) was suggested to calm and sedate the child. An energy medicine device (Radial Appliance) was prescribed to assist in coordinating the system.

Hypnotic suggestion was consistently recommended in such cases. Edgar Cayce sometimes used the expression "suggestive therapeutics" to describe a simple, natural form of suggestion to be used. Suggestion was recommended to address the habitual, involuntary hand wringing and lack of normal development:

> . . . as the body sinks to sleep—the talk, the quieting effect, the improvements through the psychopathic effect that may be created by suggestion as the body goes to sleep. Something as this, though it may be altered according to that one giving same. Do not make same as rote, or as just something to be said, but with that intense desire to be a channel of aid and help *to* the individual:
> *As you* (calling the child by *its own* name, that it responds to even by any *form* of suggestion) a*s you sink into a quiet restful sleep, the organs of the body will so function that the very best will be builded in the physical and mental being, giving that response that will be a normal activity for the organs of the sensory system.*
> 2253-2

> (Q) Is there anything we can do to get her to stop wringing her hands?
> (A) Only applying those things that will alter the present nervous reactions in the system will change same. *This* body, would be well for the suggestions to be made under the influence of hypnosis, or auto-suggestion to the body as it sleeps. This must be made by someone in sympathy with the activities of the body, and *this* would relieve such stress on the general system. 2253-3

Although we have no long-term documentation in this case, a letter from Mrs. Pope of the Rosehill School (where the child was staying) noted, "I think she has improved noticeably and more so since she has had the battery although it has been used such a short time."

Four readings were given for a nineteen-year-old male [2014] who had been "abnormal about eleven years" and who was exhibiting repetitious, involuntary movements and antisocial behaviors:

> (Q) What is the reason for, and what can be done for the habit reaction he has; such as the spitting, drawing of the mouth down, and waving of the fingers before his nose and mouth?
>
> (A) These, as indicated, are reflexes through the sensory nerve system; lack of coordination between impulses and the guided or directed forces in the mental reactions of same.
>
> Keep up the applications indicated for corrections, making the suggestions—and not attempting to control by violent means!
>
> 2014-3

> (Q) Would you advise scolding or hitting him, when he is so uncontrollable? or what method would you advise?
>
> (A) Patience, kindness, gentleness, ever; not in that of scolding or tormenting at all. But in cajoling, and in kindness and in patience, these are the manners.
>
> Remember, these conditions are for purposes. While they become very trying to the individuals who attempt to administer to the needs of the body, know that these are purposeful in thine own experience also.
>
> (Q) Is this stubborn, fresh and disobedient attitude due to his ailment?
>
> (A) Due to the ailment; else there would be other measures indicated. And in the building up of the body, there must be the response to kindness and gentleness and love—more than to force, power, might, hate or scolding.   2014-2

Again, this series of readings described nervous system incoordination involving the sensory nervous system. Pressures along the spine and in the abdominal nerve plexus associated with the digestive system were noted. Abdominal castor oil packs and spinal manipulations were suggested to relieve the pressures and coordinate the nervous systems. The Radial Appliance was also recommended to assist with the coordination. A mild laxative tea was prescribed to improve eliminations through the colon as chronic constipation was a problem.

For the behavioral problems and general pathological conditions, suggestive therapeutics was recommended:

(Q) What type of suggestion would you recommend?
(A) As just indicated, the type that is to be given continually; of the creative forces or God,—love manifesting through the activities of the body. These as helpful forces will bring the bettered conditions for this body.   2014-3

The minimal follow-up correspondence does not indicate whether the recommendations were applied consistently or what was the eventual outcome in this case.

A series of twelve readings were given for a young girl (1179) who was seven years old when she received her first reading. Her readings and follow-up correspondence suggest possible mild autism. Her readings described a "supersensitive" system with psychic or imaginative tendencies:

These conditions are rather of the unusual nature; or the body physically and mentally is supersensitive and the psychic forces are developing much faster than the bodily functionings. Or the body functionings are of such a nature that the sensitiveness of same precludes some activities through the nominal physical developments.
1179-1

There are periods when there are unusual activities in the psychic forces of the body. The imaginative reactions to the sensory and the external forces in the experience of the body at times find physical expression in moods.   1179-7

The child was somewhat withdrawn and difficult. Her mother's comment immediately following 1179-1: "Now I know better how to cope with this child, who reacts so differently from my other children—she is so unusual in so many ways."

The mother's difficulty in dealing with the child's antisocial behaviors was noted:

> *Do not* make it an issue with the body! Advise with, but do not rave at nor scold nor make the entity conscious of same by constant nagging, or insistency! And this will be better, it will be found, in *all* the ways of *impressing* the body in *any* manner for any activity. As has been indicated, the body is supersensitive, and is made aware of self's shortcomings or self's virtues by a continual impressing on same. Listen to the entity's arguments, always. Never tell her to shut up or stop, but hear it out! Then, parallel same by counsel as respecting what *might* be better if paralleled in *that* direction.
>
> 1179-6

Social withdrawal and interpersonal deficits were cited in the correspondence. The child also apparently had some difficulty with reading.

Edgar Cayce described problems with the digestive system that were contributing to the difficult psychosocial development of this child. Various digestive aids and nutritional supplements were recommended, including Ventriculin, a dietary supplement made from the gastric tissue of hogs.

As with the other cases cited above, the Radial Active appliance was suggested to assist with nervous system coordination. Spinal manipulations were recommended. A basic diet, focusing on body building foods, was emphasized. In one reading, when asked about substituting other grains for wheat, Edgar Cayce responded:

> (Q) Should the body discontinue the use of wheat products, substituting *rye break, white rice, oatmeal cereal, buckwheat and cornmeal pancakes?*
> (A) It would be well to discontinue the greater portion of the wheat products, if these others are used—and they are all very well to be used.   1179-5

Although suggestive therapeutics was not directly mentioned, the readings did insist on the importance of providing spiritual guidance to the child through Bible stories.

According to correspondence from her mother, Ms. 1179 became a school teacher at age twenty-two and married thirteen years later.

Although the above cases vary greatly with regard to symptoms and severity, some common themes are worth noting. In all these cases Edgar Cayce focused on nervous system incoordination involving the sensory nervous system. All these individuals were described as over sensitive (even "super-sensitive"). Nerve pressures were cited as causative factors. Spinal manipulation was consistently recommended, as was the use of the Radial Appliance to assist with balancing and coordinating the system.

Problems with the digestive system and intestinal tract were significant in two of these cases (1179 and 2014). Therapies such as abdominal castor oil packs, diet, and dietary supplements were suggested.

The mental and spiritual aspects of healing were prominent in all three cases. Suggestive therapeutics was usually recommended. The spiritual focus of the family and caregivers was strongly emphasized.

Thus a blending of treatments into a well-integrated treatment plan was often recommended by Edgar Cayce for the treatment of autism. Here is a summary of some of the most common treatment recommendations.

TREATMENT RECOMMENDATIONS

Conceptually, the Cayce approach to autism focuses on assisting the body in healing itself by the application of a variety of therapies intended to address the *underlying causes* of the condition. The mental and spiritual aspects of healing are strongly emphasized.

Here are some general therapeutic recommendations intended to address the *underlying causes* of autism:

1. **MANUAL THERAPY (SPINAL MANIPULATION):** Cayce often recommended spinal manipulations to correct specific problems that may be a primary cause of autism. It is difficult to obtain the osteopathic adjustments specified by Cayce. However, a chi-

ropractor may be of help. The frequency of the adjustments will depend on the recommendations of the individual chiropractor or osteopath. The use of an electric vibrator may also be helpful for individuals unable to obtain regular spinal adjustments.

2. **ELECTROTHERAPY:** Regular use of the Radial Appliance to coordinate nerve functioning and circulation is recommended.

3. **INTERNAL CLEANSING:** Because autistic symptoms were sometimes linked to problems with the alimentary canal, resulting in poor eliminations, hydrotherapy was recommended to improve eliminations through the colon. Hydrotherapy includes drinking six to eight glasses of pure water daily and obtaining colonic irrigations to cleanse the bowel. Following the diet should also assist with internal cleansing. Hot castor oil packs applied over the abdomen are recommended to improve circulation (especially lymphatic) and eliminations through the alimentary canal.

4. **DIET:** The Basic Cayce Diet is intended to improve assimilation and elimination. The diet focuses heavily on keeping a proper alkaline/acid balance, while avoiding foods which produce toxicity and drain the system. Essentially, the diet consists mainly of fruits and vegetables, while avoiding fried foods and refined carbohydrates ("junk food"). Certain food combinations are emphasized.

5. **SUGGESTIVE THERAPEUTICS:** The use of positive suggestions during the presleep period and during therapy sessions (such as massage and the Radial Appliance) is recommended to awaken the inner healing response. The spiritual attunement of the caregiver is essential.

6. **MEDICATION:** The use of a mild natural sedative (such as Passion Flower fusion) may be helpful for excitable children. Laxatives and dietary supplements may be helpful, particularly for individuals with significant gastrointestinal symptoms. Although Ventriculin is no longer available, similar products such as Secretin (made from hog gastric tissue and available only by physician's prescription) have proven helpful for some persons suffering from autism.

http://www.edgarcayce.org/health/database/chdata/data/prauti3.html

CASTOR OIL PACKS

My husband has had great relief from castor oil packs. He used to end up at the hospital with his severe pain in the abdominal area from complications with adhesions, etc. Now when he feels the pain coming on, we apply the castor oil packs. He no longer has to go on the pain killers or have the tube put down his nose to relieve the pressure on his stomach.

HEALING EPILEPSY

Jody's Journey
By Linda Caputi

In 1986, when Jo was eight years old, we moved to Virginia Beach. Regretfully, it became a traumatic event, since she missed her friends and the New York energy in which she thrived. Over time, her unhappiness developed into emotional overeating, and by age fourteen, my petite daughter was more than seventy-five pounds overweight. One thing, however, consoled her. She would be driving before her sixteenth birthday, much earlier than New York allowed. As 1993 drew near, her dream came true, as she began driving and lost the extra weight she had put on.

Yet within six months, Jo began having infrequent but strange episodes. They would begin with feelings of nausea and "zoning out." At first the incidents were easily ignored. No external problems were evident and visits to the doctor were fruitless. But with more noticeable symptoms, we were referred to a neurologist in 1995 and received a diagnosis of complex partial seizures.

Though this type of seizure appears milder than the grand mal type, it's more difficult to control with medication. The episodes were actually mild seizures called "auras." The usual electroencephalogram (EEG) and magnetic resonance imaging tests (MRI) were performed but showed nothing abnormal. We traveled to the University of Virginia Medical Center in Charlottesville and another medical center in New Jersey that specialized in the treatment of epilepsy. More tests; same results of idiopathic (of unknown origin) epilepsy.

The medical establishment looks upon epilepsy as a problem originating in the brain. Attempts are made to subdue the seizures with medication, brain surgery (to remove the "problem" area), or the insertion of the Vagus Nerve Stimulator. However, none of these treatments deal with any identifiable, underlying cause.

At the New Jersey epilepsy center, I spoke with a nurse who worked closely with the surgeons. She said they were finding that some patients would be seizure-free following surgery, but within a few years, the epilepsy would return, originating in another part of the brain. Although Jody and John, her dad, felt surgery might be an option, the information the nurse shared suggested to me that surgery would be only a temporary solution.

Edgar Cayce's perspective of idiopathic epilepsy was unique. Commonly cited reasons for seizures were directed to two areas below the brain: incoordination of the nervous systems owing to lesions along the spine or adhesions of the lateral ducts within the abdomen. The remedies most frequently suggested were osteopathic adjustments and abdominal castor oil packs.

In September 1995 Jo turned eighteen. Like many others dealing with epilepsy, she hoped to find the right medication to prevent the seizures from occurring. This offers the possibility of an easy solution, though it wasn't the case for Jody. Through her first year at Norfolk's Old Dominion University (ODU) and the years following, Jo tried a number of different medications. Side effects were numerous but none diminished the seizures after an initial "honeymoon" phase, when the medications were most sedating.

Then I found something that seemed promising. I started to explore Cayce's epilepsy remedies and found a simple suggestion that proved to be of immediate help. It was regarding the use of ice for seizures and always worked well for Jody. When Cayce had been asked, "What can be done to allay attack once it has started?" He replied: "Place a piece of ice at the base of the brain and it will stop immediately." (1001-5)

Despite the uncontrolled seizures and side effects of the medications, by September 1996, Jody did well enough at ODU to transfer to the University of Virginia (UVA) in Charlottesville. She was now only minutes away from the group of neurologists she had been seeing. During the intervening summer months, I researched Cayce's epilepsy readings more intensely and attempted to share their holistic approach with my daughter. But Jo's interest was minimal, since dietary changes and time for castor oil packs, among other things, would be necessary.

In addition to Jody's health challenges, I was facing my own. Within that last year, I had been diagnosed with muscular dystrophy (MD) and was very weak. But after discovering the epilepsy remedies for Jody, I became curious to see if anything was available in the readings for MD. There was, but as with the remedies for epilepsy, the ones for MD would take some time and effort on my part. In a way, I was relieved that Jody wasn't going to pursue the remedies right then, so I could focus on the ones for MD first. Thank God they helped. I compiled my experience in an article entitled: "Remedies Found to Fight Muscular Dystrophy," *Venture Inward,* Jan/Feb 2000.

In the fall of 1998 Jody called from the hospital in Charlottesville. She had started school again and attended a party that weekend at a friend's apartment. It was warm so Jo and her friends danced outside on an elevated deck (equal to a 2–story drop). Unexpectedly, she started having a seizure and fell off the deck backwards. The angels must have been at work because, incredibly, she landed in a padded chair in the yard below. Her friends took her to the emergency room to make sure she was all right. Other than some bruises and a sprained hand, she was.

Soon after this occurrence, Jo realized the pupil of her right eye was dilated—light didn't affect it at all. But when the neurologist examined her, he could find nothing wrong. However, he made an appointment for her with a neuro–ophthalmologist whose first question surprised her. "Are you using Afrin nasal spray?" Actually, she was. She used it frequently during fall and spring because of allergies. The doctor explained he had seen this condition before, and it generally cleared up within six months of discontinuing the spray.

It was such a relief when Jody told me this that I didn't really hear (or want to hear) that the neurologist had also suggested having another MRI. I was looking at the expense ($1,400) and thought it was unnecessary. Besides, it had only been three years since the last MRI and it seemed as if the neuro–ophthalmologist diagnosed the problem correctly. However, Jody had the final say and decided to skip the test and wean herself off the spray. With her usual resolve, that's just what she did.

March of 1999 Jo unexpectedly called to say she'd be home the next day. She had decided to take a medical leave of absence because the seizures were worse. She also said she was going to give the Cayce remedies a serious try.

Jody received the treatment plan on epilepsy from A.R.E. and looked it over. Though its one-size-fits-all approach didn't incorporate all possible treatments or individualize them, it was convenient to have an organized package outlining Cayce's general treatments.

Attempting to be of help, John and I also focused on Jo's well-being. This is not to say that John and I were in agreement about how to approach Jody's condition; we weren't. But each of us still knew that the other wanted the best for our daughter. Devotion and detachment were both needed on our part, just as the best of both allopathic and complementary/alternative approaches would eventually be needed.

April 19, 1999, Jody officially started using the remedies and set up a schedule: three consecutive days a week for abdominal castor oil packs, followed by an abdominal and spinal massage (my job); daily doses of Passion Flower Fusion; weekly spinal adjustments; and the Cayce diet.

On my own, I continued researching the epilepsy readings. Though they seemed to follow a certain pattern from one reading to another, there were many variations in what caused the problem, the effect on the body, and the treatment for it.

Old-fashioned osteopathic adjustments were consistently recommended for epilepsy, but finding that type of an osteopath in our area was nearly impossible. That left chiropractors: the best alternative, I thought, and so many to choose from.

Jody agreed to these treatments, but they seemed ineffectual and gave her no relief from the chronic tightness in her neck. However, there was a young man, Francois, who had trained in France and did bodywork similar to spinal adjustments. His treatments integrated visceral (abdominal) manipulation and massage to help relax the muscles that hold the spine in alignment. After his treatments, Jody could feel the difference in her abdomen and neck. Unfortunately, he was moving and only planned on visiting occasionally.

But Jody was determined. Gradually she made the necessary dietary changes and, after a while, even found them agreeable. More importantly, the uncomfortable sensations in her stomach diminished, as did the frequency of the seizures.

By late May 1999, Jody started going three, four, or five days without a seizure, and by July, she went eleven days straight seizure-and-aura-free! This was cause to celebrate; yet when she did have a seizure, she could still have several in a day.

Early September 1999 Jody had a routine appointment with her local neurologist. He asked how she was doing, and without mentioning the Cayce remedies, she replied that she had changed her diet and was feeling better. He said that was encouraging and to keep it up. They then discussed lowering her medication, since it didn't seem to make a difference one way or the other. However, he wanted her to have another MRI because her right pupil was still dilated. This time, Jody didn't resist the suggestion and neither did I. The seizures this last year had been more severe and frequent except when Jody carefully followed the Cayce remedies. (It was now four years since her last MRI.)

Jody went for the MRI a couple of weeks after Labor Day. A few days later, the phone rang. It was the nurse from the neurologist's office, asking us all to come in the next day to see the doctor. Alarmed, I said, "We'll be there tomorrow, but please have the doctor call us today."

The neurologist called back while Jody was out with friends. John and I listened in on different extensions as the physician explained that a tumor had been found—though this might prove to be good news. It was very possible, he thought, that the tumor was the cause of the seizures. In any case, he said he would talk with us in greater detail tomorrow.

John was optimistic, if not ecstatic. The tumor was the culprit all along and could simply be removed. Yet to me, the tumor was like a death sentence, since my mother had died from one fifteen years before.

September 22, 1999. The three of us sat down with the neurologist. He said the tumor was located in the right temporal lobe of Jody's brain. Benign or malignant, aggressive or not, these answers wouldn't be known until a biopsy was performed. Did this mean she needed a biopsy before it could be removed? No, not necessarily. This wasn't his specialty but he could refer us to a neurosurgeon at UVA.

Where was the best place to go? Would radiation or chemotherapy be recommended for this type of tumor? Why hadn't it shown up in the earlier MRIs? Questions were many—answers were few, I realized as we left the office.

By the time we arrived back home, I had been nominated to make the necessary decisions and medical arrangements. Fine. Where to start? First things first: heavy–duty praying. Then I started looking for the right neurosurgeon. (To condense: Jody had surgery at UCLA. The tumor was completely removed, but because of complications, Jo suffered a stroke that paralyzed her left side. Thankfully, she improved rapidly and was sent home within a few weeks from UCLA's well-known rehabilitation center to resume treatments in Virginia Beach.)

Originally, I thought Jody would be returning home in a wheelchair and wondered how she would get around her room without major renovations. But because of Jody's progress and her ability to ambulate with a cane, John only needed to make minor changes for reasons of safety.

Determined as ever, Jo set up a schedule for exercising inside and began taking short walks with us outside. Once more Jody was aiming high. Besides regaining use of the left side of her body, she was hoping to restart college by the fall of 2000. In order to accomplish this, she would need to build up enough strength and coordination to carry herself and a heavy backpack the required distances between classes and an apartment on campus. This would be no small feat, but I had no doubt that she would achieve her goals if only to get away from us!

November 1999. This Thanksgiving, more than ever before, was a time for gratitude. An added bonus was that Jo had been seizure-free for two months—the longest yet. We were all delighted by this and by her healing in general. To many, it seemed inevitable that it would be just a matter of time before she could resume a normal life.

However, despite how it appeared, I still had doubts about what the future might bring concerning the seizures. There were still too many unanswered questions. What if the tumor wasn't the cause of the seizures but the result? Maybe the tumor wasn't seen on the first MRI because there was nothing to see. But the most perplexing question to me was, if the tumor had triggered the seizures, as the doctors implied, why had the Cayce remedies helped the way they did?

It was my greatest hope that the seizures were over, but I kept thinking about what the nurse at the New Jersey epilepsy center had said about the recurrence of seizures after surgery. If this was true, the seizures could return at any time, because the original cause, which existed below the head, not in it, had not been alleviated.

Mid–December 1999, nearly three months since Jody's last seizure. It was morning. Jo was in her room preparing to shower. John I were nearby in the kitchen when we heard a loud yell and a thud. Thinking that Jody might have slipped and fallen, we ran in to find the bathroom door slightly ajar, with Jo lying on the floor behind it. It took only a moment to realize she hadn't fallen accidentally. She was having a seizure.

After speaking with her neurologist, Jo considered her choices and shortly before Christmas resumed the Cayce remedies. It was easy for her to pick up where she left off once she set her mind to it. She was already eating well, which was half the battle the first time around. Castor oil packs, abdominal and spinal massages, and chiropractic adjustments were started again as well. All this was in addition to an exercise program Jo's therapists had outlined for her and could be followed independently.

January 1, 2000 came and went. Days passed, and then a few weeks without another seizure. We all kept our fingers crossed, hoping for the best. But disappointingly, they returned again with her next menstrual cycle. Once more, John talked about exploring hormonal therapy. I favored Cayce. Jody was in the middle. The only positive thing we all noticed was that having one seizure a month was quite different from having ten or more.

May 2000. Over the years in my quest to help my daughter, as well as myself, I looked into a number of psychics, trying to find someone who might be able to give as good a "physical" reading as Edgar Cayce. It had been a futile search until I found Jim Branch. (Note: Jim Branch died in 2002.)

With Jody's permission, I requested a physical reading for her. However, I was cautious and deliberately gave no indication of Jody's condition prior to the reading or in the questions I submitted for the reading. What I had submitted was Jody's date, time, and place of her birth. The time and day of the reading was prearranged. All that Jim needed was her location—just like Cayce. When the time came, Jo and I waited quietly together. I looked forward to Jody's reading with anticipation—hoping with all my heart that Jody would find some help. As it turned out, I wasn't disappointed.

Within a week, we received an audiotape and transcript of the reading. The answers were nothing short of astounding. While in trance, Jim described Jody's condition—the symptoms, cause, and remedies to be followed—with an uncanny awareness of what was already being done on Jody's behalf.

I read the transcript and was humbled. What a gift! Jim's reading was no different from what Cayce might have suggested. He did what I had hoped someone could do: he individualized the remedies to Jody's particular needs. We were to continue with the Cayce diet and abdominal castor oil packs but add alternating packs of castor oil and Glyco-Thymoline (a product frequently recommended by Cayce for a variety of reasons) to the spine. Minute amounts, taken orally, of Glyco-Thymoline and atomidine, a form of iodine, were also suggested. Then Jo was to have cranial–sacral/osteopathic adjustments to help the "incoordination in the nervous system" and the "rearrangement . . . of cranial forces" between these series of packs. The chiropractic adjustments she had been receiving just weren't doing the trick.

Adding the spinal packs to Jo's regimen wouldn't be difficult, but finding the right person for the cranial sacral adjustments was a different matter. I learned that there were two different types of cranial–sacral adjustments, both conceived by osteopaths. [Note: Dr. John Upledger, founder of CranioSacral Therapy (CST) discusses the differences between the two techniques on his Web site: www.upledger.com/news/9505b.htm.] Jo tried both types of treatments, which cost anywhere from $45 to $75, depending on who was doing it. But the effects were so subtle, she found it hard to tell if the treatments were helping.

Since I had no experience with this type of bodywork, I requested a follow-up reading with Jim. The second reading emphasized that the therapist's intention and attitude were as important as the technique. This, too, went along with what Cayce had repeatedly reminded caregivers when administering to the person in need.

From Jody's second reading: "So much here then is determined by the interaction of the body with those influences laid upon the body, and in such, the acts of intention and those who do practice the same are probably the best through this period."

It was just this "interaction" that caused a problem for Jo. Besides the treatment's subtleness and cost, there was the element of time. A session usually lasted an hour, and Jo needed to lie relatively still for it. This wasn't an easy thing to ask of her, since Jody even looked upon sleep as a regrettable intrusion into her life.

But through the ensuing summer months, Jody worked with the updated remedies. This included the recommended adjustments approximately every two weeks from an osteopath we had just located—his specialty was cranial osteopathy. However, despite our best efforts, Jody continued to experience monthly seizures.

September 2000 Jo started back at ODU on her own two feet. It was a struggle but she knew it was worth it. In the meantime, Jo came home on weekends and kept up with her studies, exercises, and all of the Cayce/Branch remedies.

Through the fall months, the seizures persisted, even with Jo's bi-weekly visits to the osteopath. Maybe it was time for a change? I made inquiries and found a woman's name mentioned several times as someone who was good with CST. She was a massage therapist who had traveled to the Upledger Institute for intensive training. Jody agreed to try someone new but between everyone's schedules, trips, and studies. It took quite a while to arrange a convenient appointment.

In early December 2000, the CST therapist finally saw Jody and worked on her for more than an hour. As Jo dressed, the therapist mentioned that during the session she felt a major shift take place. She hoped it would be beneficial but said that a few more treatments would probably be needed.

However, in the car ride back to ODU, Jody informed me that she wouldn't be returning because she wasn't comfortable there. I understood, but when Jo went through a menstrual cycle in a few days without a seizure, I asked her to reconsider. Not having a seizure at this time of the month was the ultimate test—and the first time this had occurred in seven long years. But feeling the way she did, Jo rightfully wouldn't return, and I resumed the search for another CST therapist.

During Jody's recovery, I began volunteering in the A.R.E. library, which eventually turned into a full-time position. I loved being there despite my reservations about being able to work in a metaphysical library. Having dyslexia and dealing with all those unfamiliar words was a challenge. (What in the world was an "ephemeris" and how could I look it up if I couldn't even spell it?) But my supervisor, Claudeen Cowell, was generous with her encouragement and appreciated my enthusiasm for the Cayce health remedies.

It also seemed that the right people came into the library just when you needed them. That was the case when I began looking for another CST therapist. Beau Johnson walked in. He was somewhat of a modern-day Johnny Appleseed, who traveled around the country talking to people about Biodynamic agriculture and healing ways of living. Beau, as it turned out, was also a good friend of Jim's, and went on to tell me about Mark Shean, a friend to both of them who did CST when he wasn't working on his organic farm. I took Mark's number and called him. It sounded as if he didn't have as much training as the previous therapist, but he had had enough. I hoped Jody would find Mark's treatments tolerable and she did. She actually found them very relaxing. Jody saw Mark three or four times in the next couple of months. After not having a seizure in December, she had one in January and another in February. Once again, doubts clouded my mind.

Yet, looking back, it worked out all for the best just the way it was. Jo had her last CST session and last seizure in February—February 18, 2001, to be exact. Of course, she didn't know at the time that that was the last one.

As each month passed without incident, I casually asked if she had had a seizure, and she just as casually answered "no." She didn't share her feelings with me, but I had to control my own growing excitement that this might be "it," yet walk a fine line in case the next month proved me wrong.

The summer passed uneventfully. Jody circled August 18 on her calendar—the date that would signify six months had passed without a seizure—and scheduled an appointment with her neurologist. But when the time arrived, she was disappointed to learn the doctor wanted her to wait an extra month because of her medical history. Though she had no choice in the matter, she understood. So she waited, seizure-free, and started driving once again. September 18—her twenty-fourth birthday—was a long-awaited gift for all of us. Our efforts paid off. To this day, Jody continues to be seizure- and medication-free.

The author, a retired registered nurse, is on staff at the A.R.E. Library and has been involved with the Cayce material for the last twenty years. E-mail her at Linda_cputi@yahoo.com.

This article is adapted from the book *Epilepsy—Jody's Journey: An Inspiring True Story of Healing With The Edgar Cayce Remedies.*

EYES: HEMORRHAGE AND FLOATERS

January 2, 2009
Re: Herbal Tonic Vibra Tonic 3810/Optikade

I had just turned 80 in December 2007 when I started to experience 60-70 black floaters, large, medium, and small, coming from my right eye. I was referred to a doctor who specialized in the retina. Upon examination I was diagnosed with hemorrhaging behind the right retina.

I was told that there is no known treatment for this condition except group therapy.

The first week in February 2008, I attended a conference in Virginia Beach at Edgar Cayce's Foundation. I went to the library and read materials pertaining to my eye condition.

I spoke with a librarian who told me of Vibra Tonic 3810 [also sold under the name Optikade Eye Tonic], found in Edgar Cayce's readings. I purchased it right away and started to use it since February 2008 up to the present January 2009, one tablespoon three times a day before meals and at bedtime.

One month after taking Vibra Tonic 3810 I was seen again by my doctor, who was surprised to see the great change since December 2007. He stated, 'No one has recovered that quickly.'

I am now being checked every three months. The bleeding and floaters are down to a small amount and at times none appears.

My thanks and appreciation to Edgar Cayce's foundation [A.R.E.] and to the librarian who so lovingly told me of the tonic.

Love and many Blessing,
M.E.M.; A.R.E. Member
Bronx, New York

P.S. Cause of hemorrhage: occlusion of vein between heart and eye.

IRRITABLE BOWEL SYNDROME

I'm an 84-year-old geezer with a couple of Cayce method healing experiences.

Way back when I was in my thirties, I had skin problems that manifested with a hivelike rash on my chest after showers, and thin skin on my hands. The hands cracked and bled slightly from hard use. The hand problem showed when I used a golf club for a couple of hours or other such continual grip-type use.

I also had trouble with IBS at that time, which I considered a minor disturbance,—— gas and irregular bowel movements.

We moved to Virginia Beach in 1976, and the problem became more acute. So I began having colonics and that helped somewhat, so I added psyllium husks once daily to my diet. The problem remained a little, so I ultimately consulted a gastroenterologist (non-Cayce), who suggested increasing the psyllium husks to twice daily. That, along with occasional colonics, cleared up the problem completely. I now follow this routine fairly closely, with the colonics only about once a year.

During the past ten years, I've had other health problems (peripheral neuropathy and inoperable spine deterioration) and have been taking medications. I developed a severe rash on my buttocks which I assumed was caused by the medications, so I went to a skin doctor, who prescribed a cortisone cream. It made the rash worse. That doctor said the problem may have been psoriasis, so I had about four colonics in a row. This didn't solve the problem, so I went on the Pagano diet (which is based mainly on the Cayce readings), and the rash eventually disappeared.

Other than having a diet that's adheres mostly (we indulge occasionally) to the Cayce recommendations and keeps me relatively healthy, I don't have any other healings to report.

CAYCE LUNG THERAPIES

The Oak Keg-Apple Brandy Therapy
http://www.edgarcayce.org/health/database/chdata/data/thoakkeg.html

Source for the Apple Brandy
Use Laird's *Straight* Apple Brandy, 100-proof. If you can't get 100-proof, 80-proof is acceptable. (Don't use the Laird's Apple Jack Brandy, which is only 35-proof.) Cayce did recommend the Laird's brand by name.

Call Canal's Bottleshop at 856-983-4991 and say that you want to purchase the Laird's brandy for medicinal purposes. They ship nationally as long as it's legal in the destination state. Laird & Company gave me this number and said if there is any problem obtaining it, call them. Here's their contact information:

http://www.lairdandcompany.com/contact.htm.

Here's some more information. (The most recent pricing information I have is $19.99 a bottle from Canal's, plus shipping.)
http://www.caycecures.com/pdf/apple%20brandy.pdf

Source for the Oak Keg
http://www.baar.com/Merchant2/merchant.mvc?Screen=PROD&Product_Code=320&AFFIL=frg

How to Use the Keg
http://www.cayce.com/oakkeg.htm

Cayce on Lung Cancer

This link is to a concise summary of Cayce's approach to lung cancer.
http://www.edgarcayce.org/health/database/health_resources/
lung_cancer.asp

The full treatment plan can be purchased. The cost is $50, plus shipping.
http://www.edgarcayce.org/health/hrc_treatmentplan1.asp

Misc. Other Information from The Cayce Health Database

http://www.edgarcayce.org/caycehealthdatabase.html

The Charred Oak Keg

Use of the charred oak keg containing apple brandy was recommended in about 50 readings for respiratory problems, particularly tuberculosis. Charred oak kegs are used commercially in storage of aging liquors, since the charcoal absorbs impurities from the liquor. This is probably why Cayce stressed keeping the brandy in this type of keg. Even so, the keg must be periodically rinsed with warm (only!) water to remove acids that have accumulated. In this way "there is less of that influence or force which arises from the acids that come from such infusions.

To prepare the keg for use:
Soak keg in water to swell; tighten metal bands as much as possible beforehand.

- Place one or two bottles of the apple brandy in the keg and allow to sit overnight. The keg should be about ½ full.
- Keep the keg warm (about 85 degrees F.) by placing near a heating vent or on a heating pad.

To use the keg:

- Using a tube, ½" in diameter, inhale the vapor in the upper part of the keg through the nostrils or mouth for three or four breaths.
- Repeat the sessions about 3 or 4 times each day.
- Keep the tube above the liquid so as to inhale the apple brandy fumes, not the brandy itself.

CAYCE QUOTES

First we would give that the body begin inhaling the fumes from pure apple brandy in a charred oak keg. Put half a gallon of pure apple brandy (such as Hildick's) in at least a gallon or a gallon and a half of charred keg. Prepare the keg so that two vents may go into one head of the keg after it has been corked. To one vent attach a little hose or a connection so that the fumes from the vacuum may be inhaled deeply into the lungs. The other vent is to allow air to enter, so that there is not the attempt to inhale against a vacuum. At least two or three times a day inhale these fumes into the lungs, blowing out through the nostrils when it is practical. Keep the keg in a warm place so that evaporation may occur easily.

Do this and it will change those activities in the lungs that once in a while do break through. Use these fumes regularly.   3154-1

The activity on this is not only for the destruction of live tubercule tissue, but it acts as an antiseptic for all irritated areas; also giving activity to cellular force of the corpuscle itself. It acts as a stimuli to the circulation, then, recharging each cell as it passes through areas so affected by the radiation of the gases from this fluid itself.

3176-1

For the properties inhaled will work with the activity of the respiratory system, as well as the properties contained therein will act upon the influences of the liver and kidneys in their ability to be purified—in the assimilating of these forces that arise from the infusion of these influences indicated.   1557-1

This will act not only as an antiseptic, but will so change the lung tissue as to bring about healing of the tissues, and will also increase the abilities of assimilation, and we will have improvements.

5053-1

These [inhalations] will irritate at first, but use through the nostril for the stopping of cough, as well as inhaling into the lungs. 3594-1

Do not attempt to inhale too much in the beginning, or it will be
inclined to produce too much intoxication for the body.   2448-1

Keep the keg. This is as life itself.   1548-4

Note: The above information is not intended for self–diagnosis or self–
treatment. Please consult a qualified health care professional for assistance in applying the information contained in the Cayce Health
Database.

REMEDIES FOUND TO FIGHT MUSCULAR DYSTROPHY

By Linda Caputi

It was January 1996. The need to know had finally outweighed my
fear of knowing. As I sat in the neurologist's office, waiting to be seen, I
reviewed how I had arrived at this point. I was forty–eight years old,
with symptoms that had begun when I was thirty. Needless to say, I had
certainly taken my time in making an appointment. So even though my
father, brother, and uncle were doctors and I was a registered nurse,
doctors were always an avenue of last resort for me. My philosophy
regarding them was "use only in an emergency." But there was denying
it no more; something was wrong. Perhaps part of it had been denial,
but the gradual, progressive onset of symptoms had made it easy to
dismiss them. When my hand couldn't release an object it had grasped
(myotonia—temporary rigidity after muscular contraction), I explained
it as nerve damage from working hard on our old house.

When I could no longer lap swim for an hour or more, it was keeping
up with two children and the stronger chlorine in the pool.

When the grocery bags seemed to be getting heavier, it was because
I needed to do some weight training.

When my eye couldn't open (posies—dropping of an organ or part)
sometime after sleep or meditation, it was because I was so deeply relaxed.

When it was easy to bend down but nearly impossible to get up, it
was from age.

But when it reached the point where I couldn't walk very far without getting out of breath and my legs locked trying to get out of a chair, I realized I had to have some kind of neurological disorder. I knew little of neurology, just enough to know that any label—and a prognosis that went with that label given "it" by a physician—was not something I looked forward to. But here I was in the neurologist's office, waiting for the verdict. Without any great fanfare, "it" came as myotonic muscular dystrophy (MD), which was later officially updated to myotonic dystrophy.

The neurologist explained it wasn't just a children's illness—as in "Jerry's Kids"—but a slow, continuous deterioration of functions that could go on for decades. How slowly or swiftly it happened was an individual process—with no remissions, as in multiple sclerosis, to hope for. Other than medication (which I declined), to alleviate some of the myotonic symptoms there was nothing that could be done.

The doctor said to schedule my next appointment in six months, and I went home to try to come to terms with the diagnosis.

It was difficult. A part of me couldn't fathom that I'd never bike ride, swim, or take long walks in the park again.

Intellectually, however, I dealt with it by approaching things from the practical standpoint. The stairs to my bedroom were getting difficult to maneuver, so a move downstairs was a consideration. The illness had to be explained to my children (18 and 24 years old), so I calmly sat down with them and answered any questions they had, but in an optimistic manner. I asked them to pitch in more if I was doing less. They agreed.

I even discussed the possibility of divorce with my husband, concerned that my condition would eventually ruin us both financially. But he seemed to be in denial, and any attempt at practical conversation regarding the illness went nowhere. Emotionally, his attitude was strangely comforting, because it allowed me to either slip into denial myself or remember, "I am more than my body!"

Six months passed without much of a difference at home, although I switched to plastic plates and cups, which were so much lighter and easier to hold than china and glass. I did notice on a few frightening occasions, however, that I was choking when I tried to swallow.

When it was time for my next appointment with the neurologist, and
I slowly sat down across from him, he asked, "Have the symptoms become any worse?" Pause. It was like one of those intensified moments in
life where time almost stands still. It finally sank in. I realized he expected me to be getting worse. Nausea washed over me.

"No," I lied. "I'm about the same." He repeated some neuromuscular
testing and asked me to schedule another appointment in six months. I
knew, however, that unless it was "an emergency," I would not be returning.

Still in shock, I went home until once more I lost myself in the daily
routine and busyness of family life.

There was also a mental fog and a lethargy that had come with the
illness—more so as it progressed. It took concentrated effort to complete
tasks or explain a thought. As time passed, I had begun not even to try.

The Association for Research and Enlightenment (A.R.E.) is just three
short blocks from my home. I've been a member off and on since 1985
and had joined a Search for God study group when I lived in Brooklyn,
New York. Even after moving to Virginia Beach in 1986, three of us
"charter members" continued meeting by conference call once a week,
although in time we moved on to other studies.

In other words, I was very familiar with the readings and remedies
Edgar Cayce had given for various physical conditions. But it hadn't
occurred to me to research muscular dystrophy. Resignation, acceptance, or the increasing mental fog had definitely set in somewhere
along he line—very atypical of me, an outspoken, opinionated, take-
charge type of New Yorker with Jewish blood flowing in my veins.

Thank God for Karen Davis, a dear and wise friend who gently but
insistently told me there were Cayce readings on MD that I could try.
She said part of it involved a *wet-cell battery* that Cayce gave directions for
constructing. Surprisingly, I now found myself struggling with the possibility of having hope again, just as I had struggled with the
neurologist's lack of it. But hope springs eternal, even through the fog,
fear of failure, and exhaustion.

Karen then suggested I speak to Jeanette Thomas at the Edgar Cayce
Foundation, who was extremely knowledgeable about practically anything pertaining to the readings. Thank God for Jeanette. When I ex-

plained my situation, she invited me to her office or offered to come to my home. Two hours later, sitting with me at her desk, Jeanette laid out a graph she had created and an assortment of readings Cayce had given to different individuals diagnosed with MD or symptoms similar to it. They varied in content, but most involved the use of the wet-cell battery.

Jeanette had one in her office and showed me in a general way how it was used. Maybe sensing my confusion as well as my reticence at the idea of working with something electrical, she explained that the wet-cell generated less current than a flashlight battery. In fact, most people using the device are unable to feel any electrical sensation whatsoever. Again, she kindly offered to come to my home in order to set one up if I needed help.

Theoretically, anyone can make his or her own wet-cell battery from the instructions given by Cayce, but most people purchase one already made. I looked into three different models, including the one constructed by Bruce Baar that Jeanette demonstrated in her office and is for sale in the A.R.E. Bookstore. I purchased the model made by Bruce Baar.

With Jeanette's encouragement, I went to the A.R.E. Library and checked out the Circulating Files (research reports compiled from selected readings on a topic) on muscular dystrophy and read them. I then went to the readings index files to copy down all the numbers for each individual's reading. As my research continued, I became very involved and more and more helpful.

Discovering a reading given to a woman in her 50s with symptoms similar to mine, I decided to follow the instructions given to her by Cayce for the wet-cell usage. The reading suggested placing the wet-cell's copper disc on two different spinal vertebrae on alternating days and using two different solutions for 30 minutes each, one only to be used each day. During the time spent with the discs attached to the body, the individual was to remain in a peaceful, meditative state, keeping a receptive mental attitude.

Then with the help of my chiropractor, who marked the specific vertebrae's locations on my back; and my husband, who sawed wooden sticks precisely measured from floor to vertebrae points, so that I would always be able to find the correct points myself; I was ready to begin using the wet-cell.

However, the readings stated that before implementing the physical remedies, the proper spiritual and mental attitude needed to be cultivated. Specific passages from the Bible were given and were to be read, contemplated, and sometimes even memorized. I interpreted those passages to mean choose whose will you will follow—yours or God's. I have learned that it's not a sacrifice to choose God's will (when I can "hear" it), as I used to believe. It's what makes me happy.

People caring for the individual are also told that they need to hold the right attitude of love and expectancy. Consistency and persistency are key words used over and over, since it could possibly take years to see improvement. But I was thankful to hear from people who stuck with the readings' suggestions that they could see results in six months.

As I read and did my spiritual homework, I also inquired at the Cayce/Reilly School of Massotherapy to see if there might be one or two students who would come to my home for the 30-minute spinal massage I would need on a regular basis. This is a necessary part of the approximately two-hour daily routine when using the wet-cell battery on the spine. The energy needs to be distributed by massage along the spine and down and out to the extremities in a circular manner. Three students or former students were available and dependable. All of them were special angels in my life.

Cayce's readings also covered dietary recommendations, which for me were relatively easy to incorporate into my life. But be forewarned: alcohol consumption (or the formation of it in the body by the overgrowth of Candida yeast and the presence of sugar) and the wet-cell are not compatible. Regular eliminations, spinal adjustments, affirmations, and karma were also frequently mentioned.

The karmic aspect was the least helpful to me. I could hardly remember what I had for breakfast, much less recall events from 10 lifetimes before. But I think karma is less punishment from God than self-imposed suffering. We judge, condemn, and crucify ourselves for the "sins" we committed that we believe are unpardonable. Yet God, I feel, would say to each and every one of us, "This is my beloved son/daughter in whom I am well pleased." Why else would God, through Cayce, allow these remedies to be given for the "incurable" ills we struggle with, if not to help us get down off the cross?

With everything attended to, I finally began my daily routine with the wet-cell and the other recommendations. This would have been impossible without a journal or notebook just to keep track of the chemical solutions in the jars, times used, and the need for battery changing. I also found it extremely helpful to record dreams, events, thoughts, and symptoms I was experiencing. It is so easy to forget, especially when functioning in a fog, and become discouraged if unable to see improvements, which can take place so-o-o gradually in any case.

I remember when I wrote down my first dream in the journal a week after starting the Baar Battery. This small event was an important milestone, since I hadn't been able to recall a dream for the past year, even though dreams had been an important part of my life, thanks to Mark Thurston's conference on dream interpretation 10 years previously.

As for some other symptoms, within one month the mental fog began to clear. Within two months, the choking episodes subsided and I was able to walk a bit farther without tiring. In fact, Jeanette reminded me recently that the first thing I said to her after being on the Baar wet-cell for a short time was, "I can breathe again!"

In general, I found that the last symptoms I had developed were the first ones to leave.

It's been a year and a half now since I began with the Cayce remedies. I'd love to say it's been smooth sailing, but it hasn't. I didn't have the "sleeping prophet" to give me an individualized reading, just trial and error and occasional guidance, from within and without, that I wish had been clearer and more consistent. But in spite of everything, I'd estimate I'm about 70 percent improved. I don't tell people I have MD; I say that I was diagnosed with it. Say what you will, there's a distinction.

Maybe I should have waited to write this until I could say I was 100 percent cured, but being from New York and always in a rush, I couldn't wait any longer to share my experience in case it could help someone in the meantime. Thank God for Edgar Cayce.

RSD! DOOMED? HEAVEN'S NO!
I HAD THE CAYCE REMEDIES

By Darlene Bodnar

While at an Arizona retreat center in February 2008, I had the unfor-
tunate experience of having a sudden fall and acquiring three fractures
in my elbow, involving the ulna and radius bones. Drat! Through a
comedy of errors, I was not able to get a cast on for five days; but things
were cool. I really wanted to come back home to Denver to my own
doctor, but after talking with Dr. Gladys McGarey, she asked my husband to please not drive me home and wait for the doctors in Arizona.
She said if the bones would shift at all, I could be in real trouble. So we
waited it out, and I did get casted. I was told that if the bones did not
shift, I would not require surgery and could have x-rays when I was
back in Denver. Believe me, I did not want surgery.

During the six weeks of tolerating the cast—no shift of the bones, no
surgery—I noticed that my hand was extremely painful and becoming
immobile. I kept telling my husband the pain was not in my elbow but
in my hand. My cast was removed on April 1, but I had lost complete
function of my hand. Painful, painful, painful. My hand and fingers
were very swollen, translucent red, and immobile. The pain was excru-
ciating, and I couldn't bear to have even a towel touch my arm or hand.
The diagnosis: A full blown case of Reflex Sympathetic Dystrophy (RSD).
This happens with about 3% of traumas such as surgery or fractures. I
had no idea what I was dealing with at that point; all I knew was that
the pain was intolerable. When I mentioned this to several of my friends,
one told me they knew about RSD because their neighbor had it and
has been disabled for 20 years; another friend said her cousin is totally
disabled and needs to carry a pain injection with her at all times.

After seeing the physical therapist, I went home to research this RSD
on the Internet. What I found was devastating. From the Internet:

> Everyday you face the same relentless pain. Moments of relief are
> few and far between. It takes everything you have to fight through
> the pain and depression and keep going. What causes this chronic

pain? It is Reflex Sympathetic Dystrophy (RSD) and the battle has only just begun. RSD is a severe condition that causes chronic pain. It usually involves a leg or arm. It is a chronic, painful and progressive neurological condition that affects skin, muscles, joints and bones.

It proceeded to say that it was a progressive disorder with no known cure, extremely painful and debilitating, and the affected extremity could become frozen and disfigured. The pictures that accompanied this info were frightening. There was no known treatment or cure, and it would eventually get worse. It stated that many victims become clinically depressed, require anti-depressants, and contemplate and/or commit suicide to end the pain. Well, now, this was definitely a predicament. What do I do now?

I went to the physical therapist twice a week, as the one method of possibly controlling the disorder was exercise, painful exercise. I can say I did these exercises diligently (for five months). *But most important,* I knew there would be information in the Cayce readings that would give me hope and an avenue of treatment. I researched the readings in depth on fractures, wrists, hands, deformities, etc. I wrote down the various suggestions, wondering what would be the best for me. As it turned out, I decided to try every avenue possible.

The readings talked about damage to the sympathetic nervous system involving the brachial plexus area and cerebrospinal system. They suggested salt and vinegar packs to the brachial area, down the arm, and into the hand. They talked about massage that concentrated on the cerebrospinal and brachial plexus areas. They talked about olive oil and tincture of myrrh, peanut oil rubs, castor oil packs on the affected area, violet-ray applications, Epsom salts baths, heat treatments, prayer and meditation, and good attitude. I knew I had to get busy.

As it turned out, I don't know what exactly helped me the most because I tried them all, *but something worked!* I was blessed beyond blessings to have a wonderful massage therapist who loves the Cayce material and spent the whole hour with me, working with the areas suggested in the readings. She had me come twice a week for several months. Also, my wonderful friend Barry Ryan, who is a graduate of the

Cayce-Reilly Massotherapy School, worked with me with massage, energy, cranial sacral, and the violet ray treatments. I worked assiduously with the salt and vinegar packs, the different oils, heat treatments, Epsom salts baths, etc. A study group member brought me essential oils. My physical therapist was knowledgeable and knew how to work with me. My wonderful husband had to dress me for three months and cut up my food. My daughter had to wash and fix my hair and apply my makeup. But something was happening, and we could tell. My physical therapist told me I had come farther faster than any patient she had ever seen with RSD. She couldn't believe the progress. I was exhilarated. Eventually I could do my own hair and makeup. My big breakthrough came when I could tear off a piece of toilet paper, put on my own bra, and button my clothes. Small progresses? No, huge steps towards healing.

Six months later, I had 90% function of my hand back and very little pain. I can shake hands with people without fear of intense pain. I can take total care of myself—cook and clean, etc. I have always had faith in the Cayce readings, but this info was exceptional, simple, and gave me back the use of my hand. *These treatments and remedies work!!!* By the way, the fracture area at my elbow is perfectly healed, and I have no pain or motion restriction whatsoever.

I will be forever thankful to the man who laid down his life for his fellowman to give those readings and for every effort the A.R.E. puts forth to make this wonderful volume of knowledge accessible and workable for anyone who seeks. We only have to seek. I am forever grateful.

Here is an excerpt from the reading that talks about salt and vinegar packs. I include this as a fantastic example of what these readings contain. It is just one paragraph from some 14,000+ readings, and it helped give me back the use of my hand. There are so many jewels of information for all of us, just for the asking. Taken from reading 51-1.

> As to the specific conditions as are already existent in forearm, or wrist—right side—these, we will find that with the building up of the system in the manner as has been outlined, for at least three to five weeks, we may then begin with the massaging of same each evening before retiring with that of a saturated solution of plain

salt, *preferably* that that has not been clarified, or in as near raw state as may be had, or with sea salt evaporated, or evaporated salt from sea water. These would be the preferable, making same with a saturated solution of pure apple vinegar. Heat, not to be *hot,* but as to be warm even for the body, and for ten to fifteen minutes each evening *massage* this thoroughly into the wrist and hand. This *followed* in the next cycle or afternoon, with an application of the plain *violet ray,* and every third day we would take that of the sinusoidal in its high frequency, from the flexors of the *brachial* plexus and that in the elbow in the internal side. This given for at least one and a half minutes, and we will find this will be a much *better* manner of *relieving* the conditions than by operative measures; for with the *massage,* not *only* is each bone, or each segment put in its proper position one with another, but their *relations,* of the cushions, or of the cartilage lying between each, are magnified or retarded; that is, built up or removed from, in such a manner as to bring the better activity for the body.

VARIOUS REMEDIES

I want to share some other success stories with you.

1. Having Charcot–Marie–Tooth Disease (CMT) I used to be plagued with killer leg cramps at night in my calf muscles. I had to wake my husband up so he could push down on my knee to force my heel back down to the floor. The cramps were so strong and painful that I couldn't work them out myself. Dr. Genevieve Haller told me that I needed to take more minerals. Taking the Cayce product Calcios, which is a highly absorptive mineral paste, a couple of times a week has worked miracles. It completely banished the cramps. This was about 25 years ago and the cramps have never returned.

2. For years I suffered recurrent sinus infections. For example, from 2002 to 2004 I had four sinus infections that required antibiotics. Wanting to cure this problem without taking medication, I turned to a gargle that Edgar Cayce frequently recommended, Glyco

Thymoline, as an alkalizer. I was already gargling with it daily and knew that Cayce had recommended it for all of the mucous membrane linings in the body, so I thought it would be helpful to my sinuses. I began sniffing a few drops of Glyco diluted with a small amount of water from the palm of my hand up into my nostrils each morning and evening. I also tilted my head back and gently rolled it around to distribute the liquid into as many sinus passages as possible. Since that time, I've not had another major sinus flareup.

3. Like many middle-aged, overweight Americans, my doctor told me that I was hypoglycemic, which meant I was a candidate for diabetes. I had seen my father-in-law lose both legs to this insidious disease, and I knew that I definitely did not want this to happen to me. Again I turned to a suggestion in the Cayce readings—Jerusalem artichokes. They are not actually artichokes but are part of the sunflower family, so they are often called sunchokes in health food stores. Cayce said they contain insulin, which would help the pancreas to resume its normal function. I began to snack on raw sunchokes a couple of times each week. They are rather bland and look like small potatoes or ginger root. They can also be cooked. As a vegetable, I assumed they were harmless. I thought that they might help my body chemistry in some subtle way, but I never expected to feel so much better. I was often at the mercy of blood sugar swings where, if I didn't eat soon, I felt like I would faint. After eating a couple of sunchokes each week for about six months, I realized one day that I was feeling hungry, but it was a "normal" hungry feeling, not a frightening sense that I might faint. This return to normal hunger also meant that I could eat less often and therefore diet to lose weight.

Sincerely,
Ann Jaffin

APPENDIX E

This is what you need to know about Anatomy and Physiology. These are the correct answers for the Anatomy and Physiology Exam, which **must be taken without notes!!**

Anatomical Part	Function
Eyes	Facilitates vision and helps with balance.
Ears	Facilitates hearing and helps with balance.
Nose	The beginning of the upper respiratory system; helps with the control of temperature, the control of humidity, and the elimination of dust and infectious organisms. Facilitates the sense of smell.
Mouth	Entrance to both the respiratory and gastrointestinal tracts. Houses the teeth for chewing and holds the receptors for taste in the tongue.
Throat	Works as a common chamber for the respiratory and digestive tracts. The upper part lets air pass through, while the lower parts permit air, foods, and fluids to pass. The throat facilitates breathing and swallowing.
Left arm	Body limb on the upper left side of the body that facilitates a wide range of motion and dexterity.
Right arm	Body limb on the upper right side of the body that facilitates a wide range of motion and dexterity.
Chest	The part of the body that holds the heart, lungs, esophagus, aorta, ribs, and breast, the chief organs of the circulatory and respiratory systems.
Breasts	Allows for feeding newborns in women and for sexual arousal in both sexes.
Lungs	Provide oxygen from inhaled air to the capillaries and to exhale the carbon dioxide delivered from them.
Heart	A muscle that acts as two coordinated pumps, continuously sending blood around the body.

Esophagus	A muscular tube that passes food down from the mouth to the stomach.
Bronchi	The two primary divisions of the trachea that lead into the right and left lungs that facilitates breathing.
Thymus	Plays a role in the body's defenses in that it turns an immature T lymphocyte from the bone marrow into a fully mature T cell. It also produces a group of hormones involved in differentiating and stimulating cells of the immune system.
Liver	Produces cholesterol and bile from the breakdown of dietary fat and old red blood cells. Using amino acids, it makes proteins and stores iron, glycogen, and vitamins. It also removes substances such as poisons and waste products from the blood, excreting or converting them to safer substances. Major manufacturer of cholesterol.
Pancreas	Secretes insulin and related carbohydrate metabolic factors, and facilitates digestion through enzymes and sodium bicarbonate. Secretes trypsin, amylase and lipase to assist digestion.
Gall Bladder	Stores excess bile.
Right Kidney	Produces urine and filters the blood to remove the cellular wastes, as well as some water, salts, and bile pigments.
Left Kidney	Produces urine and filters the blood to remove the cellular wastes, as well as some water, salts, and bile pigments.
Stomach	A key organ of digestion and also acts as a gland in that it secretes pepsin and hydrochloric acid used during digestion and intrinsic factor for B 12 absorption
Small Intestine	Does the majority of the work in the digestion process. Secretes hormones.
Large Intestine	Mostly digested food enters the large intestine, where water and salt and remaining digested food are absorbed by the intestinal lining. The residue, together with water pigments, dead cells, and bacteria, are pressed into feces and then stored for ejection.
Spleen	Removes and destroys worn-out red blood cells and helps fight infection.

Colon—same as large intestine!!	Main function is to conserve water by absorbing it from the bowel contents.
Rectum	Holds the feces until elimination.
Bladder	Serves as the temporary retention of urine and releases it at intervals into the urethra.
Ovaries	Store primary ovarian follicles, release the mature ova, and produce the female sex hormones, particularly estrogen and progesterone.
Fallopian Tubes	Where the ovum travels to the uterus, after release from the ovary.
Uterus	Where the fetus grows and is nourished until birth. Where the lining desquamates to cause menstruation.
Vagina	Passageway that stretches during sexual intercourse and childbirth.
Prostate	Responsible for secreting most of the fluid in semen.
Penis	Functions as the male copulatory organ and as the channel by which urine leaves the body.
Testes	Produces sperm and hormones, particularly testosterone and DHEA.
Pituitary	Secretes hormones that control and regulate influence on other endocrine organs, control growth and development, or modify the contraction of smooth muscle, renal function, and reproduction.
Thyroid	This gland's major hormone controls metabolism, including heart rate and the rate of energy use. Also produces calcitonin, which insures calcium transfer into bones.
Adrenals	Secrete hormones that affect the body's response to stress, metabolic rate, growth, blood glucose concentration and the retention and loss of minerals. Most particularly epinephrine, aldosterone, DHEA and small amounts of testosterone.
Parathyroid	Makes parathormone, which balances blood calcium levels by the increase of intestinal calcium absorption, release of calcium stores from bones, and reduction of calcium excretion from the kidneys.
Arteries	Elastic, muscular-walled tubes that transport blood away from the heart to all other parts of the body.

Veins	Thin-walled blood vessels that return blood at low pressure to the heart.
Bones	The hard parts of the skeleton that serve as levers to move a body part.
Maxilla	Upper jaw that holds the teeth and meets with mandible to assist chewing and speaking.
Mandible	Lower jaw that holds teeth and allows one to hold or bite food and assists speaking.
Auditory Ossicles	Allow for sound transmission across the middle ear and acts as a mechanical transformer.
Clavicle	Links the scapula and the sternum (collarbone).
Scapula	Bones that provide articulation for the humerus and articulating with the corresponding clavicle (shoulder blade).
Humerus	Longest bone in the upper arm, from the shoulder to the elbow. Provides various processes and modified surfaces for the attachment of muscles.
Radius	The bone on the thumb side of the human forearm that is moveably articulated with the ulna at both ends so as to permit partial rotation about that bone.
Ulna	The bone on the little-finger side of the human forearm that forms with the humerus and the elbow joint and, serves as a pivot in rotation of the hand.
Ilium	The upper and largest one of the three bones composing the lateral half of the pelvis.
Sacrum	The part of the spinal column that is directly connected with or forms a part of the pelvis by articulation with the ilia and that forms the dorsal wall of the pelvis.
Femur	Also called the thigh bone, articulates with other neighboring bones and provides for the attachment of muscles.
Tibia	Known as the shin bone, this bone is the inner and usually larger of the two bones of the leg between the knee and ankle that articulates above with the femur and below with the talus.

Fibula	Calf bone, which is the slenderest bone of the human body in proportion to its length.
Metatarsals	Any bone of the metatarsus of the human ankle.
Metacarpals	Any bone of the metacarpus of the human wrist.
Muscles	Fibers held together by fibrous connective tissue that apply force to move a body part.
Pectoral	Muscles that connect the ventral walls of the chest with the bones of the upper arm and shoulder.
Biceps	The large flexor muscles of the front of the upper arms.
Triceps	The large extensor muscles that are situated along the back of the upper arms.
Gluteal	Any of three muscles of the buttocks that act to rotate the thigh.
Quadriceps	The large extensor muscles of the front of the thigh, divided above into four parts which unite in a single tendon to enclose the patella and allow flexion of the thigh.
Hamstrings	Any of three muscles at the back of the thigh that function to extend and rotate the leg and extend the thigh.
Gastrocnemius	The largest and most superficial muscle of the calf of the leg that has its tendon of insertion incorporated as part of the Achilles tendon. It extends the foot.
Right frontal brain	Emotional control center and personality; non-verbal abilities. This lobe is associated with higher-level cognitive functions like reasoning and judgment. Most importantly for speech pathologists, the frontal lobe contains several cortical areas involved in the control of voluntary muscle movement, including those necessary for the production of speech and swallowing. In a small percentage of people, the speech center is in the right frontal lobe
Left Frontal Brain	Emotional control center and personality; controlling language-related movement. This lobe is associated with higher-level cognitive functions like reasoning and judgment. Most importantly for speech pathologists, the frontal lobe contains several cortical areas involved in the control of voluntary muscle movement, including those necessary for the production of speech and swallowing. In over 90% of people, the speech center is in the left frontal lobe.

Right Temporal Brain	Selective attention to visual or auditory input; recognition of tonal sequences and many musical abilities; recognition of visual content.
Left temporal brain	Selective attention to visual or auditory input; recall of verbal and visual content, including speech perception and recognition of words.
Right parietal brain	Impacts such things as dressing and washing, personality, and non-verbal memory; and integrates sensation.
Left parietal brain	Deals with writing, mathematics, perception of objects and language, verbal memory, and ability to recall strings of digits. Final site for sensory integration.
Right occipital brain	This area detects and interprets visual images.
Left occipital brain	This area detects and interprets visual images.
Cerebellum	Neurons of the cerebellum link with other regions of the brain and the spinal cord, facilitating smooth, precise movement, and controlling balance and posture. It also plays a role in speech.
Hypothalamus	The hypothalamic nuclei monitor and regulate body temperature, food intake, water/salt balance, blood flow, the sleep/wake cycle, and the activity of the hormones secreted by the pituitary gland. The nuclei also mediate the responses to emotions such as anger and fear.
Pineal	This tiny gland secretes melatonin, a hormone that controls body rhythms such as sleeping and waking and may influence sexual development.
Diencephalon	The posterior subdivision of the forebrain.
Brain stem	The brain stem contains centers that regulate several functions that are vital for survival; these include blood pressure, heartbeat, respiration, digestion, and certain reflex actions, such as swallowing and vomiting.
Right leg	Legs contain arteries, bones, muscles, and nerves which allow for a wide range of motion and dexterity.
Left leg	Legs contain arteries, bones, muscles, and nerves which allow for a wide range of motion and dexterity.

Spinal Cord	Through 31 pairs of spinal nerves, the spinal cord is connected to the rest of the body and relays information received via these nerves about its internal and external environment to and from the brain.
Spinal vertebrae	The spine holds the head and body upright and allows the upper body to bend and twist. There are 24 ringlike bones called the vertebrae linked by a series of mobile joints, and terminate in the sacrum. Consists of 5 fused vertebrae, followed by the coccyx.
Cervical (how many)	Located in the neck, there are 7 vertebrae.
Thoracic (how many)	Located in the upper back, there are 12 vertebrae.
Lumbar (how many)	Located in the lower back, there are 5 vertebrae.
Sacral (how many)	Located toward the base of the spine, there are 5 fused vertebrae. At the very base of the spine is the coccyx, 4 fused vertebrae.
Sympathetic Nervous System	A division of the autonomic nervous system, the sympathetic nervous system is principally an excitatory system that prepares the body for stress.
Parasympathetic Nervous System	A division of the autonomic nervous system, the parasympathetic nervous system maintains or restores energy. Balances the sympathetic system.
Skin	The body's protective outer boundary. Regulates body temperature; a variety of sensory receptors make many parts of this organ sensitive to the lightest touch. Because its appearance can alter with body emotional states and general health, skin reveals signs of a wide range of disorders.
Major enzymes produced by stomach	Hydrochloric acid, pepsin, gastrin, and intrinsic factor.
Major enzymes produced by pancreas	Trypsin, peptidase, muclease, lipase, pancreatic amylase, lactase, sucrase, and maltase.
Major enzymes produced by Salivary Glands	Salivary amylase

Melatonin	From the pineal gland, targets a variety of tissue to mediate control of biorhythms, the body's daily routine.
Serotonin	A neurotransmitter that plays a role in the regulation of anger, aggression, body temperature, mood, sleep, vomiting, sexuality, and appetite.
Dopamine	A neurotransmitter that plays a role in behavior and cognition, motor activity, motivation, and reward, sleep, mood, attention, and learning.
Norepinephrine	Stimulates the heart muscle and other muscles during the fight or flight response; increases the amount of glucose in the blood to provide quick energy to fight or flee. Main hormone of the sympathetic system.
Epinephrine	Stimulates the heart muscle and other muscles during the fight or flight response; increases the amount of glucose in the blood to provide quick energy to fight or flee.
Neurotensin	A 13 amino acid peptide found in the brain and spinal cord that affects pituitary hormone release and gastrointestinal functions and is a neuroleptic and pain reliever.
Cholinesterase	An enzyme found primarily at nerve endings that catalyzes the hydrolysis of acetylcholine into acetic acid and choline.
Acetylcholine	A neurotransmitter that allows neurons to communicate with each other. The major hormone of the parasympathetic system.
GABA	An inhibitory neurotransmitter found in the nervous system that binds specific receptors.
Beta Endorphins	An endorphin produced by the pituitary gland that is a potent pain suppressant
ACTH	From the pituitary gland, stimulates growth or cortex in the adrenal gland and secretion of corticosteroids by the cortex of the adrenal gland, increased during stressful periods.
Cortisone	A naturally occurring corticosteroid that functions in carbohydrate metabolism and is a major immune regulator.

Aldosterone	A steroid hormone of the adrenal cortex that functions in the regulation of the salt and water balance of the body.
DHEA	Produced from cholesterol; an intermediate in the biosynthesis of testosterone. Major balancer of cortisone and regulator of immune function.
Calcitonin	From the thyroid gland, targets the bones, kidneys, and intestines to reduce the level of calcium in the blood and maintain it in bone. Potent pain reliever.
Platelets	Released from the bone marrow into the blood; assists in blood clotting.
White blood cells	Cells of the immune system which defend the body against both infectious disease and foreign materials.
Lymphocytes	Originate from stem cells that are the typical cellular elements of lymph and constitute 20 to 30 percent of the white blood cells of normal human blood which function in cellular immunity.
Neutrophils	An abundant type of granular white blood cell that is highly destructive of microorganisms.
Eosinophils	White blood cells of the immune system that are responsible for combating infection by parasites. Also control mechanisms associated with allergy and asthma.
Lymph system	An extensive network of transparent lymph vessels and lymph nodes. It returns excess tissue fluid to the circulation and helps combat infections and cancer cells.
Categories of Diseases	1. Addiction 2. Autoimmune 3. Benign tumor 4. Biochemical, metabolic 5. Degenerative 6. Electrical 7. Endocrine 8. Hematological 9. Hereditary/congenital 10. Immunological 11. Infectious: bacterial, viral, fungal, protozoan, amoebic 12. Inflammatory 13. Psychological/emotional/ spiritual 14. Malignant tumor 15. Surgical 16. Traumatic 17. Vascular
Major intracellular minerals	Potassium, magnesium

Major extracellular minerals	Sodium, calcium
Beneficial effects of cholesterol	Cholesterol is required to build and maintain cell membranes; it regulates membrane fluidity over a wider range of temperatures. Cholesterol also aids in the manufacture of bile and is also important for the metabolism of fat-soluble vitamins. Major foundation for most hormones and for brain tissue.

ANATOMY AND PHYSIOLOGY FOR SPIRITUAL HEALING/ ENERGY MEDICINE

COURSE NUMBER 754. EXAMINATION

Name: _____ Date: _____

I. On the sketch of the body, please place in the appropriate ana-tomical location as exactly as possible the area of each of these physical components. To the right of each of these anatomical parts, please list as many of the physiological functions as pos-sible.

1. Eyes _____

2. Ears _____

3. Nose _____

4. Mouth _____

5. Throat _____

6. Left arm _____

7. Right arm _____

8. Chest _____

9. Breast _____

10. Lungs _____

11. Heart _____

12. Esophagus _____

13. Bronchi _____

14. Thymus _____

I 5. Liver _____

16. Pancreas _____

17. Gall bladder _____

18. Right kidney _____

19. Left kidney _____

20. Stomach _____

21. Small intestine _____

22. Large intestine _____

23. Spleen _____

24. Colon _____

25. Rectum _____

26. Bladder _____

27. Ovaries _____

28. Fallopian Tubes _____

29. Uterus _____

30. Vagina _____

31. Prostate _____

32. Penis _____

33. Testes _____

34. Pituitary _____

35. Thyroid _____

36. Adrenals _____

37. Parathyroid _____

38. Arteries _____

39. Veins _____

40. Bones

    A. Maxilla _____

B. Mandible _____

C. Auditory Ossicles _____

D. Clavicle _____

E. Scapula _____

F. Humerus _____

G. Radius _____

H. Ulna _____

I. Ilium _____

J. Sacrum _____

K. Femur _____

L. Tibia _____

M. Fibula _____

N. Metatarsals _____

O. Metacarpals _____

41. Muscle

A. Pectoral _____

B. Biceps _____

C. Triceps _____

D. Gluteal _____

E. Quadriceps _____

F. Hamstrings _____

G. Gastrocnemius _____

42. Right frontal brain _____

43. Left frontal brain _____

44. Right temporal brain _____

45. Left temporal brain _____

46. Right parietal brain _____

47. Left parietal brain _____

48. Right occipital brain _____

49. Left occipital brain _____

50. Cerebellum _____

51. Hypothalamus _____

52. Pineal _____

53. Diencephalon _____

54. Brain stem _____

55. Right leg _____

56. Left leg _____

57. Spinal cord _____

58. Spinal vertebrae _____

    Cervical (How Many) _____

    Thoracic (How Many) _____

    Lumbar (How Many) _____

    Sacral (How Many) _____

59. Sympathetic Nervous System _____

60. Parasympathetic Nervous System. _____

61. Skin _____

ADDITIONAL PHYSIOLOGICAL QUESTIONS:

List the major enzymes produced by:

1. Stomach _____

2. Pancreas _____

3. Salivary Glands _____

List the major physiological function of the following:

1. Melatonin _____

2. Serotonin _____

3. Dopamine _____

4. Norepinephrine _____

5. Epinephrine _____

6. Neurotensin _____

7. Cholinesterase _____

8. Acetylcholine _____

9. GABA _____

10. Beta Endorphins _____

11. ACTH _____

12. Cortisone _____

13. Aldosterone _____

14. DHEA _____

15. Calcitonin _____

16. What is the function of platelets _____

17. What are the functions of:

    A. White blood cells _____

    B. Lymphocytes _____

C. Neutrophils _____

D. Eosinophils _____

E. Lymph system _____

18. List the categories of diseases _____

_____

_____

_____

19. List the major intracellular minerals _____

20. List the major extracellular minerals _____

21. List the beneficial effects of cholesterol _____

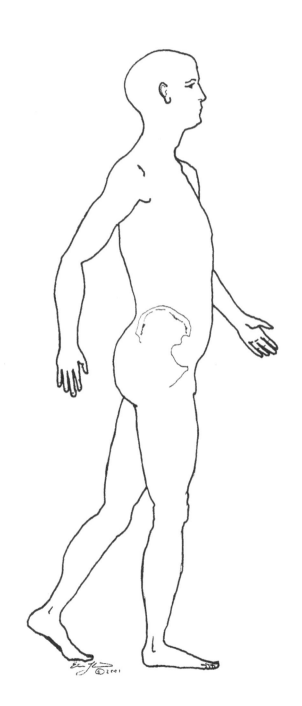

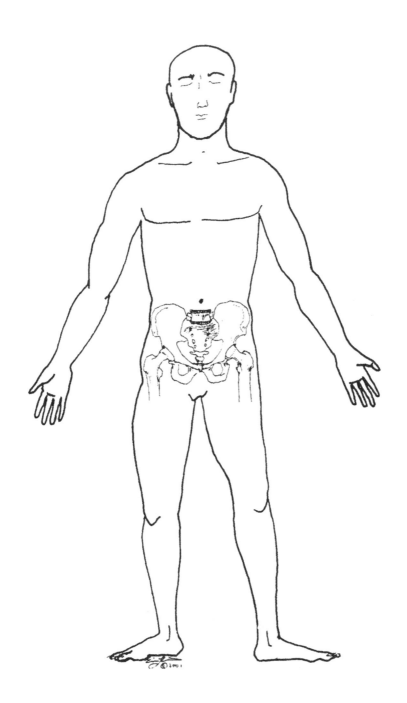

4TH DIMENSION PRESS

An Imprint of A.R.E. Press

4th Dimension Press is an imprint of A.R.E. Press, the publishing division of Edgar Cayce's Association for Research and Enlightenment (A.R.E.).

We publish books, DVDs, and CDs in the fields of intuition, psychic abilities, ancient mysteries, philosophy, comparative religious studies, personal and spiritual development, and holistic health.

For more information, or to receive a catalog, contact us by mail, phone, or online at:

4th Dimension Press
215 67th Street
Virginia Beach, VA 23451-2061
800-333-4499

4THDIMENSIONPRESS.COM

Who Was Edgar Cayce?
Twentieth Century Psychic and Medical Clairvoyant

Edgar Cayce (pronounced Kay-Cee, 1877-1945) has been called the "sleeping prophet," the "father of holistic medicine," and the most-documented psychic of the 20th century. For more than 40 years of his adult life, Cayce gave psychic "readings" to thousands of seekers while in an unconscious state, diagnosing illnesses and revealing lives lived in the past and prophecies yet to come. But who, exactly, was Edgar Cayce?

Cayce was born on a farm in Hopkinsville, Kentucky, in 1877, and his psychic abilities began to appear as early as his childhood. He was able to see and talk to his late grandfather's spirit, and often played with "imaginary friends" whom he said were spirits on the other side. He also displayed an uncanny ability to memorize the pages of a book simply by sleeping on it. These gifts labeled the young Cayce as strange, but all Cayce really wanted was to help others, especially children.

Later in life, Cayce would find that he had the ability to put himself into a sleep-like state by lying down on a couch, closing his eyes, and folding his hands over his stomach. In this state of relaxation and meditation, he was able to place his mind in contact with all time and space—the universal consciousness, also known as the super-conscious mind. From there, he could respond to questions as broad as, "What are the secrets of the universe?" and "What is my purpose in life?" to as specific as, "What can I do to help my arthritis?" and "How were the pyramids of Egypt built?" His responses to these questions came to be called "readings," and their insights offer practical help and advice to individuals even today.

The majority of Edgar Cayce's readings deal with holistic health and the treatment of illness. Yet, although best known for this material, the sleeping Cayce did not seem to be limited to concerns about the physical body. In fact, in their entirety, the readings discuss an astonishing 10,000 different topics. This vast array of subject matter can be narrowed down into a smaller group of topics that, when compiled together, deal with the following five categories: (1) Health-Related Information; (2) Philosophy and Reincarnation; (3) Dreams and Dream Interpretation; (4) ESP and Psychic Phenomena; and (5) Spiritual Growth, Meditation, and Prayer.

Learn more at EdgarCayce.org.

What Is A.R.E.?

Edgar Cayce founded the non-profit Association for Research and Enlightenment (A.R.E.) in 1931, to explore spirituality, holistic health, intuition, dream interpretation, psychic development, reincarnation, and ancient mysteries—all subjects that frequently came up in the more than 14,000 documented psychic readings given by Cayce.

The Mission of the A.R.E. is to help people transform their lives for the better, through research, education, and application of core concepts found in the Edgar Cayce readings and kindred materials that seek to manifest the love of God and all people and promote the purposefulness of life, the oneness of God, the spiritual nature of humankind, and the connection of body, mind, and spirit.

With an international headquarters in Virginia Beach, Va., a regional headquarters in Houston, regional representatives throughout the U.S., Edgar Cayce Centers in more than thirty countries, and individual members in more than seventy countries, the A.R.E. community is a global network of individuals.

A.R.E. conferences, international tours, camps for children and adults, regional activities, and study groups allow like-minded people to gather for educational and fellowship opportunities worldwide.

A.R.E. offers membership benefits and services that include a quarterly body-mind-spirit member magazine, *Venture Inward*, a member newsletter covering the major topics of the readings, and access to the entire set of readings in an exclusive online database.

Learn more at EdgarCayce.org.